THE BEDFORD SERIES IN HISTORY AND CULTURE

# The 9/11 Commission Report

## with Related Documents

D0974258

Related Titles in
# THE BEDFORD SERIES IN HISTORY AND CULTURE
*Advisory Editors:* Lynn Hunt, *University of California, Los Angeles*
David W. Blight, *Yale University*
Bonnie G. Smith, *Rutgers University*
Natalie Zemon Davis, *Princeton University*
Ernest R. May, *Harvard University*

---

*The Age of McCarthyism: A Brief History with Documents,*
Second Edition
Ellen Schrecker, *Yeshiva University*

*American Cold War Strategy: Interpreting NSC 68*
Edited with an Introduction by Ernest R. May, *Harvard University*

*The Rise of Conservatism in America, 1945–2000: A Brief History with Documents*
Ronald Story, *University of Massachusetts Amherst* and Bruce Laurie, *University of Massachusetts Amherst*

*The Movements of the New Left, 1950–1975: A Brief History with Documents*
Van Gosse, *Franklin and Marshall College*

*My Lai: A Brief History with Documents*
James S. Olson, *Sam Houston State University*, and Randy Roberts, *Purdue University*

*The Oil Crisis of 1973–1974: A Brief History with Documents*
Karen R. Merrill, *Williams College*

*Jimmy Carter and the Energy Crisis of the 1970s: The "Crisis of Confidence" Speech of July 15, 1979: A Brief History with Documents*
Daniel Horowitz, *Smith College*

THE BEDFORD SERIES IN HISTORY AND CULTURE

# The 9/11 Commission Report

## with Related Documents

*Abridged and with an Introduction by*

## Ernest R. May

*Harvard University*

BEDFORD/ST. MARTIN'S          Boston   ◆   New York

*For Bedford/St. Martin's*

*Publisher for History*: Mary V. Dougherty
*Director of Development for History*: Jane Knetzger
*Developmental Editor*: Shannon Hunt
*Editorial Assistant*: Laurel Damashek
*Production Supervisor*: Andrew Ensor
*Executive Marketing Manager*: Jenna Bookin Barry
*Project Management*: Books By Design, Inc.
*Text Design*: Claire Seng-Niemoeller
*Indexer*: Books By Design, Inc.
*Cover Design*: Billy Boardman
*Cover Art*: *National Security Adviser Condoleezza Rice Is Sworn in before Testifying to the Independent Commission Investigating the September 11 Attacks, Thursday, April 8, 2004, in Washington, D.C.* AP Images.
*Composition*: Stratford Publishing Services, Inc.
*Printing and Binding*: RR Donnelley & Sons Company

*President*: Joan E. Feinberg
*Editorial Director*: Denise B. Wydra
*Director of Marketing*: Karen Melton Soeltz
*Director of Editing, Design, and Production*: Marcia Cohen
*Manager, Publishing Services*: Emily Berleth

Library of Congress Control Number: 2006932544

Manufactured in the United States of America.

2   1   0   9   8   7
f    e    d    c    b    a

*For information, write*: Bedford/St. Martin's, 75 Arlington Street, Boston, MA 02116 (617-399-4000)

ISBN-10: 0-312-45099-0
ISBN-13: 978-0-312-45099-1

# Foreword

The Bedford Series in History and Culture is designed so that readers can study the past as historians do.

The historian's first task is finding the evidence. Documents, letters, memoirs, interviews, pictures, movies, novels, or poems can provide facts and clues. Then the historian questions and compares the sources. There is more to do than in a courtroom, for hearsay evidence is welcome, and the historian is usually looking for answers beyond act and motive. Different views of an event may be as important as a single verdict. How a story is told may yield as much information as what it says.

Along the way the historian seeks help from other historians and perhaps from specialists in other disciplines. Finally, it is time to write, to decide on an interpretation and how to arrange the evidence for readers.

Each book in this series contains an important historical document or group of documents, each document a witness from the past and open to interpretation in different ways. The documents are combined with some element of historical narrative—an introduction or a biographical essay, for example—that provides students with an analysis of the primary source material and important background information about the world in which it was produced.

Each book in the series focuses on a specific topic within a specific historical period. Each provides a basis for lively thought and discussion about several aspects of the topic and the historian's role. Each is short enough (and inexpensive enough) to be a reasonable one-week assignment in a college course. Whether as classroom or personal reading, each book in the series provides firsthand experience of the challenge—and fun—of discovering, recreating, and interpreting the past.

Lynn Hunt
David W. Blight
Bonnie G. Smith
Natalie Zemon Davis
Ernest R. May

# Preface

The terrorist attacks of September 11, 2001, traumatized the United States. Like the Japanese attack on Pearl Harbor in World War II or the assassinations of President John F. Kennedy, his brother Senator Robert Kennedy, and civil rights leader Martin Luther King Jr., the event left a permanent scar on the memories of all Americans who read about or saw pictures of the toppling towers of New York City's World Trade Center, the smashed-in south face of the Pentagon, the smoldering remains of the plane crash in Pennsylvania, or the agonized faces of first responders trying to effect rescues and men and women looking for lost loved ones. College students learning about 9/11, though they may have a clear recollection of the event itself, may be less familiar with its historical context—the bitter political divisions in the United States at the time, the motivations of Islamist terrorists, the CIA's early actions against al Qaeda, and the military defense strategies prepared in the aftermath of the attacks.

One of the best ways of understanding the political, cultural, and economic circumstances surrounding 9/11 is to read *The 9/11 Commission Report*. The report's sources include hundreds of thousands of documents and transcripts of more than a thousand closed-door interviews, most of which were highly classified and will remain sealed for a long time to come. The report is remarkable for being professional and bipartisan at a time when partisanship was unusually ferocious. It is even more remarkable—perhaps unique among official documents—for being written in vivid and accessible language. *Time* magazine described the report as "one of the most riveting, disturbing and revealing accounts of crime, espionage and the inner workings of government ever written." It is the only government report ever to be nominated for a National Book Award.

What limits the usefulness of the report for teachers is its size and some of its technicality. It is 567 pages long—about 300,000 words.

Portions reconstructing exactly what happened at the sites attacked and in the hijacked planes, air traffic control centers, and military headquarters make fascinating reading but overflow with detail. This volume condenses the report to about 50,000 words, making it a feasible assignment for a college course. I was the 9/11 Commission's senior adviser and had a hand in writing the report. For this reason, I think I have been able to shorten it without distorting the original or making it less riveting. I have aimed to give students an understanding of the whole event, including its background in Islamist extremism and all the ultimately ineffective counterterrorist activities of the CIA, the FBI, and other parts of the U.S. government.

In the introduction, I describe the inner workings of the Commission and how the report was composed. Background information on the stormy political climate of the time serves to provide context for the reader. I also identify some questions to prompt students to critically examine both the event and the document.

A cast of characters and a list of acronyms help the reader navigate the text itself, and maps of Afghanistan and of western Africa and the Middle East depict important places mentioned in the narrative. A chronology of 9/11, questions for consideration, a selected bibliography, and an index round out this volume's pedagogical features.

Working on *The 9/11 Commission Report* was one of the high points of my long career of writing and teaching history. It is my strong hope that this edition will both cast a new light on 9/11 for those who lived through it and bring to those too young to remember 9/11 some understanding of the event's indelible mark on America.


## ACKNOWLEDGMENTS

It is hard to know where to begin or end expressions of thanks. I am indebted, personally and in every other way, to the 9/11 commissioners, to my associates in their "front office," and to their splendid staff. Charles Christensen, the former president of Bedford/St. Martin's, came up with the idea of a classroom version of the report. His successor, Joan Feinberg, along with Mary Dougherty, publisher for history; Jane Knetzger, director of development for history; and Emily Berleth, production manager, helped make the book a reality. Shannon Hunt, my editor at Bedford/St. Martin's, did wonders with my text; editorial assistant Laurel Damashek helped prepare the manuscript for production.

We were all aided by critical readings of my original drafts by seven historians whom Bedford asked to serve as reviewers: Petra Goedde, Temple University (Pennsylvania); Matthew Jacobs, University of Florida; Meg Jacobs, Massachusetts Institute of Technology; Andrew Johns, Brigham Young University (Utah); Patrick D. Reagan, Tennessee Technological University; Catherine Rymph, University of Missouri; and Sayuri Shimizu, Michigan State University.

In addition, I received oral and written comments from another twenty-four teacher/scholars who came to Harvard in June 2005 for a three-day seminar sponsored by the Council of Independent Colleges and the Gilder Lehrman Institute of American History. The historians among them were Ryan J. Carey, Simon's Rock College of Bard (New York); Lawrence W. Cobb, Oklahoma City University; Joe P. Dunn, Converse College (South Carolina); Thomas C. Ellington, Wesleyan College (Georgia); Raymond Frey, Centenary College (New Jersey); Jolyon Girard, Cabrini College (Pennsylvania); Larry Hartenian, Curry College (Massachusetts); John S. Hill, Immaculata University (Pennsylvania); Marie E. Hooper, Oklahoma City University; Maurice Isserman, Hamilton College (New York); Ken Jones, St. John's University/College of St. Benedict (Minnesota); Jeremy Lewis, Huntingdon College (Alabama); Julia Liss, Scripps College (California); Barbara McGowan, Ripon College (Wisconsin); Philip G. Payne, St. Bonaventure University (New York); Edythe Anne Quinn, Hartwick College (New York); Kimberly A. Redding, Carroll College (Wisconsin); Hyman Rubin, Columbia College (South Carolina); Edward G. Warren, Nichols College (Massachusetts); and David Witwer, Lycoming College (Pennsylvania). The four who practiced other disciplines were Timothy J. O'Neill, Department of Political Science, Southwestern University (Texas); Kristen Rafferty, Department of Government and International Studies, Berry College (Georgia); Timothy Rawson, Department of Liberal Studies, Alaska Pacific University; and Eileen Scully, Department of Social Sciences, Bennington College (Vermont).

I am indebted to Richard Ekman of the Council of Independent Colleges; Lesley S. Herrmann, executive director of the Gilder Lehrman Institute; and Sasha M. Rolon, Lesley's fellowship and seminar coordinator. They recruited me to run the seminar and agreed to let me enlist the participants as reviewers of this volume in draft form. I owe a debt additionally to Professors Maurice Vaïsse and Pierre Mélandri of the École Libre des Sciences Politiques in Paris. At their invitation I was able to present a version of this book's introduction to an international audience. Their comments, those of members of the audience, and particularly those of Dr. Samuel Wells, associate director of the Woodrow Wilson Center in Washington, D.C., who was then a visiting scholar at "Sciences Po," were extremely helpful. Daniel Sargent, a doctoral student at Harvard, helped me with the seminar and not only made notes on the classroom discussion but also recorded the proceedings on DVD. Ben Zimmer, a Harvard undergraduate, has been my research assistant for much of the past three years and helped on this project as on many others.

## A NOTE ON THE TEXT

We considered indicating all places where the report had been compressed but decided that elision marks would make the abridgment less readable. Strings of asterisks do show where large segments of the original text have been omitted. Otherwise, ellipses in this abridgment are ellipses that appear in the original. Additions to the original text are enclosed in brackets.

Ernest R. May

# Contents

**Foreword**   v

**Preface**   vii

PART ONE
**Introduction: The Making of *The*
*9/11 Commission Report***                                        **1**

The Politics of the 9/11 Era                                      2

The Creation of the 9/11 Commission                              6

Battles between the Commission and the Administration           10

The Public Hearings of the Commission                           13

The Commission Report                                           15

Shortcomings of the Report                                      19

What's Missing?                                                 25

**Cast of Characters**                                          **27**

**Glossary of Acronyms**                                        **32**

**PART TWO**

**The Document:** *The 9/11 Commission Report*  **35**

 Preface  35

**1. "We Have Some Planes"**  **37**

 Inside the Four Flights  37
  *Boston: American 11 and United 175, 37* • *Washington*
  *Dulles: American 77, 38* • *Newark: United 93, 39* • *The*
  *Hijacking of American 11, 39* • *The Hijacking of United*
  *175, 42* • *The Hijacking of American 77, 43* • *The Battle*
  *for United 93, 44*

 Improvising a Homeland Defense  47

 National Crisis Management  48
  *The President and the Vice President, 49* • *United 93 and*
  *the Shootdown Order, 50*

**2. The Foundation of the New Terrorism**  **52**

 A Declaration of War  52

 Bin Ladin's Appeal in the Islamic World  54
  *Islam, 54* • *Bin Ladin's Worldview, 55* • *History and*
  *Political Context, 57* • *Social and Economic Malaise, 57* •
  *Bin Ladin's Historical Opportunity, 58*

 The Rise of Bin Ladin and al Qaeda (1988–1992)  58
  *Attacks Known and Suspected, 61*

 Al Qaeda's Renewal in Afghanistan (1996–1998)  62
  *The Embassy Bombings, 64*

**3. Counterterrorism Evolves**  **65**

 From the Old Terrorism to the New: The First World
 Trade Center Bombing  65

 Adaptation—and Nonadaptation—in the Law
 Enforcement Community  67
  *The Justice Department and the FBI, 67* • *Legal Constraints*
  *on the FBI and "the Wall," 68* • *Other Law Enforcement*
  *Agencies, 69*

 . . . and in the Intelligence Community  70
  *The CIA, 71* • *Clandestine and Covert Action, 71* •
  *Analysis, 72* • *Early Counterterrorism Efforts, 72*

 . . . and in the State Department and the Defense
 Department  73
  *The State Department, 73* • *The Department of Defense, 74*

... and in the White House 74

... and in the Congress 76

**4. Responses to al Qaeda's Initial Assaults** **77**

Before the Bombings in Kenya and Tanzania 77
*Early Efforts against Bin Ladin, 77* • *The CIA Develops a Capture Plan, 78*

Crisis: August 1998 80
*A Follow-on Campaign? 84*

Covert Action 85

Searching for Fresh Options 88
*"Boots on the Ground?" 88* • *The Desert Camp, February 1999, 90* • *Looking for New Partners, 90* • *Kandahar, May 1999, 91*

**5. Al Qaeda Aims at the American Homeland** **93**

Terrorist Entrepreneurs 93
*Khalid Sheikh Mohammed [KSM], 93*

The "Planes Operation" 95
*The Plan Evolves, 97*

The Hamburg Contingent 98
*Mohamed Atta, 98* • *Ramzi Binalshibh, 99* • *Marwan al Shehhi, 100* • *Ziad Jarrah, 101* • *Requirements for a Successful Attack, 104*

**6. From Threat to Threat** **104**

The Millennium Crisis 105
*"Bodies Will Pile Up in Sacks," 105* • *Ressam's Arrest, 106* • *Emergency Cooperation, 106* • *A Lost Trail in Southeast Asia, 108*

Post-Crisis Reflection: Agenda for 2000 109
*"Afghan Eyes," 109*

The Attack on the USS *Cole* 110
*Considering a Response, 111*

Change and Continuity 113
*Early Decisions, 115* • *Starting a Review, 116*

The New Administration's Approach 116
*September 2001, 117*

**7. The Attack Looms** **118**

First Arrivals in California 118

The 9/11 Pilots in the United States                    120
*The Fourth Pilot: Hani Hanjour, 121*

Assembling the Teams                                     122
*Dissent within the al Qaeda Leadership, 126  •  Moving to
Departure Positions, 127*

**8.  "The System Was Blinking Red"                      128**

The Summer of Threat                                     128
*Zacarias Moussaoui, 131  •  Time Runs Out, 134*

**9.  Heroism and Horror                                 134**

Emergency Response at the Pentagon                       137

**10.  Wartime                                           138**

Immediate Responses at Home                              139

Planning for War                                         142

"Phase Two" and the Question of Iraq                     145

**11.  Foresight—and Hindsight                           148**

Imagination                                              149
*Historical Perspective, 149  •  Understanding the
Danger, 150  •  Institutionalizing Imagination: The Case
of Aircraft as Weapons, 152*

Policy                                                   154

Capabilities                                             157

Management                                               159
*Operational Management, 159  •  Institutional
Management, 161  •  The Millennium Exception, 162*

**12.  What to Do? A Global Strategy                     163**

**13.  How to Do It? A Different Way of Organizing
Government                                               165**

**PART THREE**

**Related Documents                                      167**

1.  *Declarations by Usama Bin Ladin*, August 23, 1996;
May 10, 1997; February 23, 1998                          169

2. From *The President's Daily Brief*, December 4, 1998, and
   August 6, 2001                                                            173
3. The 9/11 Commission, *Final Report on 9/11 Commission
   Recommendations*, December 5, 2005                                        177


**APPENDIXES**
   A 9/11 Chronology (1978–2005)        185
   Questions for Consideration       190
   Selected Bibliography        191


**Index**    195

# PART ONE

# Introduction:
# The Making of *The 9/11 Commission Report*

The 9/11 Commission came into being because Americans found the events of September 11, 2001, incomprehensible. On that perfect autumn morning, the United States had around 280 million people, was the richest country in history, and spent hundreds of billions of dollars a year on national security. Yet nineteen young Arabs from al Qaeda, a Muslim extremist network trained in Afghanistan, evaded checks in three major U.S. airports, hijacked four planes, brought down the 110-story World Trade Center, smashed one side of the Pentagon and targeted another building in Washington, D.C. (probably the Capitol but possibly the White House), and killed about three thousand people.

Relatives and friends of the victims demanded an all-out investigation by an independent commission. Others seconded their appeal. It took fourteen months for President George W. Bush and the U.S. Congress to establish such a commission, and even then, the street prediction was failure. The Commission was to have five Republicans and five Democrats, all chosen by party leaders, and they were expected to quarrel and never give a satisfactory account of what had happened and why.

I became the Commission's senior adviser soon after its birth. In this introduction, I try to explain why failure seemed so likely, how the ten commissioners managed eventually to achieve unanimity, and why commentators judged the Commission report to be not only a gripping narrative but also unlike any previous government report. Despite pride in having helped to write the report, I believe that it has shortcomings, and in the last section of this introduction, I try to identify them.

## THE POLITICS OF THE 9/11 ERA

The ferocious partisanship of the 1990s and early 2000s made the eventual bipartisanship of the 9/11 Commission seem almost miraculous. Over the previous decades, Republican-Democratic conflict had come to be less about interests—farmers vs. businesses vs. labor and so on—than about moral beliefs. The "sixties" (really the period from the early 1960s to the mid-1970s) had seen campaigns for civil rights and gender equality, the introduction of the Pill, and the near disappearance of many taboos, such as those on premarital sex and the use of four-letter words. It was a time of destructive riots in urban ghettos and sometimes violent demonstrations over the Vietnam War, and its waning days brought the Watergate burglary and cover-up, President Richard Nixon's forced resignation, and soul-shriveling footage of Americans kicking their erstwhile South Vietnamese allies overboard as their helicopters abandoned Saigon.

These upheavals transformed American politics. In the South, which had been Democratic since the Reconstruction era following the Civil War—earning it the nickname "the Solid South"—conservative whites became Republicans. Other once solidly Democratic ethnic and religious blocs fragmented. Irish, Italian, and Jewish Americans could no longer be counted on to vote for Democrats. The Republican party came more and more to represent social conservatives as well as traditional fiscal conservatives, and these social conservatives abhorred much of what was associated with the sixties.

In the 1980s, this new alignment gave Republican Ronald Reagan two terms as president and allowed his vice president, George H. W. Bush, to succeed him. In 1992, however, Bush lost his campaign for reelection, and Democrat Bill Clinton moved into the White House. At forty-six, Clinton belonged to the post–World War II baby boom generation and had matured during the sixties. Born into a working-class family, he had gone on to graduate from college, become a Rhodes scholar at Oxford University in England, and graduate from Yale Law

School. With a sunny smile, a powerful intellect, and a passion for politics, Clinton had returned to his home state of Arkansas and was soon elected governor. He learned to capitalize on his southernness—to be the "Bubba of Bubbas"[1]—a quality that helped him win enough votes from the conservative South to become president.

But Clinton symbolized everything that social conservatives deplored. As a young man, he had evaded military service during the Vietnam War by using loopholes in student deferment regulations. Photos from Oxford showed him with long hair and a beard, looking almost like a "hippie."[2] Rumors about his sexual escapades were rife. As president, he tried (but failed) to end the military's ban on homosexuals. He proposed federal gun control legislation and limitations on the death penalty. He raised gas taxes and income taxes and backed a plan by First Lady Hillary Rodham Clinton that was attacked as a move toward the government takeover of the medical insurance system.

Hillary Rodham Clinton's involvement in her husband's presidency drew conservative criticism. Born in 1947 to an upper-middle-class family and brought up as a conservative Republican, she had become a liberal feminist while attending Wellesley College and Yale Law School, where she was a year ahead of Clinton. Despite evident strains in their marriage, President Clinton spoke of his wife as a virtual co-president, and this irritated conservatives to no end. A popular 1993 bumper sticker read, "Impeach President Clinton—and her husband too."[3]

In the 1994 off-year elections, Newt Gingrich, a Republican congressman from Georgia, mobilized conservatives of all stripes to oppose Clinton. Also a baby boomer, Gingrich had been educated at a succession of U.S. military bases and then at Emory University and Tulane University, where he earned a Ph.D. in history. From a teaching post in Georgia, he launched a political career. Brimming with facts, ideas, and aphorisms, Gingrich was both a sensitive reader of political trends and a brilliant polemicist. Even though he believed that many voters saw Clinton as "a lying, adulterous draft dodger," he suspected that the Republicans might lose the presidency in 1996 because they would not bring to the polls enough of the Americans repelled by the sixties.[4] Gingrich's much publicized 1994 Republican Contract with America promised, among other things, an end to the "cycle of scandal and disgrace" presumably symbolized by Clinton. As a result of his campaign, Republicans gained fifty-four seats in the House and eight in the Senate, overturning the Democratic majorities there. The biggest gains in Republican support were among southern whites and evangelical Christians. Gingrich himself became Speaker of the House.

In the next two years, struggles between Gingrich and Clinton threatened to shut down the federal government. Meanwhile, Clinton, displaying astonishing ideological flexibility, appropriated elements of Gingrich's Contract with America, replaced his earlier commitment to reform with a commitment to fiscal austerity, and adopted the slogan "The era of big government is over." As a result of this reaching out to the political right, Clinton won reelection in November 1996, while Republicans retained control of Congress. Ironically, Gingrich had been careless in banking excessive royalties from books he had sold to the party faithful. Rather than undergo further ethics investigations, he stepped down as Speaker and resigned from the House.

The conservatives' campaign against Clinton, however, was far from over. For years, opponents had charged him and his wife with financial wrongdoing. They focused particularly on a complicated Arkansas real estate deal known as Whitewater. Clinton agreed to have the deal investigated by a special prosecutor. The task fell to Kenneth Starr, a former federal appeals court judge who, it turned out, believed that Clinton was not only corrupt but actually evil. Starr pursued every lead, no matter how tenuous.

By 1997, Starr had chanced on Monica Lewinsky. His staff leaked reports that Clinton had had sex with her when she was a White House intern. Looking into the television cameras, Clinton declared angrily to the nation, "I never had sexual relations with that woman, Miss Lewinsky." A few months later, in August 1998, while testifying under oath, he recanted, admitting that Lewinsky had engaged in oral sex with him.

In October 1998, the House of Representatives voted 258 to 176 to open impeachment proceedings against the president. In December, by a party-line vote, the House charged Clinton with perjury and obstruction of justice and called for his removal from office. In early 1999, the Senate became a jury, with Chief Justice William Rehnquist presiding in the impeachment trial. Since the Constitution requires a two-thirds majority for conviction, there was never much chance that the Senate would remove Clinton from office, but a full 50 percent of the senators voted that he had indeed obstructed justice.

A successor to Starr eventually pronounced the Clintons guilty of no financial wrongdoing in the Whitewater matter. Republicans nevertheless continued to denounce the administration as immoral, and

Vice President Al Gore, who became the Democratic presidential candidate in 2000, distanced himself from Clinton. Gore said publicly that Clinton's behavior in the Lewinsky affair had been "inexcusable," and his campaign managers kept Clinton away from states such as Tennessee and New Hampshire, where many Democrats were social conservatives. Gore received half a million popular votes more than his Republican opponent, George W. Bush, but he lost Tennessee, New Hampshire, and enough other states that the outcome in the electoral college turned on scores of disputed ballots in Florida. A 5–4 decision by the Supreme Court ultimately awarded Florida—and the presidency—to Bush.

The new Republican president was yet another baby boomer, the same age as Clinton but from a much more affluent family. The son of former president George H. W. Bush, the grandson of a Connecticut senator, and descended from other eastern and midwestern millionaire bankers and industrialists, he had attended an exclusive New England prep school, Yale University, and Harvard Business School. Like Clinton, he had evaded active service in Vietnam, but instead of staying out of uniform, he had wangled a commission in the Texas Air National Guard, where he had faced almost no chance of being sent into combat and had even been allowed to take long leaves of absence.[5] In 1986, at the age of forty, Bush stopped drinking and became a born-again Christian, remaking himself as a down-to-earth Texas rancher. In 1994, running primarily against Clinton, he won the governorship of Texas. In 1998, he repeated the victory, taking advantage of polls that showed large segments of the electorate "repulsed" by the Clinton scandals.[6] In 2000, he sought the presidency with promises to restore dignity to the White House and to pursue "compassionate conservatism."

Following Bush's victory, the Democrats accused the Republicans of stealing the election. They charged Bush and his vice president, Dick Cheney, with tailoring energy and environmental policies to suit the big oil companies. They condemned the administration's foreign policy as arrogant and unilateralist. They denounced the centerpiece of Bush's domestic program—tax cuts to stimulate investment—as a giveaway to the rich.

The nation briefly united after 9/11, but the Democrats would go on the offensive again when the administration launched a war against Iraq in March 2003 despite failing to get a mandate from the UN. Meanwhile, little had come to light to explain the surprise attack of 9/11 or to suggest what could be done to avert such attacks in the future. In this climate of partisan politics, the 9/11 Commission's bipartisan unanimity was truly remarkable.

## THE CREATION OF THE 9/11 COMMISSION

In November 2002, President Bush and leaders in Congress finally consented to establish a ten-member National Commission on Terrorist Attacks upon the United States to investigate all "facts and circumstances relating to the terrorist attacks of September 11, 2001." The president would choose the chair. Democratic leaders in Congress would choose a vice chair. The Republican Speaker of the House and the Senate majority leader would each name two commissioners. The Democratic minority leaders in the two houses would do likewise. The Commission would consist of five Republicans and five Democrats.

Few expected this Commission to succeed. The House and Senate committees charged with overseeing intelligence agencies had already run a "joint inquiry" on whether 9/11 had resulted from an intelligence failure. The administration and Republican leaders in Congress had frustrated this investigation, fearing that it would provide Democrats with ammunition for the next election. Senator John McCain of Arizona, a Republican but a rival of Bush's for the 2000 nomination and often out of step with the president, complained that the administration had "slow-walked and stonewalled" the inquiry.[7] The new Commission had little reason to expect a different fate.

The president chose former secretary of state Henry Kissinger to chair the Commission. The families of 9/11 victims demanded that Kissinger disclose the names of his consulting firm's clients, suspecting that some might be airlines or Arabs. After the Senate ethics committee seconded the families' demand, Kissinger resigned. In mid-December 2002, Bush named Thomas Kean (pronounced "Cane") to take Kissinger's place. At the time, it did not seem a promising appointment. Kean had been a two-term governor of New Jersey in the 1980s but had since been out of public life, serving as president of Drew University. He had never worked in Washington or dealt with national security matters. It would take until March 2003 for Kean to obtain the security clearances he needed to read the highly classified documents being assembled by the Commission staff.

The Democratic vice chair was Lee Hamilton, who had served as a congressman from Indiana for thirty-four years and now headed the Woodrow Wilson International Center for Scholars in Washington,

D.C. During his time in the House, Hamilton had chaired committees overseeing the State Department and CIA. He was a member of several sensitive government advisory panels and had all the clearances that Kean lacked. He could both get a running start on Kean and act as his tutor.

The statute required that the Commission produce a report before the end of May 2004, giving it little more than a year to complete its task. Kean would later say that the Commission had been "set up to fail." He explained, "If you want something to fail, you take a controversial topic and appoint five people from each party. You make sure they are appointed by the most partisan people from each party—the leaders of the party. And, just to be sure, let's ask the Commission to finish the report during the most partisan period of time—the presidential election season."[8]

The remaining eight commissioners had records of firm party loyalty. The Republicans were Fred Fielding, a soft-spoken Washington lawyer who had been White House counsel under both Nixon and Reagan; Slade Gorton, a former three-term senator from Washington State; John Lehman, a financier from Philadelphia who had served as Reagan's Navy secretary and was a prolific and proficient writer on government issues and naval history; and James Thompson, the longest-serving governor in the history of Illinois.

Fielding, Gorton, and Thompson were lawyers. So were two of the Democrats. Richard Ben-Veniste, when scarcely out of law school, had headed the Watergate task force whose findings had driven Nixon from office. More recently, he had defended the Clintons in the Whitewater investigation. Jamie Gorelick had been deputy attorney general under Clinton. A third Democrat, trained in political science rather than law, was Tim Roemer, a young but recently retired congressman from Indiana who had participated in the joint inquiry and been one of the legislative sponsors of the 9/11 Commission. The fourth Democrat was originally former Georgia senator Max Cleland, also not a lawyer. A Vietnam veteran who had lost his legs and an arm to a grenade, he still seethed at being ousted from his seat in 2002, in part because of trumped-up attacks on his patriotism. Had he remained on the Commission, it is most unlikely that its report could have been unanimous. When Cleland resigned from the Commission in December 2003 to take a paid government post as a director of the Export-Import Bank, his replacement was former Nebraska senator Bob Kerrey, a onetime businessman and also a wounded and decorated Vietnam War veteran. Now president of the New School in New York

City, he was as partisan as Cleland but not as bitter toward the Bush administration.

The fact that the Commission did not splinter along party lines or otherwise fail in its mission was due to at least four factors. One was effective lobbying by representatives of the victims' families, which sustained interest in and support for the Commission in Congress and the news media. The second was leadership by Kean, Hamilton, and a few commissioners who agreed with them on the importance of bipartisan unanimity. The third was adroit day-to-day management by the Commission's executive director, Philip Zelikow; his deputy, Christopher Kojm; and the Commission's general counsel, Daniel Marcus. The fourth was surprising cooperation on the part of the Bush administration and executive agencies such as the CIA, which had refused to give any help to the congressional joint inquiry.

Several individuals, particularly the widows known as "four moms from New Jersey," produced research that challenged official versions of 9/11. They and other friends and family of the victims became familiar figures on Capitol Hill and on television. Day in and day out, they pleaded to learn why and how their loved ones had died. Carie Lemack, whose mother was killed on the first plane to hit the World Trade Center, joined with other victims' families to create the Family Steering Committee.

Kean and Hamilton, who had not been acquainted before becoming chair and vice chair, proved to have complementary strengths. Neither had any ambition for further public office. Both were determined to overcome the odds against the Commission's success. The contrast between the two served them both, as Kean's inexperience gave him license to ask questions that sometimes seemed naive, while Hamilton's wide-ranging experience made it difficult for these or other questions to be answered offhandedly.

Kean and Hamilton decided at once to function almost as if they were one person. They conferred frequently, usually by phone. Neither would say anything to anyone—including other commissioners and staff—unless he was sure the words were agreeable to the other. Luckily, from the beginning, Gorton and Gorelick supported Kean and Hamilton's determination to prevent the Commission from dividing. When Kerrey replaced Cleland, he also proved an ardent ally in this cause.

To steer the commissioners and staff toward consensus—or at least away from an open split—Kean, Hamilton, and their allies had to walk a thin line. They had to avoid a break with both the families and the administration. If the families deserted the Commission, its chances of success would plummet. If the administration decided to slow-walk and stonewall, as with the congressional joint inquiry, the Commission's reporting deadline would arrive without its being close to accomplishing its mission.

Kean and Hamilton managed relations with the families by meeting with family representatives and, whenever possible, acknowledging the families' grief in public. They designated two Commission staff members as liaisons. Roemer also served as a bridge, sometimes letting the families know that he had been outvoted on an issue of importance to them but consistently encouraging hope that, in the end, they would be satisfied.

Managing relations with the administration called for great finesse. Kean took the first step when he insisted that the president promise full cooperation in enabling the Commission's staff to obtain documents and testimony. Hamilton took an important second step when he persuaded Zelikow to become executive director. A onetime trial lawyer in Texas, then a fast-track Foreign Service officer and a faculty member at Harvard, Zelikow was now a professor of history at the University of Virginia. Like Kean and Hamilton, Zelikow, a Republican, and Kojm, a Democrat, operated as if they were one person.

While in the Foreign Service, Zelikow had worked on the National Security Council staff alongside Condoleezza Rice, now President Bush's national security adviser. He and Rice had coauthored a scholarly study on the post–cold war unification of Germany, and he was well regarded in the White House. He would not agree to be the Commission's executive director until he had assurances from Rice and White House chief of staff Andrew Card similar to those Bush had given Kean.[9] Eventually, Card and White House counsel Alberto Gonzales would send letters to all agency heads unambiguously directing them to supply any documents or testimony requested by the Commission.

Kean, Hamilton, Zelikow, and Kojm recognized that White House cooperation could be undone in an instant by any leak of classified information. If that happened, all the administration's doors would slam shut. Zelikow told staff members in the sternest terms possible that the Commission had a "zero tolerance" policy. His message was clear: "There are no innocent conversations with reporters. . . . If you talk to a reporter, and you haven't been authorized to do so, you'll be fired."[10] Happily, not a single damaging leak occurred during the Commission's twenty-month life span.

The extent of cooperation from the White House and various government agencies was not visible to the public or the news media (or indeed to all commissioners or Commission staff), for knowledge of it would almost certainly have fed family representatives' suspicions that the Commission was colluding in an administration cover-up. The commissioners and a few staff members—myself among them—received authorization to see all National Security Council staff records bearing on counterterrorism policy from the Clinton and Bush administrations. As far as I can tell, the White House staff showed us every document they turned up, and the CIA was similarly forthcoming.

The one serious exception was that although the CIA gave the Commission detailed summaries of interrogations of al Qaeda detainees and even put to them some of the Commission's questions, commissioners and staff members had no direct access to them. We never even knew where they were, who their interrogators were, or what methods the interrogators used. Along with a minority of the Commission and a number of staff members, I found this regrettable because it weakened our reconstruction of the terrorist side of the story. Otherwise, I do not think the report can be faulted on the ground that the Commission did not get the evidence it wanted.

## BATTLES BETWEEN THE COMMISSION AND THE ADMINISTRATION

Despite the administration's overall willingness to cooperate, there were moments of real tension. Gonzales and his staff worried constantly about precedents injurious to executive privilege—the legal right of a president not to reveal to Congress the advice he received in the process of making decisions. Often getting concessions from Gonzales required steady pressure from the families, the news media, and the Commission. The Republican commissioners were particularly effective in this regard. They would call friends in the White House or Congress, who would then advise Gonzales that stubbornness could be politically costly. He eventually gave way in every dispute, but rarely without a struggle.

The first open dispute concerned the President's Daily Brief (PDB), a document carried to the White House each morning by the director of central intelligence. In the Bush administration, the PDB went to fewer than a score of high officials, most of whom were not allowed to keep copies. Usually around twenty single-spaced pages, each PDB reported the most recent information obtained from signal intercepts, satellite imagery, spies, and foreign intelligence services.

In May 2002, CBS News reported that an August 2001 PDB had warned President Bush of a possible al Qaeda attack inside the United States,[11] and at least one favored journalist, Bob Woodward of the *Washington Post*, seemed to have been shown PDBs.[12] Yet the CIA insisted that PDBs were sacrosanct—the agency's advice to the president—and could never be made public. Gonzales had successfully prevented the congressional joint inquiry from seeing PDBs or even taking testimony about them. When the 9/11 Commission asked for access to them, Gonzales took the same position. Family representatives and many in the news media saw the Commission's ability to gain access to PDBs as an acid test of its independence and power.

In the midst of one public hearing, the commissioners recessed for a long private huddle. When they returned, Kean issued a terse statement. A New Jersey newspaper, used to covering Kean, reported, "His jaw set and his trademark jovial demeanor evaporating as each word spilled from his lips, Kean put fellow Republicans in the administration on notice that the Commission could wait no longer for key documents that provide a hint about why America was caught off guard [on] Sept. 11."[13]

The media speculated about a possible Commission subpoena for PDBs. The following day, they learned that the Commission had issued its first subpoena—for records of the Federal Aviation Administration (FAA). This was clearly a warning shot. In a later interview with the *New York Times*, Kean said, "Any document that has to do with this investigation cannot be beyond our reach. I will not stand for it."[14]

With most of the news media supporting Kean, the White House retreated, eventually agreeing that Gorelick and Zelikow—one Democrat and one Republican—be allowed to see the full run of PDBs. They would identify portions bearing on 9/11, then Kean and Hamilton would join in reviewing those portions. All four would take notes, and their notes would be shared with the other commissioners. Although Ben-Veniste, Roemer, and some family representatives said that all the commissioners ought to be able to see the PDBs, a bipartisan majority of the commissioners approved the deal.

A second contest occurred in January 2004, when the Commission voted to request a two-month extension of its reporting deadline. The White House and Republican leaders in Congress were initially unsympathetic. They wanted the Commission's report out of the way well before the presidential election. House Speaker Dennis Hastert seemed adamant in this regard. A spokesman for him said, "I can't imagine a situation where they get an extension."[15] The families, however, supported the plea for additional time, as did many in the news media. CNN's Aaron Brown called the Speaker's position "unconscionable and indefensible."[16] With Senator McCain threatening a legislative maneuver that would tie up appropriations unless an extension was granted, the Speaker finally relented. At the beginning of March 2004, the House extended the Commission's reporting deadline by sixty days, to July 26.

March 2004 also saw a third struggle. The Commission staff had taken closed-door testimony from National Security Advisor Condoleezza Rice; now the Commission asked that she follow up with a public appearance. Gonzales ruled that such public testimony would jeopardize executive privilege. All the commissioners, Republicans as well as Democrats, pointed out that Rice made frequent appearances on television talk shows, which presumably also jeopardized this privilege. Once again, the White House backed off. Rice gave public testimony less than ten days after having declined to do so.

The last open dispute concerned testimony by President Bush and Vice President Cheney. Early on, Clinton and Gore had agreed in principle to meet privately with the Commission. Bush and Cheney had been more hesitant, with Gonzales again warning of a dangerous precedent. After Clinton and Gore each gave the commissioners and staff three hours of interview time, pressure from the families and the news media wore down administration resistance. Bush ultimately agreed to meet with all ten commissioners; Cheney was also to be present. At the meeting, Bush not only answered all the Commission's questions but surprised everyone by taking the dominant role. Cheney, often characterized as the White House puppet master, spoke only about his specific actions on 9/11 while the president was absent from Washington visiting an elementary school in Florida.

Kean and Hamilton thus appeared to have won every round. The net effect was to make the families and their friends in Congress more tolerant of the Commission's desire to minimize confrontation. The Card and Gonzales directives, together with friendly informal contacts between members of the Commission staff and government insiders, were thus able to ensure both closed-door testimony and the flow of documents.

## THE PUBLIC HEARINGS OF THE COMMISSION

Public hearings helped Kean, Hamilton, and their allies hold the support of the families while at the same time capturing wider public attention. During one such hearing in late January 2004, the Commission reviewed details of what had happened on the four hijacked planes. The live audience—and television and radio audiences for days afterward—heard tapes of in-flight reports from crew members. One begins with Betty Ong, a flight attendant, saying to Nydia Gonzalez, at an American Airlines ground facility, "The cockpit's not answering. Somebody's stabbed in business class." The tape ends with Gonzalez's plea: "Betty, talk to me. Betty, are you there? Betty?"

The biggest audiences for Commission hearings were in late March and early April, when the highest officials of the Clinton and Bush administrations testified. Though ranking well below most of these officials, Richard Clarke, counterterrorism coordinator on the National Security Council under both Clinton and Bush, proved to be the star. Stocky, gray-haired, and with almost immobile features, Clarke was a veteran civil servant and looked the part. In fact, however, his outward calm concealed a passion that, just the week before, had been revealed in a memoir titled *Against All Enemies* and in an appearance on the widely watched CBS News program *60 Minutes*.[17]

Clarke began by saying that he welcomed the hearing: "It is finally a forum where I can apologize to the loved ones of the victims of 9/11. . . . Your government failed you, . . . and I failed you. . . . And for that failure, I would ask—once all the facts are out—for your understanding and for your forgiveness." The audience applauded loudly, and family representatives said afterward that they had been waiting to hear these words ever since 9/11.

In response to questions, Clarke reiterated two points central to his book. The first, as he put it in answer to a question from Roemer, was that the Bush administration "considered terrorism an important issue but not an urgent issue." The second, stated with vehemence, was that the Bush administration's war against Iraq was wrongheaded. The administration, he charged, had shelved the campaign against Usama

Bin Ladin and al Qaeda in order to go after Saddam Hussein, and in his view this action had not only taken resources away from the fight against al Qaeda but had actually brought al Qaeda new recruits.

Some Republican commissioners came down hard on Clarke. Later news reports alleged that they had been fed questions by the White House. After the hearing, Kean and Hamilton held a press conference in which, in effect, they apologized for the Commission's behavior, promising that "in the hearings that'll follow, you'll see a different tone and fewer partisan shots."[18]

The public hearing with Rice tested this promise. There were, to be sure, some edgy exchanges. When Rice asked to finish a point, for example, Ben-Veniste said, "I didn't know there was a point." Mostly, however, politeness marked both sides. The event led the news cycle for several days, as Rice at last admitted that there had been an August 2001 PDB item titled "Bin Ladin Determined to Strike in U.S." (Document 2). Although she dismissed it as "historical information based on old reporting," insisting that there had been "no new threat information," she agreed to declassify the item and release it to the news media.

A few days later, the Commission took testimony from Attorney General John Ashcroft. The staff statement delivered ahead of time quoted a former acting director of the FBI as saying that he had tried to brief Ashcroft about terrorism but had been told that the attorney general "did not want to hear this information anymore." Ashcroft said that this was untrue, then went on to say, "We did not know an attack was coming because for nearly a decade our government had blinded itself to its enemies." Laying special stress on "the wall"—rules that inhibited communication between FBI agents investigating crimes and those investigating terrorism or espionage—Ashcroft said that he had declassified and was presenting an internal memorandum of 1995 setting forth these rules. He continued, "Full disclosure compels me to inform you that the author of this memorandum is a member of the Commission"—namely Gorelick, who had been deputy attorney general in 1995.

After the hearing, several Republicans in Congress called for Gorelick's resignation, but the other commissioners supported her without qualification. Gorelick's intelligence, charm, sense of humor, and hard work as a commissioner had made her a favorite among her colleagues and the Commission staff. By giving informal dinner parties at her Washington home, she had helped the commissioners bond with one another. Lehman termed criticism of her "baloney"; Gorton called it "garbage." Thompson characterized Ashcroft's revelation as "an underhanded, unfair shot." Ashcroft's attack on Gorelick may have been the tipping point, after which Commission unanimity became likely, not just possible.

## THE COMMISSION REPORT

While most of the commissioners and most of the Commission's managers focused on bargaining with the administration, dealing with the families and the news media, and staging nineteen days of public hearings, a few, along with most of the staff, studied documents, interviewed witnesses, and drafted sections of the final report.

This report was unusual in concept and design. For that, Zelikow and I were partly responsible. We had taught together at Harvard and had collaborated on a book and a number of case studies.[19] Our families had become close friends. After Zelikow had been approached about becoming executive director, he and I had had a long telephone conversation. Although we both thought that the Commission's prospects of success were dim, we agreed that if it could succeed, it had a chance of doing something that had never been done before.

Previous commission reports, largely the work of lawyers, politicians, and bureaucrats, had tended to set forth findings of fact tailored for either accusations of blame or recommended remedies. Zelikow and I, both historians, believed that the 9/11 Commission's report could be quite different. The various reports on the attack on Pearl Harbor were examples of what we did not want to do. They resembled courtroom presentations, focusing on the indictment or defense of U.S. officials. Only decades later had scholars gone back over the evidence to analyze the Japanese side of the story and the processes that had blinded Americans to Japan's preparations for the attack. Zelikow and I agreed that there was at least a chance that the 9/11 Commission could write a history dealing with both al Qaeda and the U.S. government, probing the planning of the attack and why the United States had been so unprepared.

When Zelikow talked with Kean, he discovered that Kean had developed a view much like ours. Having done graduate work in history and politics at Columbia University, he tended to think like a historian and to be more interested in getting the story right than in looking for immediate lessons. Kean would later state, "We want a report that our grandchildren can take off the shelf in 50 years and say, 'This is what happened.'"[20] There was never a gap between his conception of an ideal Commission report and ours.

Hamilton also accepted this concept, although he attached less importance to the story of 9/11 than to the Commission's recommendations. Long experience had taught him that officials and members of Congress rarely focus on anything else. But he grasped at once that couching the report as a history might help delay a partisan split: If the commissioners debated details about what had happened at specific places and times, they might postpone quarrels about whom to blame and what morals to draw. In the process, they might bond and begin to focus more on their common mission than on their differences.

After Zelikow agreed to become executive director and I to sign on as a senior adviser, we worked up a detailed outline. As staff were recruited, they were organized into teams partly determined by the Commission's charter but also partly by our outline. Because of the tight timetable, the need for high-level security clearances, and the customs of Washington, most available staffers were young lawyers, former congressional aides, or persons lent to us by the CIA, the FBI, the military services, or other agencies. But we managed to include historians on the critical teams working on al Qaeda, the plot, and U.S. counterterrorism in the Clinton and Bush administrations.

We hit one home run while the Commission was still searching for office space. One day we telephoned Douglas MacEachin in Nice, France. A former head of the CIA's Directorate of Intelligence, he had spent his first postretirement years working with us at Harvard, where he had produced several elegant monographs on intelligence history.[21] He agreed to lead the team writing about al Qaeda. In this one move, the Commission gave reassurance to the intelligence community and secured better access to its documents. MacEachin not only worked fourteen hours a day, seven days a week but also developed rolling chronologies that challenged all the other teams to do the same. Zelikow used MacEachin as a model, and soon even veteran litigators found themselves thinking as much about sequences as about patterns.

Once our outline had received official approval from Kean, Hamilton, and Kojm, we all agreed to treat it as if it were our most highly classified document. We feared that premature debate about the structure of the report could produce rifts within the Commission and the staff. By the time the outline was exposed for general viewing, in early 2004, the idea of telling a complete story instead of simply arraying findings had gained enough acceptance that there was minimal grumbling.

The final report differed from our original outline in only one important respect. The outline had called for opening with a chapter on al Qaeda, perhaps even beginning with the birth of Islam. Late in the process of drafting the report, Roemer recommended that the first chapter describe what happened on 9/11. Fielding seconded Roemer's proposal, and all the other commissioners quickly agreed. It was an inspired recommendation that added to the report's narrative power.

The actual drafting of the report was very much a collective undertaking. I wrote some early drafts, not much of which survived intact. Each team produced more drafts. Each draft went to every staff member with the requisite security clearances. The "front office"—essentially Zelikow, Kojm, Marcus, and me, along with Stephanie Kaplan, our tireless administrator/editor—revised those drafts, sometimes as a result of sitting together and looking at text projected on a screen in the conference room. We tried very hard to use an arbitrary word limit to discipline the staff, but the limit kept moving upward as staff members battled for the inclusion of particular evidence or a particular point. The limit nevertheless helped persuade drafters to keep the narrative flowing and to shift into footnotes bits of evidence or argument that were not clearly indispensable.

Collective work on staff statements to be read as prefaces to important public hearings contributed importantly to the development of a common voice. The sessions that produced these statements sometimes went through the night. But the effect was an agreed-upon language, some of which could be—and was—borrowed for the final report. The process heightened everyone's sensitivity to terms and meanings. For example, one seemingly endless debate concerned the question of whether *Islamism* and *Islamic extremism* were synonymous. And since each staff statement had to be cleared for public release, the process also helped reduce the number of later clearance issues in the report itself.

The last phase of the Commission's formal work was hectic. Some of the commissioners worked through drafts as they emerged from negotiations between teams and the front office. Gorelick performed an exacting line-by-line review of every chapter. Gorton faxed Zelikow page after page of handwritten commentary on particular passages. Kerrey and I had extended e-mail exchanges about other passages. Roemer, Ben-Veniste, and Lehman made a number of textual suggestions. In some instances, we were able to persuade commissioners that the staff-written text was preferable. In most instances, we yielded—more often than not because the commissioners' changes were improvements.

Earlier, Kean and Hamilton had accepted Zelikow's suggestion that the Commission test the possibility of the report's being brought out by a commercial publisher. The Government Printing Office, the customary publisher of official reports, planned a volume that would sell for $65 and be available chiefly through its own outlet stores. After seeking bids from several publishers, the Commission signed a contract with W. W. Norton in mid-May 2004. It stipulated that the report was to be put on sale in paperback form in most American bookstores on the day of its public release and that the price was not to exceed $10. Norton agreed that if the book made a substantial profit, at least some of it would go to charity. (Neither the government nor the Commission could accept royalties.) The Commission's spokesperson, former House staff member Al Felzenberg, made sure that all the news media learned about the contract.

During the last phase, the Commission had two sets of offices in Washington and another office in New York. The report was produced at Commission headquarters, one floor of an office building on K Street in Washington that Hamilton had persuaded the CIA to lend to the Commission. It was a Sensitive Compartmented Information Facility (SCIF, pronounced "skiff"), essentially a thirteen-room safe with numerous smaller safes inside. A copy editor cleared for access to classified data went to work there. Staff technicians set up computers from which page-proof copy could be transmitted directly to the printer.

Delegations from the CIA, the Pentagon, the FBI, and other agencies also worked at the already crowded SCIF. These delegations combed the text for any disclosures of classified information. From writing his collaborative book with Rice, Zelikow had learned that, except in very rare cases, the data identifying a classified document is not itself classified. The uncleared, classified draft of the report had thousands of entries citing documents that were not only top secret but that also carried some of the dozens of code words that give a text a higher and more exclusive classification. But if all indications of classification were removed, the agency reviewers could object only if they found something in the Commission report itself that would jeopardize national security or reveal intelligence sources and methods. Thus the report could reference a multiple-code-word memorandum from Director of Central Intelligence George Tenet to Richard Clarke as long as the citation was simply "Tenet to Clarke" with the date and whatever file number would enable some researcher to find it later in the National Archives.

Negotiations occasionally resulted in rewriting a passage so as not to risk identifying a clandestine human source or a particular code-breaking (or other such) capability. There was no instance to my knowledge in which an agency suggested any change relating to a policy debate within the U.S. government.

During the final days, Kean and Hamilton wanted to brief the White House and leaders in both houses of Congress on the report, but they did not want to give anyone an advance copy, as they were sure it would be leaked. Norton, therefore, had to hold up printing so that Kean and Hamilton could say truthfully, on the day before release, that they had not themselves seen copies of the final report. Almost miraculously, Norton managed to print 600,000 copies overnight and express them to bookstores across the country so that they could go on sale more or less precisely at noon eastern time on July 22, 2004. (I won some money betting colleagues that Norton would carry this off.) But a dreadful moment came on the day before publication, when an aide to Speaker Hastert telephoned the Commission asking angrily about a rumor that the report would be issued by a private publisher. "It's a report to Congress," the aide thundered. The person on our end of the line remarked that stories about the Commission's publication plans had been featured in the *New York Times* weeks earlier. "We don't read the fucking *New York Times*," the aide replied. Fortunately, the Speaker's staff decided not to pursue the complaint.

## SHORTCOMINGS OF THE REPORT

All histories have biases as a matter of course. The simple act of choosing one piece of evidence and setting aside another tilts interpretation. But readers of this volume ought to take particular notice of three respects in which *The 9/11 Commission Report* may have bias beyond the normal. The first is narrowness of focus. The second is the skirting of firm verdicts on institutions or individuals. The third is delicate treatment of the motives for the 9/11 attack—the report's answer to the often-asked question, Why do they hate us so?

### Is the Focus Too Narrow?

As the report's preface says, the commissioners or the staff examined approximately two and a half million documents and interviewed more than twelve hundred witnesses. The closed-door interviews, often under oath, were almost always more candid and productive than the testimony given in public. Tenet answered questions for two full days. Clarke did so for almost three. Members of the Commission staff fanned out to FBI field offices across the United States and to foreign capitals, including some in the Middle East, to take testimony from both Americans and non-Americans.

Our research was extraordinarily deep but also extraordinarily narrow. We saw only documents relating to terrorism and counterterrorism. What we read in National Security Council files, for example, told us much about Clarke, the counterterrorism coordinator, but almost nothing about others on the National Security Council staff. We had no idea what else was on the agenda of the national security advisor or whether terrorism was there at all. A story written solely from this documentary record would have centered on Clarke even more than does his memoir.

The evidence was equally skewed for the Pentagon. We saw records from an office for Special Operations and Low-Intensity Conflict (SO/LIC, pronounced "so-lick"). They told us what both civilians and people in the military had known or done about terrorism. They told us almost nothing about other concerns of the military establishment or how terrorism had ranked among those concerns.

Interviews helped to correct the imbalance. It seemed significant, for example, when a witness had no recollection at all of a document or meeting. We had seen, for example, an elaborate "Plan Delenda" developed by Clarke in 1998, which outlined a program of active measures against al Qaeda. In his private and public testimony for the Commission, Clarke made much of this plan, as he does in his book. But neither President Clinton nor anyone high in his administration recalled ever having heard of it.

Similarly, we learned that most SO/LIC files had made no impression on individuals at high levels in the Department of Defense. Pentagon witnesses reminded us that they had had a lot of other matters on their minds, including military operations in Bosnia and Kosovo and the reshaping of forces to fit a post–cold war world.

For me, a telling moment came in October 2003 when we interviewed Army major general Russel Honoré. He told us that although he had been vice director of operations for the Joint Chiefs of Staff, he had known next to nothing about al Qaeda. He "commented to us that intelligence and planning documents relating to al Qaeda arrived in a ziplock red package and that many flag and general officers never had the clearances to see its contents."[22] Readers should reflect on how much the report may distort the history by its exclusive focus on terrorism and counterterrorism.

## Why Did the Commission Avoid Firm Verdicts?

The Commission report describes the evolution of U.S. counterterrorism under Clinton and Bush and in a wide variety of government agencies. Because of preoccupation with achieving bipartisan accord, the Commission and the front office—myself included—bent over backward to balance any point potentially reflecting unfavorably on one administration with a point reflecting unfavorably on the other. Similarly, although we criticized the practices and procedures of a number of agencies, we also took pains not to personalize the criticism and not to denigrate men and women in the civil service or the uniformed services. Throughout, we removed words with interpretive connotations.

The report sometimes pairs contradictory assertions. Chapter 4, for example, discusses the U.S. cruise missile strikes on Afghanistan and Sudan in 1998, which were the Clinton administration's response to al Qaeda's bombing of U.S. embassies in East Africa. The text concedes that the strikes coincided with the worst moments of the Lewinsky affair and notes public skepticism about the rationale for their use. It goes on to say both that these strikes might have had "a cumulative effect" discouraging later decisions on the possible use of force and that Clinton's national security adviser said there was no "sense of constraint." The report leaves the conclusion wholly up to the reader.

Bipartisanship encouraged especially indulgent treatment of the two presidents and their intimate advisers. The text does not describe Clinton's crippling handicaps. Although he had an imaginative grasp of the threat posed by al Qaeda, he lacked support within the parts of his government capable of addressing this threat. His Vietnam War record and tolerance of gays in the military, among other things, made him an object of scorn in much of the Pentagon. Almost everyone in the CIA turned against him when he failed to attend a ceremony for two employees gunned down by a terrorist at the entrance to agency headquarters, sending the first lady in his place. His relations with the FBI started out bad and became worse. In the end, he and FBI director Louis Freeh did not speak to each other, but Clinton could not fire Freeh because of the ongoing Whitewater investigation. Of course, any official in any agency would have snapped to a command from Clinton, but few were enthusiastic about helping him figure out what commands he ought to give. The report veils these limitations in Clinton's real authority. It also avoids even whispered endorsement of Clarke's manifestly accurate charge that the Bush administration considered terrorism important but not urgent.

## Why Do They Hate Us So?

The report details the development of al Qaeda and its plots. Its explanation of al Qaeda's motives is, however, ambiguous. In effect, the report says that the United States was al Qaeda's target because of what America was, not because of anything it did. The commissioners agreed to say no more. They feared disagreeing among themselves and also raising the hackles of Americans with strong views about U.S. support for Israel or other aspects of U.S. Middle East policy. Students and teachers discussing the report should not be so inhibited.

Usama Bin Ladin, the dominant figure in al Qaeda, had openly declared war on the United States. In February 1998, he and two other extremists had issued a fatwa, or religious decree, saying that "to kill the Americans and their allies—civilians and military—is an individual duty for every Muslim who can do it in any country in which it is possible to do it" (Document 1).

In this and other declarations, Bin Ladin always alleged that he was calling for retaliation for "crimes and sins committed by the Americans." One such crime was support of Israel. Another was the presence of American military bases in Saudi Arabia near the holy cities of Mecca and Medina. Yet another was the maintenance of economic sanctions against Iraq since the Persian Gulf War of 1991. Bin Ladin detested the secular regime of Saddam Hussein, but he alleged that the sanctions had killed a million Iraqis.

Bin Ladin's accusations were not baseless. The United States was indeed a strong supporter of Israel. Even though Israel had a population of only around three million, it had since World War II received more U.S. foreign aid than any other country in the world. The aid involved fewer restrictions and less U.S. oversight than in any other country. Europeans as well as Arabs persistently reproached the United States for underwriting Israel without setting any conditions regarding Israel's treatment of Arabs in occupied territories, including Jerusalem, which was a Muslim, as well as a Jewish and Christian, holy city.

Although the U.S. government also had sought friendly relations with Arab states, its main concern had been access to oil. More often than not, it had supported dictators who had suppressed all reform movements, including those of Islamists. The close U.S. relationship with Saudi Arabia particularly outraged Bin Ladin because the Saudi government, after the Persian Gulf War, imprisoned leading Islamist clerics and deprived Bin Ladin himself of his Saudi citizenship and part of his personal fortune.

What Bin Ladin said about the suffering of Arabs was mostly true. Palestinian Arabs experienced daily humiliation under Israeli occupation. Many who had gone into exile lived in crowded and poorly supplied refugee camps. And in Iraq, in part because Saddam Hussein diverted for his own use resources intended to relieve the effects of UN sanctions, many Iraqis died needlessly as a result of hunger or disease.

The key question, however, is not whether Bin Ladin's accusations had a grain or more of truth. It is whether Bin Ladin would not have staged a murderous attack inside the United States had U.S. dealings with the Middle East been different. One possible argument is that Bin Ladin would have regarded the United States as a criminal no matter what its actions. Another is that alternative courses of action that might have changed Islamist opinion were, as a practical matter, out of the question.

To think through the first of these arguments, consider Bin Ladin's perspective: He was hardly typical. His father was an immensely rich Saudi contractor, he had been brought up to run large businesses, and he had studied at Saudi Arabia's premier university, King Abdul Aziz University in Jeddah. There he had come under the influence of Islamists, particularly the learned Palestinian cleric Abdullah Yusuf Azzam.

Islamists such as Azzam and Bin Ladin have in common a few basic beliefs. One is that the seventh century c.e. was a golden age for Islam. This is no myth. In the early seventh century, the prophet Mohammed emerged from the villages of Mecca and Medina in the Arabian desert. He professed to have been chosen by God to bring humankind the final truths completing the partial messages sent earlier through the Hebrew and Christian prophets Abraham and Jesus. Mohammed's followers called on all people to submit. (*Islam* literally means "submission," and a Muslim is a true believer in submission.) The great medievalist Henri Pirenne, who sought to integrate the history of the Middle East with that of Europe, writes: "In the whole history of the world there has been nothing comparable . . . with the expansion of Islam. . . . Wherever it had passed[,] the ancient States . . .

were overturned as by a cyclone. . . . Henceforth, all these regions were subject, in religion and political obedience, to the most powerful potentate who had ever existed, the Caliph of Baghdad."[23] For more than a century, this new Islamic empire bubbled not only with religious fervor but with creativity, contributing to the world, among other things, algebra, chess, and the fables in *The Thousand and One Nights* (supposedly composed for Harun ar-Rashid, caliph from 786 to 809).

A second major Islamist belief is that failure to follow the teachings of the Prophet caused the fragmentation of the caliphate. Successors to Mohammed quarreled, and to their lands came a succession of conquerors, including the Christian crusaders of the eleventh to thirteenth centuries and most recently European colonialists and Zionists, who created the state of Israel.

A third belief, corollary to the others, is that meticulous observation of laws and customs derived from Mohammed's words will not only bring back the golden age of Islam but also permit Islam to become the faith of the world. Sharia, a strict Islamic code of law and custom, will then govern all humans, and a new caliph will exercise universal dominion.

As Bin Ladin reached maturity, he and other Islamists thought that they saw a new golden age dawning. Islamists scored victories in Iran, Afghanistan, and elsewhere. In 1978, Muslims in Iran overthrew a secular monarch and established an Islamic republic. When the Soviet Union invaded Afghanistan in 1979, Afghan Muslims resisted with the help of mujahideen, or guerrilla warriors, from other Muslim countries. By the end of the 1980s, the Soviet Union announced that it would abandon the struggle. Meanwhile, Islamists became increasingly strong forces in, among other places, Somalia, Sudan, Algeria, and Egypt. Bin Ladin himself fought in Afghanistan. At the end of the jihad against the Soviets, he formed al Qaeda, an organization through which the mujahideen could continue to battle for an eventual universal caliphate.

When Bin Ladin decided to direct his jihad primarily against the United States, Bill Clinton was president. The United States had long promoted negotiations between Israel and the Palestinians; Clinton continued this effort. In the last year of his presidency, he thought he was near success. But the head of the Palestine Liberation Organization (PLO), Yasir Arafat, balked. Clinton wrote later, "Arafat never said no; he just couldn't bring himself to say yes. . . . It was an error of historic proportions."[24]

One question that readers of *The 9/11 Commission Report* ought to ask is whether the United States could or should have done more to dampen Arab antagonism and, if so, whether Bin Ladin and al Qaeda might have been deflected from their murderous plans. The question merits closer debate than is to be found in the report.

## WHAT'S MISSING?

This condensed report sacrifices much of the detail of the original— for example, the elaborate detective work that traces the credit card charges of the hijackers as they moved into position for the attacks, and the movements of individuals, floor by floor, in the World Trade Center. Something else severely cut is fine-grained description of the workings of the U.S. bureaucracy. Chapter 3 begins with this observation: "As in any study of the U.S. government, some of the most important characters are institutions." The full report follows up this observation with particulars about the inner workings of the CIA, the FBI, and other agencies and their relations with one another. This condensed version has only broad-stroke portraits of these institutions.

The original report has 118 pages of fine-print endnotes. To try to hold down bulk, we kept reducing the size of the footnote font, and even members of the Commission staff complained of eyestrain. But the footnotes show, as the text cannot, the full range of supportive source material. Before challenging any assertions in the text, one must look closely at the footnotes to discover their evidentiary base.

The most severe cuts here are in the two chapters containing the Commission's recommendations. In the original report, these two chapters run to sixty-seven pages. Here they get only two pages. One reason is that the commissioners made adaptations as the recommendations were debated publicly and incorporated into legislation signed by President Bush on December 17, 2004. Principally, this legislation created a new director of national intelligence as a coordinator for the CIA, the FBI, and other elements of the U.S. intelligence community. Meanwhile, although the Commission had formally disbanded, the ten commissioners created the private Public Discourse Project. Through it, they periodically commented on progress in implementing their proposals. In early December 2005, they closed down the project, issuing a year-after report card, giving both Congress and the executive branch mostly failing grades. This report card appears as Document 3, and it is perhaps a better vehicle than the concluding chapters of the report itself for discussion of lessons to be drawn from 9/11.

# NOTES

[1] Kevin Phillips, *American Dynasty: Aristocracy, Fortune, and the Politics of Deceit in the House of Bush* (New York: Viking, 2004), 82.

[2] See David Maraniss, *First in His Class: A Biography of Bill Clinton* (New York: Simon and Schuster, 1995), photograph 14.

[3] John F. Harris, *The Survivor: Bill Clinton in the White House* (New York: Random House, 2005), 145.

[4] Mel Steely, *The Gentleman from Georgia: The Biography of Newt Gingrich* (Macon, Ga.: Mercer University Press, 2000), 239–40; Sidney Blumenthal, *The Clinton Wars* (New York: Farrar, Straus and Giroux, 2003), 125.

[5] Phillips, *American Dynasty*, 89.

[6] Ibid., 84, 220.

[7] See John Prados, "Slow-Walked and Stonewalled," *Bulletin of the Atomic Scientists* (March/April 2003): 28–37.

[8] Mike Kelly, "Kean: Some Wanted 9/11 Panel to Fail," *Bergen County Record*, July 20, 2004.

[9] "Piloting a Bipartisan Ship: Strategies and Tactics of the 9/11 Commission," Case No. C15-05-1813.0, Kennedy School of Government Case Program, Harvard University, Cambridge, 2005, 10.

[10] Ibid., 18.

[11] *Television News Archive*, May 15–20, 2002, Vanderbilt University.

[12] Bob Woodward, *Bush at War* (New York: Simon and Schuster, 2002), 39–41, 132, 161.

[13] Mike Kelly, "Agency Has Kean Feeling Frustrated," *Bergen County Record*, October 15, 2003.

[14] Philip Shenon, "9/11 Commission Could Subpoena Oval Office Files," *New York Times*, October 25, 2003.

[15] Dan Eggen, "9/11 Panel Unlikely to Get Later Deadline," *Washington Post*, January 17, 2004.

[16] Aaron Brown, "The Whip," CNN Evening News, Television News Archive, February 26, 2004, Vanderbilt University.

[17] Richard A. Clarke, *Against All Enemies: Inside America's War on Terror* (New York: Free Press, 2004); Erich Lichtblau, "President Asked Aide to Explore Iraq Link to 9/11," *New York Times*, March 27, 2004.

[18] Dana Milbank and Dan Eggen, "Bush Counsel Called 9/11 Panelist before Clarke Testified," *Washington Post*, April 1, 2004.

[19] The book is *The Kennedy Tapes: Inside the White House during the Cuban Missile Crisis* (Cambridge: Harvard University Press, 1997). A sample of the case studies appears in our *Dealing with Dictators: Dilemmas of U.S. Diplomacy and Intelligence Analysis* (Cambridge, Mass.: MIT Press, 2006).

[20] John T. Ward, "Citizen Kean," *New Jersey Monthly*, May 27, 2004.

[21] See, for example, *The Final Months of the War with Japan: Signals Intelligence, U.S. Invasion Planning, and the A-Bomb Decision* (Washington, D.C.: Center for the Study of Intelligence, 1998), and *U.S. Intelligence and the Confrontation in Poland, 1980–1981* (University Park: Pennsylvania State University Press, 2002).

[22] *The 9/11 Commission Report* (New York: W. W. Norton, 2005), 351.

[23] Henri Pirenne, *A History of Europe*, trans. Bernard Miall (New York: University Books, 1956), 25–26.

[24] Bill Clinton, *My Life* (New York: Alfred A. Knopf, 2004), 944–45.

# Cast of Characters

**Albright, Madeleine**  U.S. secretary of state, 1997–2001.

**Allen, Charles**  Career U.S. intelligence officer; assistant director of Central Intelligence for collection, 1998–2005.

**Armitage, Richard**  U.S. deputy secretary of state, 2001–2005.

**Ashcroft, John**  U.S. attorney general, 2001–2005.

**Atef, Mohammed**  Also known as Abu Hafs al Masri. Chief of al Qaeda's military committee and principal deputy to Bin Ladin. He was killed during U.S. air attacks on Afghanistan in October 2001.

**Atta, Mohamed**  Egyptian-born, German-educated pilot hijacker of American Airlines flight 11.

**Aziz Ali, Ali Abdul**  Native and resident of the United Arab Emirates who transmitted funds to Hani Hanjour and other 9/11 hijackers.

**Azzam, Abdullah Yusuf**  Palestinian-born Islamic scholar who was one of Bin Ladin's teachers at King Abdul Aziz University in Jeddah, Saudi Arabia. He took part in the 1979–1989 jihad in Afghanistan, cofounded al Qaeda with Bin Ladin, and was killed in 1989 by a bomb of unknown origin.

**Banihammad, Fayez**  United Arab Emirates muscle hijacker on United Airlines flight 175.

**Bara al Yemeni, Abu**  Member of al Qaeda who was almost one of the 9/11 hijackers.

**Ben-Veniste, Richard**  Washington lawyer; Democratic member of the 9/11 Commission.

**Berger, Samuel ("Sandy")**  Deputy national security advisor, 1993–1997; national security adviser, 1997–2001.

**Binalshibh, Ramzi**  European contact for Mohamed Atta during the final stages of the 9/11 plot.

**Bin Ladin, Usama**  Saudi-born head of al Qaeda.

**Black, J. Cofer**  Career U.S. intelligence officer; director of the Counterterrorist Center, 1999–2002.

**Bush, George H. W.**   U.S. vice president, 1981–1989; U.S. president, 1989–1993.

**Bush, George W.**   U.S. president, 2001–.

**Card, Andrew, Jr.**   Chief of staff to President George W. Bush, 2001–2006.

**Cheney, Richard B.**   U.S. vice president, 2001–.

**Clarke, Richard A.**   Member of the National Security Council staff, 1992–2003; chair of the Counterterrorism Security Group, 1992–2003; national counterterrorism coordinator, 1997–2001.

**Cleland, Max**   U.S. senator from Georgia, 1997–2003; Democratic member of the 9/11 Commission who resigned in December 2003 to join the board of the Export-Import Bank.

**Clinton, William Jefferson**   U.S. president, 1993–2001.

**Cohen, William**   U.S. secretary of defense, 1997–2001.

**Deek, Khalil**   Naturalized U.S. citizen arrested in Jordan in December 1999 and later executed as a terrorist linked to al Qaeda.

**Fielding, Fred F.**   Washington lawyer; White House counsel for Presidents Nixon and Reagan; Republican member of the 9/11 Commission.

**Franks, Tommy**   U.S. Army general; commander of U.S. Central Command, 2000–2003.

**Freeh, Louis**   Director of the FBI, 1993–2001.

**Ghamdi, Ahmed al**   Saudi muscle hijacker on United Airlines flight 175.

**Ghamdi, Hamza al**   Saudi muscle hijacker on United Airlines flight 175.

**Ghamdi, Saeed al**   Candidate to be a 9/11 muscle hijacker.

**Gingrich, Newt**   U.S. Speaker of the House, 1995–1999.

**Giuliani, Rudolph**   Mayor of New York City, 1994–2001.

**Gore, Al, Jr.**   U.S. vice president, 1993–2001.

**Gorelick, Jamie S.**   Washington lawyer; Democratic member of the 9/11 Commission.

**Gorton, Slade**   U.S. senator from Washington State, 1981–1987 and 1989–2001; Republican member of the 9/11 Commission.

**Hadley, Stephen**   Deputy national security advisor, 2001–2005; national security advisor, 2005–.

**Hamilton, Lee**   Member of the U.S. House of Representatives from Indiana, 1965–1999; Democratic vice chair of the 9/11 Commission.

**Hanjour, Hani**   Saudi pilot hijacker of American Airlines flight 77.

**Hastert, Dennis**   U.S. Speaker of the House, 1999–2007.

**Hazmi, Nawaf al**  Saudi muscle hijacker on American Airlines flight 77.

**Hazmi, Salem al**  Saudi muscle hijacker on American Airlines flight 77.

**Haznawi, Ahmad al**  Saudi muscle hijacker on United Airlines flight 93.

**Hijazi, Raed**  California-born former Boston cabdriver arrested in Jordan in December 1999 and later executed as a terrorist linked to al Qaeda.

**Hussein, Saddam**  Dictator of Iraq, 1979–2003.

**Jarrah, Ziad**  Lebanese pilot hijacker of United Airlines flight 93.

**Kean, Thomas H.**  Governor of New Jersey, 1982–1990; Republican chair of the 9/11 Commission.

**Kerrey, Bob**  U.S. senator from Nebraska, 1989–2001; Democratic member of the 9/11 Commission.

**Khallad**  Real name Tawfiq bin Attash. Al Qaeda operative involved in the African embassy bombings and the attack on the USS *Cole*.

**Kojm, Christopher**  Deputy executive director of the 9/11 Commission.

**Lake, Anthony**  National security adviser, 1993–1997.

**Lehman, John F.**  U.S. secretary of the Navy, 1983–1987; Republican member of the 9/11 Commission.

**MacEachin, Douglas**  Chief of the CIA's Directorate of Intelligence, 1993–1995; staff member of the 9/11 Commission.

**Marcus, Daniel**  General counsel of the 9/11 Commission.

**Massoud, Ahmed Shah**  Leader of the Northern Alliance in Afghanistan; murdered by al Qaeda operatives on the eve of 9/11.

**McCain, John**  U.S. senator from Arizona, 1987–.

**Mihdhar, Khalid al**  Saudi muscle hijacker on American Airlines flight 77.

**"Mike"**  Pseudonym for a career U.S. intelligence officer; revealed after publication of *The 9/11 Commission Report* to be Michael Scheuer.

**Moqed, Majed**  Saudi muscle hijacker on American Airlines flight 77.

**Moussaoui, Zacarias**  Pilot trainee associated with al Qaeda; arrested in Minnesota shortly before 9/11.

**Mueller, Robert**  Director of the FBI, 2001–.

**Musharraf, Pervez**  Leader of Pakistan, 1999–.

**Nami, Ahmed al**  Saudi muscle hijacker on United Airlines flight 93.

**Omar, Mullah Mohammed**  Chief figure in the Taliban government in Afghanistan.

**Omari, Abdul Aziz al**  Saudi muscle hijacker on American Airlines flight 11.

**O'Neill, John**   FBI agent in charge of counterterrorism in the New York field office, 1997–2001; chief of security for the World Trade Center, 2001; killed on 9/11.

**Pavitt, James**   Career U.S. intelligence officer; deputy director for operations, CIA, 1999–2004.

**Pickard, Thomas**   Acting director of the FBI, June–September 2001.

**Powell, Colin**   U.S. secretary of state, 2001–2005.

**Qutb, Sayyid**   Egyptian author (1906–1966) of widely read works expressing extreme Islamist views.

**Rahman, Sheikh Omar Abdel**   Radical Islamist cleric from Egypt, known as "the Blind Sheikh," who took up residence in the United States and was arrested, tried, and imprisoned for participation in the 1993 World Trade Center bombing and the plot to destroy New York City landmarks.

**Reno, Janet**   U.S. attorney general, 1993–2001.

**Ressam, Ahmed**   Algerian arrested in 1999 for transporting explosives across the U.S.-Canadian border.

**Rice, Condoleezza**   National security advisor, 2001–2005; U.S. secretary of state, 2005–.

**Roemer, Timothy J.**   Member of the U.S. House of Representatives from Indiana, 1991–2003; Democratic member of the 9/11 Commission.

**Rolince, Michael**   Section chief of international terrorism operations, FBI, 1998–2002.

**Rove, Karl**   Chief political adviser to President George W. Bush, 2001–.

**Rumsfeld, Donald**   U.S. secretary of defense, 2001–2006.

**Salameh, Mohammed**   Participant in the 1993 World Trade Center bombing.

**Scheuer, Michael**   See "Mike."

**Schoomaker, Peter**   U.S. Army general; commander of the Special Operations Command, 1997–2000.

**Schroen, Gary**   Career U.S. intelligence officer; CIA station chief in Pakistan, 1996–1999.

**Senguen, Aysel**   Girlfriend of Ziad Jarrah.

**Shehhi, Marwan al**   United Arab Emirates pilot hijacker of United Airlines flight 175.

**Shehri, Mohand al**   Saudi muscle hijacker on United Airlines flight 175.

**Shehri, Wail al**   Saudi muscle hijacker on American Airlines flight 11.

**Shehri, Waleed al**   Saudi muscle hijacker on American Airlines flight 11.

**Sheikh Mohammed, Khalid**   Pakistani mastermind of the 9/11 attacks.

**Shelton, Hugh**  U.S. Army general; chairman of the Joint Chiefs of Staff, 1997–2001.

**Steinberg, James**  Deputy national security advisor, 1996–2000.

**Suqami, Satam al**  Saudi muscle hijacker on American Airlines flight 11.

**Tenet, George**  Director of central intelligence, 1997–2004.

**Thompson, James R.**  Governor of Illinois, 1977–1991; Republican member of the 9/11 Commission.

**Thompson, Larry**  Deputy U.S. attorney general, 2001–2003.

**Turab al Jordani, Abu**  Jordanian who trained terrorists at al Qaeda camps in Afghanistan.

**Watson, Dale**  Executive assistant director for counterterrorism and counterintelligence, FBI, 2001–2002.

**Wolfowitz, Paul**  U.S. deputy secretary of defense, 2001–2005.

**Woodward, Bob**  *Washington Post* correspondent and frequent author of insider books about Washington.

**Yousef, Ramzi**  Pakistani mastermind of 1993 World Trade Center bombing.

**Zawahiri, Ayman al**  Leader of Egyptian Islamic Jihad; deputy to Bin Ladin in al Qaeda.

**Zelikow, Philip D.**  Executive director of the 9/11 Commission.

**Zinni, Anthony**  U.S. Marine general; commander of U.S. Central Command, 1997–2000.

**Zubaydah, Abu**  Palestinian in al Qaeda leadership.

# Glossary of Acronyms

**CAP**   combat air patrol
**CENTCOM**   U.S. Central Command
**CIA**   Central Intelligence Agency
**CSG**   Counterterrorism Security Group
**CTC**   Counterterrorism Center
**DHS**   Department of Homeland Security
**FAA**   Federal Aviation Administration
**FBI**   Federal Bureau of Investigation
**FDNY**   New York City Fire Department
**FISA**   Foreign Intelligence Surveillance Act
**INS**   Immigration and Naturalization Service
**ISID**   Inter-Services Intelligence Directorate (Pakistan)
**JTTF**   Joint Terrorism Task Force
**KSM**   Khalid Sheikh Mohammed
**MAK**   Mektab al Khidmat (the predecessor of al Qaeda established in Pakistan in the 1980s by Bin Ladin and Abdullah Azzam)
**MON**   Memorandum of Notification
**NORAD**   North American Air Defense Command
**NSA**   National Security Agency
**NSC**   National Security Council
**NSPD**   National Security Presidential Directive
**NYPD**   New York City Police Department
**PAPD**   Port Authority (of New York and New Jersey) Police Department
**PDB**   President's Daily Brief
**SO/LIC**   Special Operations and Low-Intensity Conflict

**UAE**    United Arab Emirates
**UBL**    Usama Bin Ladin
**WMD**    weapons of mass destruction (chemical, biological, nuclear)
**WTC**    World Trade Center
**WTO**    World Trade Organization

# PART TWO

# The Document:
# *The 9/11 Commission Report*

## Preface

We present the narrative of this report and the recommendations that
flow from it to the President of the United States, the United States
Congress, and the American people for their consideration. Ten Commissioners—five Republicans and five Democrats chosen by elected
leaders from our nation's capital at a time of great partisan division—
have come together to present this report without dissent.

We have come together with a unity of purpose because our nation
demands it. September 11, 2001, was a day of unprecedented shock
and suffering in the history of the United States. The nation was
unprepared. How did this happen, and how can we avoid such tragedy
again?

To answer these questions, the Congress and the President created
the National Commission on Terrorist Attacks Upon the United States
(Public Law 107-306, November 27, 2002).

Our mandate was sweeping. The law directed us to investigate
"facts and circumstances relating to the terrorist attacks of September

11, 2001," including those relating to intelligence agencies, law enforcement agencies, diplomacy, immigration issues and border control, the flow of assets to terrorist organizations, commercial aviation, the role of congressional oversight and resource allocation, and other areas determined relevant by the Commission.

In pursuing our mandate, we have reviewed more than 2.5 million pages of documents and interviewed more than 1,200 individuals in ten countries. This included nearly every senior official from the current and previous administrations who had responsibility for topics covered in our mandate.

We have sought to be independent, impartial, thorough, and nonpartisan. From the outset, we have been committed to share as much of our investigation as we can with the American people. To that end, we held 19 days of hearings and took public testimony from 160 witnesses.

Our aim has not been to assign individual blame. Our aim has been to provide the fullest possible account of the events surrounding 9/11 and to identify lessons learned.

We learned about an enemy who is sophisticated, patient, disciplined, and lethal. The enemy rallies broad support in the Arab and Muslim world by demanding redress of political grievances, but its hostility toward us and our values is limitless. Its purpose is to rid the world of religious and political pluralism, the plebiscite, and equal rights for women. It makes no distinction between military and civilian targets. *Collateral damage* is not in its lexicon.

We learned that the institutions charged with protecting our borders, civil aviation, and national security did not understand how grave this threat could be, and did not adjust their policies, plans, and practices to deter or defeat it. We learned of fault lines within our government—between foreign and domestic intelligence, and between and within agencies. We learned of the pervasive problems of managing and sharing information across a large and unwieldy government that had been built in a different era to confront different dangers.

At the outset of our work, we said we were looking backward in order to look forward. We hope that the terrible losses chronicled in this report can create something positive—an America that is safer, stronger, and wiser. That September day, we came together as a nation. The test before us is to sustain that unity of purpose and meet the challenges now confronting us.

We want to note what we have done, and not done. We have endeavored to provide the most complete account we can of the events of September 11, what happened and why. This final report is only a summary of what we have done, citing only a fraction of the sources we have consulted. But in an event of this scale, touching so many issues and organizations, we are conscious of our limits. We have not interviewed every knowledgeable person or found every relevant piece of paper. New information inevitably will come to light. We present this report as a foundation for a better understanding of a landmark in the history of our nation.

## 1. "WE HAVE SOME PLANES"

Tuesday, September 11, 2001, dawned temperate and nearly cloudless in the eastern United States. Millions of men and women readied themselves for work. Some made their way to the Twin Towers, the signature structures of the World Trade Center complex in New York City. Others went to Arlington, Virginia, to the Pentagon. Across the Potomac River, the United States Congress was back in session. At the other end of Pennsylvania Avenue, people began to line up for a White House tour. In Sarasota, Florida, President George W. Bush went for an early morning run.

For those heading to an airport, weather conditions could not have been better for a safe and pleasant journey. Among the travelers were Mohamed Atta and Abdul Aziz al Omari, who arrived at the airport in Portland, Maine.

### Inside the Four Flights

BOSTON: AMERICAN 11 AND UNITED 175

Atta and Omari boarded a 6:00 A.M. flight from Portland to Boston's Logan International Airport.

Atta and Omari arrived in Boston at 6:45. Seven minutes later, Atta apparently took a call from Marwan al Shehhi, a longtime colleague who was at another terminal at Logan Airport. They spoke for three minutes. It would be their final conversation.

Between 6:45 and 7:40, Atta and Omari, along with Satam al Suqami, Wail al Shehri, and Waleed al Shehri, checked in and boarded American Airlines Flight 11, bound for Los Angeles. The flight was scheduled to depart at 7:45.

In another Logan terminal, Shehhi, joined by Fayez Banihammad, Mohand al Shehri, Ahmed al Ghamdi, and Hamza al Ghamdi, checked in for United Airlines Flight 175, also bound for Los Angeles. A couple of Shehhi's colleagues were obviously unused to travel; according to the United ticket agent, they had trouble understanding the standard security questions, and she had to go over them slowly until they gave the routine, reassuring answers. Their flight was scheduled to depart at 8:00.

In passing through [security] checkpoints, each [man] would have been screened by a walk-through metal detector calibrated to detect items with at least the metal content of a .22-caliber handgun. Anyone who might have set off that detector would have been screened with a hand wand—a procedure requiring the screener to identify the metal item or items that caused the alarm. In addition, an X-ray machine would have screened carry-on belongings. The screening was in place to identify and confiscate weapons and other items prohibited from being carried onto a commercial flight. None of the checkpoint supervisors recalled anything suspicious.

Atta, Omari, and Suqami took their seats in business class. The Shehri brothers had adjacent seats in the first class cabin. They boarded American 11 between 7:31 and 7:40. The aircraft pushed back from the gate at 7:40.

Shehhi and his team boarded United 175 between 7:23 and 7:28. Their aircraft pushed back from the gate just before 8:00.

WASHINGTON DULLES: AMERICAN 77

Hundreds of miles southwest of Boston, at Dulles International Airport in the Virginia suburbs of Washington, D.C., five more men were preparing to take their early morning flight. At 7:15, a pair of them, Khalid al Mihdhar and Majed Moqed, checked in at the American Airlines ticket counter for Flight 77, bound for Los Angeles. Within the next 20 minutes, they would be followed by Hani Hanjour and two brothers, Nawaf al Hazmi and Salem al Hazmi.

All five passed through the Main Terminal's west security screening checkpoint. The checkpoint featured closed-circuit television that recorded all passengers as they were screened. At 7:18, Mihdhar and Moqed entered the security checkpoint.

Mihdhar and Moqed placed their carry-on bags on the belt of the X-ray machine and proceeded through the first metal detector. Both set off the alarm, and they were directed to a second metal detector. Mihdhar did not trigger the alarm and was permitted through the checkpoint. After Moqed set it off, a screener wanded him. He passed this inspection.

About 20 minutes later, at 7:35, another passenger for Flight 77, Hani Hanjour, proceeded, without alarm, through the metal detector. A short time later, Nawaf and Salem al Hazmi entered the same checkpoint. Salem al Hazmi cleared the metal detector and was permitted through; Nawaf al Hazmi set off the alarms for both the first and second metal detectors and was then hand-wanded before being passed. The video footage indicates that he was carrying an unidentified item in his back pocket, clipped to its rim.

When the local civil aviation security office of the Federal Aviation Administration (FAA) later investigated these security screening operations, the screeners recalled nothing out of the ordinary. We asked a screening expert to review the videotape of the hand-wanding, and he found the quality of the screener's work to have been "marginal at best." The screener should have "resolved" what set off the alarm; and in the case of both Moqed and Hazmi, it was clear that he did not.

At 7:50, Majed Moqed and Khalid al Mihdhar boarded the flight and were seated in coach. Hani Hanjour, assigned to seat 1B (first class), soon followed. The Hazmi brothers joined Hanjour in the first-class cabin.

NEWARK: UNITED 93

Between 7:03 and 7:39, Saeed al Ghamdi, Ahmed al Nami, Ahmad al Haznawi, and Ziad Jarrah checked in at the United Airlines ticket counter [at Newark International Airport] for Flight 93, going to Los Angeles.

The four men passed through the security checkpoint. The FAA interviewed the screeners later; none recalled anything unusual or suspicious.

The four men boarded the plane between 7:39 and 7:48. All four had seats in the first-class cabin; their plane had no business-class section.

The 19 men were aboard four transcontinental flights. They were planning to hijack these planes and turn them into large guided missiles, loaded with up to 11,400 gallons of jet fuel. By 8:00 A.M. on the morning of Tuesday, September 11, 2001, they had defeated all the security layers that America's civil aviation security system then had in place to prevent a hijacking.

THE HIJACKING OF AMERICAN 11

American Airlines Flight 11 took off at 7:59. Just before 8:14, it had climbed to 26,000 feet, not quite its initial assigned cruising altitude of

29,000 feet. All communications and flight profile data were normal. About this time the "Fasten Seatbelt" sign would usually have been turned off and the flight attendants would have begun preparing for cabin service.

At that same time, American 11 had its last routine communication with the ground when it acknowledged navigational instructions from the FAA's air traffic control (ATC) center in Boston. Sixteen seconds after that transmission, ATC instructed the aircraft's pilots to climb to 35,000 feet. That message and all subsequent attempts to contact the flight were not acknowledged. From this and other evidence, we believe the hijacking began at 8:14 or shortly thereafter.

Reports from two flight attendants in the coach cabin, Betty Ong and Madeline "Amy" Sweeney, tell us most of what we know about how the hijacking happened. As it began, some of the hijackers— most likely Wail al Shehri and Waleed al Shehri, who were seated in row 2 in first class—stabbed the two unarmed flight attendants who would have been preparing for cabin service.

At the same time or shortly thereafter, Atta—the only terrorist on board trained to fly a jet—would have moved to the cockpit from his business-class seat, possibly accompanied by Omari. As this was happening, passenger Daniel Lewin, who was seated in the row just behind Atta and Omari, was stabbed by one of the hijackers—probably Satam al Suqami, who was seated directly behind Lewin. Lewin had served four years as an officer in the Israeli military. He may have made an attempt to stop the hijackers in front of him, not realizing that another was sitting behind him.

The hijackers quickly gained control and sprayed Mace, pepper spray, or some other irritant in the first-class cabin, in order to force the passengers and flight attendants toward the rear of the plane. They claimed they had a bomb.

About five minutes after the hijacking began, Betty Ong contacted the American Airlines Southeastern Reservations Office in Cary, North Carolina, via an AT&T airphone to report an emergency aboard the flight. The emergency call lasted approximately 25 minutes, as Ong calmly and professionally relayed information about events taking place aboard the airplane to authorities on the ground.

At 8:19, Ong reported: "The cockpit is not answering, somebody's stabbed in business class—and I think there's Mace—that we can't breathe—I don't know, I think we're getting hijacked." She then told of the stabbings of the two flight attendants.

At 8:21, one of the American employees receiving Ong's call in

North Carolina, Nydia Gonzalez, alerted the American Airlines operations center in Fort Worth, Texas, reaching Craig Marquis, the manager on duty. Marquis soon realized this was an emergency and instructed the airline's dispatcher responsible for the flight to contact the cockpit. At 8:23, the dispatcher tried unsuccessfully to contact the aircraft. Six minutes later, the air traffic control specialist in American's operations center contacted the FAA's Boston Air Traffic Control Center about the flight. The center was already aware of the problem.

Boston Center knew of a problem on the flight in part because just before 8:25 the hijackers had attempted to communicate with the passengers. The microphone was keyed, and immediately one of the hijackers said, "Nobody move. Everything will be okay. If you try to make any moves, you'll endanger yourself and the airplane. Just stay quiet." Air traffic controllers heard the transmission; Ong did not. The hijackers probably did not know how to operate the cockpit radio communication system correctly, and thus inadvertently broadcast their message over the air traffic control channel instead of the cabin public-address channel. Also at 8:25, and again at 8:29, Amy Sweeney got through to the American Flight Services Office in Boston and began relaying updates to the manager, Michael Woodward.

Sweeney calmly reported on her line that the plane had been hijacked; a man in first class had his throat slashed; two flight attendants had been stabbed—one was seriously hurt and was on oxygen while the other's wounds seemed minor; a doctor had been requested; the flight attendants were unable to contact the cockpit; and there was a bomb in the cockpit. Sweeney told Woodward that she and Ong were trying to relay as much information as they could to people on the ground.

At 8:38, Ong told Gonzalez that the plane was flying erratically again. Around this time Sweeney told Woodward that the hijackers were Middle Easterners, naming three of their seat numbers. One spoke very little English and one spoke excellent English. The hijackers had gained entry to the cockpit, and she did not know how. The aircraft was in a rapid descent.

At 8:41, Sweeney told Woodward that passengers in coach were under the impression that there was a routine medical emergency in first class. Other flight attendants were busy at duties such as getting medical supplies while Ong and Sweeney were reporting the events.

At 8:44, Gonzalez reported losing phone contact with Ong. About this same time Sweeney reported to Woodward, "Something is wrong. We are in a rapid descent . . . we are all over the place." Woodward asked Sweeney to look out the window to see if she could determine where they were. Sweeney responded: "We are flying low. We are flying very, very low. We are flying way too low." Seconds later she said, "Oh my God we are way too low." The phone call ended.

At 8:46:40, American 11 crashed into the North Tower of the World Trade Center in New York City. All on board, along with an unknown number of people in the tower, were killed instantly.

THE HIJACKING OF UNITED 175

United Airlines Flight 175 pushed back from its gate at 7:58 and departed Logan Airport at 8:14. By 8:33, it had reached its assigned cruising altitude of 31,000 feet. The flight attendants would have begun their cabin service.

The hijackers attacked sometime between 8:42 and 8:46. They used knives (as reported by two passengers and a flight attendant), Mace (reported by one passenger), and the threat of a bomb (reported by the same passenger). They stabbed members of the flight crew (reported by a flight attendant and one passenger). Both pilots had been killed (reported by one flight attendant). The eyewitness accounts came from calls made from the rear of the plane, from passengers originally seated further forward in the cabin, a sign that passengers and perhaps crew had been moved to the back of the aircraft. Given similarities to American 11 in hijacker seating and in eyewitness reports of tactics and weapons, as well as the contact between the presumed team leaders, Atta and Shehhi, we believe the tactics were similar on both flights.

At 8:52, in Easton, Connecticut, Lee Hanson received a phone call from his son Peter, a passenger on United 175. His son told him: "I think they've taken over the cockpit—An attendant has been stabbed—and someone else up front may have been killed. The plane is making strange moves. Call United Airlines—Tell them it's Flight 175, Boston to LA." Lee Hanson then called the Easton Police Department and relayed what he had heard.

At 8:59, Flight 175 passenger Brian David Sweeney called his mother, Louise Sweeney, told her the flight had been hijacked, and added that the passengers were thinking about storming the cockpit to take control of the plane away from the hijackers.

At 9:00, Lee Hanson received a second call from his son Peter:

It's getting bad, Dad—A stewardess was stabbed—They seem to have knives and Mace—They said they have a bomb—It's getting very bad on the plane—Passengers are throwing up and getting sick—The plane is making jerky movements—I don't think the pilot is flying the plane—I think we are going down—I think they intend to go to Chicago or someplace and fly into a building—Don't worry, Dad—If it happens, it'll be very fast—My God, my God.

The call ended abruptly. Lee Hanson had heard a woman scream just before it cut off. He turned on a television, and in her home so did Louise Sweeney. Both then saw the second aircraft hit the World Trade Center.

At 9:03:11, United Airlines Flight 175 struck the South Tower of the World Trade Center. All on board, along with an unknown number of people in the tower, were killed instantly.

### THE HIJACKING OF AMERICAN 77

American Airlines Flight 77 was scheduled to depart from Washington Dulles for Los Angeles at 8:10. The aircraft was a Boeing 757 [with] four flight attendants [and] 58 passengers.

American 77 pushed back from its gate at 8:09 and took off at 8:20. At 8:46, the flight reached its assigned cruising altitude of 35,000 feet. Cabin service would have begun. At 8:51, American 77 transmitted its last routine radio communication. The hijacking began between 8:51 and 8:54. As on American 11 and United 175, the hijackers used knives (reported by one passenger) and moved all the passengers (and possibly crew) to the rear of the aircraft (reported by one flight attendant and one passenger). Unlike the earlier flights, the Flight 77 hijackers were reported by a passenger to have box cutters. Finally, a passenger reported that an announcement had been made by the "pilot" that the plane had been hijacked. Neither of the firsthand accounts mentioned any stabbings or the threat or use of either a bomb or Mace, though both witnesses began the flight in the first-class cabin.

At 9:00, American Airlines Executive Vice President Gerard Arpey learned that communications had been lost with American 77. This was now the second American aircraft in trouble. He ordered all American Airlines flights in the Northeast that had not taken off to remain on the ground. After learning that United Airlines was missing a plane, American Airlines headquarters extended the ground stop nationwide.

At some point between 9:16 and 9:26, Barbara Olson called her husband, Ted Olson, the solicitor general of the United States. She reported that the flight had been hijacked, and the hijackers had knives and box cutters. She further indicated that the hijackers were not aware of her phone call, and that they had put all the passengers in the back of the plane. About a minute into the conversation, the call was cut off. Solicitor General Olson tried unsuccessfully to reach Attorney General John Ashcroft.

Shortly after the first call, Barbara Olson reached her husband again. She reported that the pilot had announced that the flight had been hijacked, and she asked her husband what she should tell the captain to do. Ted Olson asked for her location and she replied that the aircraft was then flying over houses. Another passenger told her they were traveling northeast. The solicitor general then informed his wife of the two previous hijackings and crashes. She did not display signs of panic and did not indicate any awareness of an impending crash. At that point, the second call was cut off.

At 9:34, Ronald Reagan Washington National Airport advised the Secret Service of an unknown aircraft heading in the direction of the White House. American 77 was then 5 miles west-southwest of the Pentagon and began a 330-degree turn. At the end of the turn, it was descending through 2,200 feet, pointed toward the Pentagon and downtown Washington. The hijacker pilot then advanced the throttles to maximum power and dove toward the Pentagon.

At 9:37:46, American Airlines Flight 77 crashed into the Pentagon, traveling at approximately 530 miles per hour. All on board, as well as many civilian and military personnel in the building, were killed.

THE BATTLE FOR UNITED 93

At 8:42, United Airlines Flight 93 took off from Newark (New Jersey) Liberty International Airport bound for San Francisco.

The hijackers had planned to take flights scheduled to depart at 7:45 (American 11), 8:00 (United 175 and United 93), and 8:10 (American 77). Three of the flights had actually taken off within 10 to 15 minutes of their planned departure times. United 93 would ordinarily have taken off about 15 minutes after pulling away from the gate. When it left the ground at 8:42, the flight was running more than 25 minutes late.

As United 93 left Newark, the flight's crew members were unaware of the hijacking of American 11. Around 9:00, the FAA, American, and United were facing the staggering realization of apparent multiple hijackings. At 9:03, they would see another aircraft strike the World

Trade Center. Crisis managers at the FAA and the airlines did not yet act to warn other aircraft. At the same time, Boston Center realized that a message transmitted just before 8:25 by the hijacker pilot of American 11 included the phrase, "We have some planes."

By all accounts, the first 46 minutes of Flight 93's cross-country trip proceeded routinely. Radio communications from the plane were normal. Heading, speed, and altitude ran according to plan.

The hijackers attacked at 9:28. While traveling 35,000 feet above eastern Ohio, United 93 suddenly dropped 700 feet. Eleven seconds into the descent, the FAA's air traffic control center in Cleveland received the first of two radio transmissions from the aircraft. During the first broadcast, the captain or first officer could be heard declaring "Mayday" amid the sounds of a physical struggle in the cockpit. The second radio transmission, 35 seconds later, indicated that the fight was continuing. The captain or first officer could be heard shouting: "Hey get out of here—get out of here—get out of here."

The terrorists who hijacked three other commercial flights on 9/11 operated in five-man teams. They initiated their cockpit takeover within 30 minutes of takeoff. On Flight 93, however, the takeover took place 46 minutes after takeoff and there were only four hijackers. The operative likely intended to round out the team for this flight, Mohamed al Kahtani, had been refused entry by a suspicious immigration inspector at Florida's Orlando International Airport in August.

At 9:32, a hijacker, probably Jarrah, made or attempted to make the following announcement to the passengers of Flight 93: "Ladies and Gentlemen: Here the captain, please sit down keep remaining sitting. We have a bomb on board. So, sit." The flight data recorder (also recovered) indicates that Jarrah then instructed the plane's autopilot to turn the aircraft around and head east.

The cockpit voice recorder data indicate that a woman, most likely a flight attendant, was being held captive in the cockpit. She struggled with one of the hijackers who killed or otherwise silenced her.

Shortly thereafter, the passengers and flight crew began a series of calls from GTE airphones and cellular phones. These calls between family, friends, and colleagues took place until the end of the flight and provided those on the ground with firsthand accounts. They enabled the passengers to gain critical information, including the news that two aircraft had slammed into the World Trade Center.

At least ten passengers and two crew members shared vital information with family, friends, colleagues, or others on the ground. All understood the plane had been hijacked. They said the hijackers wielded knives and claimed to have a bomb. The hijackers were wearing red bandanas, and they forced the passengers to the back of the aircraft.

Callers reported that a passenger had been stabbed and that two people were lying on the floor of the cabin, injured or dead—possibly the captain and first officer. One caller reported that a flight attendant had been killed.

Five calls described the intent of passengers and surviving crew members to revolt against the hijackers. According to one call, they voted on whether to rush the terrorists in an attempt to retake the plane. They decided, and acted.

At 9:57, the passenger assault began. Several passengers had terminated phone calls with loved ones in order to join the revolt. One of the callers ended her message as follows: "Everyone's running up to first class. I've got to go. Bye."

The cockpit voice recorder captured the sounds of the passenger assault muffled by the intervening cockpit door. Some family members who listened to the recording report that they can hear the voice of a loved one among the din. We cannot identify whose voices can be heard. But the assault was sustained.

In response, Jarrah immediately began to roll the airplane to the left and right, attempting to knock the passengers off balance. At 9:58:57, Jarrah told another hijacker in the cockpit to block the door. Jarrah continued to roll the airplane sharply left and right, but the assault continued. At 9:59:52, Jarrah changed tactics and pitched the nose of the airplane up and down to disrupt the assault. The recorder captured the sounds of loud thumps, crashes, shouts, and breaking glasses and plates. At 10:00:03, Jarrah stabilized the airplane.

Five seconds later, Jarrah asked, "Is that it? Shall we finish it off?" A hijacker responded, "No. Not yet. When they all come, we finish it off." The sounds of fighting continued outside the cockpit. Again, Jarrah pitched the nose of the aircraft up and down. At 10:00:26, a passenger in the background said, "In the cockpit. If we don't we'll die!" Sixteen seconds later, a passenger yelled, "Roll it!" Jarrah stopped the violent maneuvers at about 10:01:00 and said, "Allah is the greatest! Allah is the greatest!" He then asked another hijacker in the cockpit, "Is that it? I mean, shall we put it down?" to which the other replied, "Yes, put it in it, and pull it down."

The passengers continued their assault and at 10:02:23, a hijacker said, "Pull it down! Pull it down!" The hijackers remained at the controls but must have judged that the passengers were only seconds from overcoming them. The airplane headed down; the control wheel was turned hard to the right. The airplane rolled onto its back, and one of the hijackers began shouting "Allah is the greatest. Allah is the greatest." With the sounds of the passenger counterattack continuing, the aircraft plowed into an empty field in Shanksville, Pennsylvania, at 580 miles per hour, about 20 minutes' flying time from Washington, D.C.

Jarrah's objective was to crash his airliner into symbols of the American Republic, the Capitol or the White House. He was defeated by the alerted, unarmed passengers of United 93.

### Improvising a Homeland Defense

On 9/11, the defense of U.S. airspace depended on close interaction between two federal agencies: the FAA and the North American [Air] Defense Command (NORAD).

As of September 11, 2001, the FAA was mandated by law to regulate the safety and security of civil aviation. From an air traffic controller's perspective, that meant maintaining a safe distance between airborne aircraft. Before 9/11, it was not unheard of for a commercial aircraft to deviate slightly from its course, or for an FAA controller to lose radio contact with a pilot for a short period of time. In all of these instances, the job of the controller was to reach out to the aircraft, the parent company of the aircraft, and other planes in the vicinity in an attempt to reestablish communications and set the aircraft back on course. Alarm bells would not start ringing until these efforts—which could take five minutes or more—were tried and had failed.

NORAD is a binational command established in 1958 between the United States and Canada. Its mission was, and is, to defend the airspace of North America and protect the continent. That mission does not distinguish between internal and external threats; but because NORAD was created to counter the Soviet threat, it came to define its job as defending against external attacks.

Prior to 9/11, it was understood that an order to shoot down a commercial aircraft would have to be issued by the National Command Authority (a phrase used to describe the president and secretary of defense). Exercise planners also assumed that the aircraft would originate from outside the United States, allowing time to identify the target and scramble interceptors. The threat of terrorists hijacking commercial airliners within the United States—and using them as guided missiles—was not recognized by NORAD before 9/11.

The FAA and NORAD had developed protocols for working together in the event of a hijacking. The protocols in place on 9/11 for the FAA and NORAD to respond to a hijacking presumed that

— the hijacked aircraft would be readily identifiable and would not attempt to disappear;

— there would be time to address the problem through the appropriate FAA and NORAD chains of command; and

— the hijacking would take the traditional form: that is, it would not be a suicide hijacking designed to convert the aircraft into a guided missile.

On the morning of 9/11, the existing protocol was unsuited in every respect for what was about to happen.

* * *

### National Crisis Management

When American 11 struck the World Trade Center at 8:46, no one in the White House or traveling with the President knew that it had been hijacked. While that information circulated within the FAA, we found no evidence that the hijacking was reported to any other agency in Washington before 8:46. Most federal agencies learned about the crash in New York from CNN.

In Sarasota, Florida, the presidential motorcade was arriving at the Emma E. Booker Elementary School, where President Bush was to read to a class and talk about education. White House Chief of Staff Andrew Card told us he was standing with the President outside the classroom when Senior Advisor to the President Karl Rove first informed them that a small, twin-engine plane had crashed into the World Trade Center. The President's reaction was that the incident must have been caused by pilot error.

At 8:55, before entering the classroom, the President spoke to National Security Advisor Condoleezza Rice, who was at the White House. She recalled first telling the President it was a twin-engine aircraft—and then a commercial aircraft—that had struck the World Trade Center, adding "that's all we know right now, Mr. President."

At the White House, Vice President Dick Cheney had just sat down for a meeting when his assistant told him to turn on his television because a plane had struck the North Tower of the World Trade Center. The Vice President was wondering "how the hell could a plane hit the World Trade Center" when he saw the second aircraft strike the South Tower.

THE PRESIDENT AND THE VICE PRESIDENT

The President was seated in a classroom when, at 9:05, Andrew Card whispered to him: "A second plane hit the second tower. America is under attack." The President told us his instinct was to project calm, not to have the country see an excited reaction at a moment of crisis. The press was standing behind the children; he saw their phones and pagers start to ring. The President felt he should project strength and calm until he could better understand what was happening.

The President remained in the classroom for another five to seven minutes, while the children continued reading. He then returned to a holding room shortly before 9:15, where he was briefed by staff and saw television coverage. He next spoke to Vice President Cheney, Dr. Rice, New York Governor George Pataki, and FBI Director Robert Mueller. He decided to make a brief statement from the school before leaving for the airport. The Secret Service told us they were anxious to move the President to a safer location, but did not think it imperative for him to run out the door.

Between 9:15 and 9:30, the staff was busy arranging a return to Washington, while the President consulted his senior advisers about his remarks. No one in the traveling party had any information during this time that other aircraft were hijacked or missing. Staff was in contact with the White House Situation Room, but as far as we could determine, no one with the President was in contact with the Pentagon. The focus was on the President's statement to the nation. The only decision made during this time was to return to Washington.

The President's motorcade departed at 9:35, and arrived at the airport between 9:42 and 9:45. During the ride the President learned about the attack on the Pentagon. He boarded the aircraft, asked the Secret Service about the safety of his family, and called the Vice President. According to notes of the call, at about 9:45 the President told the Vice President: "Sounds like we have a minor war going on here, I heard about the Pentagon. We're at war . . . somebody's going to pay."

About this time, Card, the lead Secret Service agent, the President's military aide, and the pilot were conferring on a possible destination for Air Force One. The Secret Service agent felt strongly that the situation in Washington was too unstable for the President to return there, and Card agreed. The President strongly wanted to return to Washington and only grudgingly agreed to go elsewhere. The issue was still undecided when the President conferred with the Vice President at about the time Air Force One was taking off. The Vice President recalled urging the President not to return to Washington. Air Force One departed at about 9:54 without any fixed destination. The objective was to get up in the air—as fast and as high as possible—and then decide where to go.

At 9:33, the tower supervisor at Reagan National Airport picked up a hotline to the Secret Service and told the Service's operations center that "an aircraft [is] coming at you and not talking with us." This news prompted the Secret Service to order the immediate evacuation of the Vice President just before 9:36. Agents propelled him out of his chair and told him he had to get to the bunker. The Vice President entered the underground tunnel leading to the shelter at 9:37.

Once inside, Vice President Cheney and the agents paused in an area of the tunnel that had a secure phone, a bench, and television. The Vice President asked to speak to the President, but it took time for the call to be connected. He learned in the tunnel that the Pentagon had been hit, and he saw television coverage of smoke coming from the building.

UNITED 93 AND THE SHOOTDOWN ORDER

On the morning of 9/11, the President and Vice President stayed in contact not by an open line of communication but through a series of calls. The President told us he was frustrated with the poor communications that morning. He could not reach key officials, including Secretary [of Defense Donald] Rumsfeld, for a period of time. The line to the White House shelter conference room—and the Vice President— kept cutting off.

The Vice President remembered placing a call to the President just after entering the shelter conference room. There is conflicting evidence about when the Vice President arrived in the shelter conference room. We have concluded, from the available evidence, that the Vice President arrived in the room shortly before 10:00, perhaps at 9:58. The Vice President recalled being told, just after his arrival, that the Air Force was trying to establish a combat air patrol [CAP] over Washington.

The Vice President stated that he called the President to discuss the rules of engagement for the CAP. He recalled feeling that it did no good to establish the CAP unless the pilots had instructions on whether they were authorized to shoot if the plane would not divert.

He said the President signed off on that concept. The President said he remembered such a conversation, and that it reminded him of when he had been an interceptor pilot. The President emphasized to us that he had authorized the shootdown of hijacked aircraft.

Among the sources that reflect other important events of that morning, there is no documentary evidence for this call, but the relevant sources are incomplete. Others nearby who were taking notes, such as the Vice President's chief of staff, [Lewis (Scooter)] Libby, who sat next to him, and Mrs. [Lynne] Cheney, did not note a call between the President and Vice President immediately after the Vice President entered the conference room.

At 10:02, the communicators in the shelter began receiving reports from the Secret Service of an inbound aircraft—presumably hijacked— heading toward Washington. That aircraft was United 93. The Secret Service was getting this information directly from the FAA, [which] was not aware the plane was already down in Pennsylvania.

At some time between 10:10 and 10:15, a military aide told the Vice President and others that the aircraft was 80 miles out. Vice President Cheney was asked for authority to engage the aircraft. His reaction was described by Scooter Libby as quick and decisive, "in about the time it takes a batter to decide to swing." The Vice President authorized fighter aircraft to engage the inbound plane.

Minutes went by and word arrived of an aircraft down in Pennsylvania. Those in the shelter wondered if the aircraft had been shot down pursuant to this authorization.

At approximately 10:30, the shelter started receiving reports of another hijacked plane, this time only 5 to 10 miles out. Believing they had only a minute or two, the Vice President again communicated the authorization to "engage" or "take out" the aircraft. Eventually, the shelter received word that the alleged hijacker 5 miles away had been a medevac helicopter.

\* \* \*

The details of what happened on the morning of September 11 are complex, but they play out a simple theme. NORAD and the FAA were unprepared for the type of attacks launched against the United States on September 11, 2001. They struggled, under difficult circumstances, to improvise a homeland defense against an unprecedented challenge they had never before encountered and had never trained to meet.

At 10:02 that morning, an assistant to the mission crew commander at NORAD's Northeast Air Defense Sector in Rome, New York, was recorded remarking that "This is a new type of war."

He was, and is, right. But the conflict did not begin on 9/11. It had been publicly declared years earlier, most notably in a declaration faxed early in 1998 to an Arabic-language newspaper in London. Few Americans had noticed it. The fax had been sent from thousands of miles away by the followers of a Saudi exile gathered in one of the most remote and impoverished countries on earth.

## 2. THE FOUNDATION OF THE NEW TERRORISM

### A Declaration of War

In February 1998, the 40-year-old Saudi exile Usama Bin Ladin and a fugitive Egyptian physician, Ayman al Zawahiri, arranged from their Afghan headquarters for an Arabic newspaper in London to publish what they termed a fatwa issued in the name of a "World Islamic Front." A fatwa is normally an interpretation of Islamic law by a respected Islamic authority, but neither Bin Ladin, Zawahiri, nor the three others who signed this statement were scholars of Islamic law. Claiming that America had declared war against God and his messenger [the prophet Mohammed], they called for the murder of any American, anywhere on earth, as the "individual duty for every Muslim who can do it in any country in which it is possible to do it."

Though novel for its open endorsement of indiscriminate killing, Bin Ladin's 1998 declaration was only the latest in the long series of his public and private calls since 1992 that singled out the United States for attack.

In August 1996, Bin Ladin had issued his own self-styled fatwa calling on Muslims to drive American soldiers out of Saudi Arabia. The long, disjointed document condemned the Saudi monarchy for allowing the presence of an army of infidels in a land with the sites most sacred to Islam, and celebrated recent suicide bombings of American military facilities in the Kingdom. It praised the 1983 suicide bombing in Beirut [Lebanon] that killed 241 U.S. Marines, the 1992 bombing in Aden [Yemen], and especially the 1993 firefight in Somalia. [See Map 1 for a geographic reference.]

Bin Ladin said [in 1998] that he and his followers had been preparing in Somalia for another long struggle, like that against the Soviets in Afghanistan, but "the United States rushed out of Somalia in shame

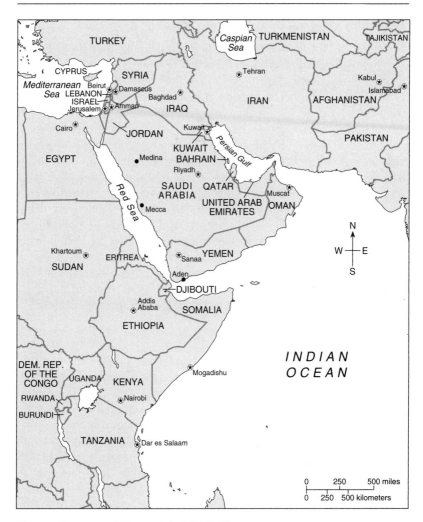

**Map 1.** *Northeast Africa and the Middle East*

and disgrace." Citing the Soviet army's withdrawal from Afghanistan [a decade earlier] as proof that a ragged army of dedicated Muslims could overcome a superpower, he told the interviewer: "We are certain that we shall—with the grace of Allah—prevail over the Americans." He went on to warn that "if the present injustice continues . . . , it will inevitably move the battle to American soil."

## Bin Ladin's Appeal in the Islamic World

How did Bin Ladin—with his call for the indiscriminate killing of Americans—win thousands of followers and some degree of approval from millions more?

The history, culture, and body of beliefs from which Bin Ladin has shaped and spread his message are largely unknown to many Americans. Seizing on symbols of Islam's past greatness, he promises to restore pride to people who consider themselves the victims of successive foreign masters. He uses cultural and religious allusions to the holy Qur'an [the primary religious text of Islam] and some of its interpreters. He appeals to people disoriented by cyclonic change as they confront modernity and globalization. His rhetoric selectively draws from multiple sources—Islam, history, and the region's political and economic malaise. He also stresses grievances against the United States widely shared in the Muslim world. He inveighed against the presence of U.S. troops in Saudi Arabia, the home of Islam's holiest sites. He spoke of the suffering of the Iraqi people as a result of sanctions imposed after the Gulf War, and he protested U.S. support of Israel.

### ISLAM

Islam (a word that literally means "surrender to the will of God") arose in Arabia with what Muslims believe are a series of revelations to the Prophet Mohammed from the one and only God, the God of Abraham and of Jesus. These revelations, conveyed by the angel Gabriel, are recorded in the Qur'an. Muslims believe that these revelations, given to the greatest and last of a chain of prophets stretching from Abraham through Jesus, complete God's message to humanity. The Hadith, which recount Mohammed's sayings and deeds as recorded by his contemporaries, are another fundamental source. A third key element is the Sharia, the code of law derived from the Qur'an and the Hadith.

Islam is divided into two main branches, Sunni and Shia. Soon after the Prophet's death, the question of choosing a new leader, or *caliph*, for the Muslim community, or *Ummah*, arose. Those who became the Shia held that any leader of the Ummah must be a direct descendant of the Prophet; those who became the Sunni argued that lineal descent was not required if the candidate met other standards of faith and knowledge. After bloody struggles, the Sunni became (and remain) the majority sect.

Many Muslims look back at the century after the revelations to the Prophet Mohammed as a golden age. Its memory is strongest among the Arabs. What happened then—the spread of Islam from the Arabian Peninsula throughout the Middle East, North Africa, and even into Europe within less than a century—seemed, and seems, miraculous. Nostalgia for Islam's past glory remains a powerful force.

Islam is both a faith and a code of conduct for all aspects of life. For many Muslims, a good government would be one guided by the moral principles of their faith. This does not necessarily translate into a desire for clerical rule and the abolition of a secular state. It does mean that some Muslims tend to be uncomfortable with distinctions between religion and state, though Muslim rulers throughout history have readily separated the two.

To extremists, such divisions, as well as the existence of parliaments and legislation, only prove these rulers to be false Muslims usurping God's authority over all aspects of life. Periodically, the Islamic world has seen surges of what, for want of a better term, is often labeled "fundamentalism." Denouncing waywardness among the faithful, some clerics have appealed for a return to observance of the literal teachings of the Qur'an and Hadith.

The extreme Islamist version of history blames the decline from Islam's golden age on the rulers and people who turned away from the true path of their religion, thereby leaving Islam vulnerable to encroaching foreign powers eager to steal their land, wealth, and even their souls.

BIN LADIN'S WORLDVIEW

Bin Ladin offers an extreme view of Islamic history designed to appeal mainly to Arabs and Sunnis. He draws on fundamentalists who blame the eventual destruction of the Caliphate on leaders who abandoned the pure path of religious devotion. He repeatedly calls on his followers to embrace martyrdom since "the walls of oppression and humiliation cannot be demolished except in a rain of bullets." For those yearning for a lost sense of order in an older, more tranquil world, he offers his "Caliphate" as an imagined alternative to today's uncertainty. For others, he offers simplistic conspiracies to explain their world.

Bin Ladin also relies heavily on the Egyptian writer Sayyid Qutb. A member of the Muslim Brotherhood executed in 1966 on charges of attempting to overthrow the government, Qutb mixed Islamic scholarship with a very superficial acquaintance with Western history and thought. Sent by the Egyptian government to study in the United States in the late 1940s, Qutb returned with an enormous loathing of Western society and history. He dismissed Western achievements as entirely material, arguing that Western society possesses "nothing that will satisfy its own conscience and justify its existence."

Three basic themes emerge from Qutb's writings. First, he claimed that the world was beset with barbarism, licentiousness, and unbelief (a condition he called *jahiliyya*, the religious term for the period of ignorance prior to the revelations given to the Prophet Mohammed). Qutb argued that humans can choose only between Islam and jahiliyya. Second, he warned that more people, including Muslims, were attracted to jahiliyya and its material comforts than to his view of Islam; jahiliyya could therefore triumph over Islam. Third, no middle ground exists in what Qutb conceived as a struggle between God and Satan. All Muslims—as he defined them—therefore must take up arms in this fight. Any Muslim who rejects his ideas is just one more nonbeliever worthy of destruction.

Bin Ladin shares Qutb's stark view, permitting him and his followers to rationalize even unprovoked mass murder as righteous defense of an embattled faith. Many Americans have wondered, "Why do 'they' hate us?" Some also ask, "What can we do to stop these attacks?"

Bin Ladin and al Qaeda have given answers to both these questions. To the first, they say that America had attacked Islam; America is responsible for all conflicts involving Muslims. Thus Americans are blamed when Israelis fight with Palestinians, when Russians fight with Chechens, when Indians fight with Kashmiri Muslims, and when the Philippine government fights ethnic Muslims in its southern islands. America is also held responsible for the governments of Muslim countries, derided by al Qaeda as "your agents." Bin Ladin has stated flatly, "Our fight against these governments is not separate from our fight against you." These charges found a ready audience among millions of Arabs and Muslims angry at the United States because of issues ranging from Iraq to Palestine to America's support for their countries' repressive rulers.

Bin Ladin's grievance with the United States may have started in reaction to specific U.S. policies but it quickly became far deeper. To the second question, what America could do, al Qaeda's answer was that America should abandon the Middle East, convert to Islam, and end the immorality and godlessness of its society and culture: "It is saddening to tell you that you are the worst civilization witnessed by the history of mankind." If the United States did not comply, it would be at war with the Islamic nation, a nation that al Qaeda's leaders said "desires death more than you desire life."

## HISTORY AND POLITICAL CONTEXT

Few fundamentalist movements in the Islamic world gained lasting political power. In the nineteenth and twentieth centuries, fundamentalists helped articulate anticolonial grievances but played little role in the overwhelmingly secular struggles for independence after World War I.

The secular regimes promised a glowing future, often tied to sweeping ideologies that called for a single, secular Arab state. However, what emerged were almost invariably autocratic regimes that were usually unwilling to tolerate any opposition.

The bankruptcy of secular, autocratic nationalism was evident across the Muslim world by the late 1970s. At the same time, these regimes had closed off nearly all paths for peaceful opposition, forcing their critics to choose silence, exile, or violent opposition. Iran's 1979 revolution swept a Shia theocracy into power. Its success encouraged Sunni fundamentalists elsewhere.

In the 1980s, awash in sudden oil wealth, Saudi Arabia competed with Shia Iran to promote its Sunni fundamentalist interpretation of Islam, Wahhabism. The Saudi government, always conscious of its duties as the custodian of Islam's holiest places, joined with wealthy Arabs from the Kingdom and other states bordering the Persian Gulf in donating money to build mosques and religious schools that could preach and teach their interpretation of Islamic doctrine. [They found] a ready audience for calls to Muslims to purify their society, reject unwelcome modernization, and adhere strictly to the Sharia.

## SOCIAL AND ECONOMIC MALAISE

In the 1970s and early 1980s, an unprecedented flood of wealth led the then largely unmodernized oil states to attempt to shortcut decades of development. They funded huge infrastructure projects, vastly expanded education, and created subsidized social welfare programs. By the late 1980s, diminishing oil revenues, the economic drain from many unprofitable development projects, and population growth made these programs unsustainable. The resulting cutbacks created enormous resentment among recipients who had come to see government largesse as their right. This resentment was further stoked by public understanding of how much oil income had gone straight into the pockets of the rulers, their friends, and their helpers.

By the 1990s, high birthrates and declining rates of infant mortality had produced a common problem throughout the Muslim world: a large, steadily increasing population of young men without any reasonable expectation of suitable or steady employment—a sure prescription for social turbulence. Many of these young men, such as the enormous number trained only in religious schools, lacked the skills needed by their societies. Far more acquired valuable skills but lived in stagnant economies that could not generate satisfying jobs. [Some] of these young men were easy targets for radicalization.

BIN LADIN'S HISTORICAL OPPORTUNITY

Most Muslims prefer a peaceful and inclusive vision of their faith, not the violent sectarianism of Bin Ladin. Among Arabs, Bin Ladin's followers are commonly nicknamed *takfiri*, or "those who define other Muslims as unbelievers," because of their readiness to demonize and murder those with whom they disagree. Yet as political, social, and economic problems created flammable societies, Bin Ladin used Islam's most extreme, fundamentalist traditions as his match. All these elements—including religion—combined in an explosive compound.

By 1998, Bin Ladin had a distinctive appeal, as he focused on attacking America. He argued that other extremists, who aimed at local rulers or Israel, did not go far enough. They had not taken on what he called "the head of the snake."

Finally, Bin Ladin had another advantage: a substantial, worldwide organization. By the time he issued his February 1998 declaration of war, Bin Ladin had nurtured that organization for nearly ten years. He could attract, train, and use recruits for ever more ambitious attacks, rallying new adherents with each demonstration that his was the movement of the future.

## The Rise of Bin Ladin and al Qaeda (1988–1992)

A decade of conflict in Afghanistan, from 1979 to 1989, gave Islamist extremists a rallying point and training field. A Communist government in Afghanistan gained power in 1978 but was unable to establish enduring control. At the end of 1979, the Soviet government sent in military units to ensure that the country would remain securely under Moscow's influence. The response was an Afghan national resistance movement that defeated Soviet forces.

Young Muslims from around the world flocked to Afghanistan [Map 2] to join as volunteers in what was seen as a "holy war"—

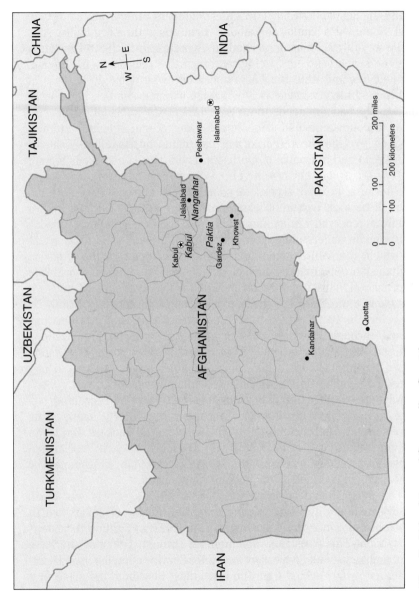

**Map 2.** *Afghanistan and Surrounding Countries*

*jihad*—against an invader. The largest numbers came from the Middle East. Some were Saudis, and among them was Usama Bin Ladin.

Twenty-three when he arrived in Afghanistan in 1980, Bin Ladin was the seventeenth of 57 children of a Saudi construction magnate. Six feet five and thin, Bin Ladin appeared to be ungainly but was in fact quite athletic, skilled as a horseman, runner, climber, and soccer player. He had attended Abdul Aziz University in Saudi Arabia. By some accounts, he had been interested there in religious studies, inspired by tape recordings of fiery sermons by Abdullah Azzam, a Palestinian and a disciple of Qutb. Bin Ladin was conspicuous among the volunteers not because he showed evidence of religious learning but because he had access to some of his family's huge fortune. Though he took part in at least one actual battle, he became known chiefly as a person who generously helped fund the anti-Soviet jihad.

Bin Ladin understood better than most of the volunteers the extent to which the continuation and eventual success of the jihad in Afghanistan depended on an increasingly complex, almost worldwide organization. This organization included a financial support network that came to be known as the "Golden Chain," put together mainly by financiers in Saudi Arabia and the Persian Gulf states. Donations flowed through charities or other nongovernmental organizations (NGOs). Bin Ladin and the "Afghan Arabs" drew largely on funds raised by this network, whose agents roamed world markets to buy arms and supplies for the mujahideen, or "holy warriors."

Mosques, schools, and boardinghouses served as recruiting stations in many parts of the world, including the United States. Some were set up by Islamic extremists or their financial backers. Bin Ladin had an important part in this activity. He and the cleric Azzam had joined in creating a "Bureau of Services" (Mektab al Khidmat, or MAK), which channeled recruits into Afghanistan.

The international environment for Bin Ladin's efforts was ideal. Saudi Arabia and the United States supplied billions of dollars' worth of secret assistance to rebel groups in Afghanistan fighting the Soviet occupation. This assistance was funneled through Pakistan: the Pakistani military intelligence service (Inter-Services Intelligence Directorate, or ISID), helped train the rebels and distribute the arms. But Bin Ladin and his comrades had their own sources of support and training, and they received little or no assistance from the United States.

April 1988 brought victory for the Afghan jihad. Moscow declared it would pull its military forces out of Afghanistan within the next nine months. As the Soviets began their withdrawal, the jihad's leaders debated what to do next.

Bin Ladin and Azzam agreed that the organization successfully created for Afghanistan should not be allowed to dissolve. They established what they called a base or foundation (al Qaeda) as a potential general headquarters for future jihad. Though Azzam had been considered number one in the MAK, by August 1988 Bin Ladin was clearly the leader (*emir*) of al Qaeda. This organization's structure included as its operating arms an intelligence component, a military committee, a financial committee, a political committee, and a committee in charge of media affairs and propaganda. It also had an Advisory Council (Shura) made up of Bin Ladin's inner circle.

Bin Ladin's assumption of the helm of al Qaeda was evidence of his growing self-confidence and ambition. He soon made clear his desire for unchallenged control and for preparing the mujahideen to fight anywhere in the world. Azzam, by contrast, favored continuing to fight in Afghanistan until it had a true Islamist government. And, as a Palestinian, he saw Israel as the top priority for the next stage.

Whether the dispute was about power, personal differences, or strategy, it ended on November 24, 1989, when a remotely controlled car bomb killed Azzam and both of his sons. The killers were assumed to be rival Egyptians. The outcome left Bin Ladin indisputably in charge of what remained of the MAK and al Qaeda.

[Bin Ladin returned to Saudi Arabia from Afghanistan but attacked the Saudi government for allowing American infidels to base military forces in the country during and after the Persian Gulf War of 1991. In 1992, he moved to Sudan at the invitation of that country's radical Islamist regime.]

\* \* \*

ATTACKS KNOWN AND SUSPECTED

After U.S. troops deployed to Somalia in late 1992, al Qaeda leaders formulated a fatwa demanding their eviction. In December, bombs exploded at two hotels in Aden where U.S. troops routinely stopped en route to Somalia, killing two, but no Americans. The perpetrators are reported to have belonged to a group from southern Yemen headed by a Yemeni member of Bin Ladin's Islamic Army Shura; some in the group had trained at an al Qaeda camp in Sudan.

Al Qaeda leaders set up a Nairobi cell and used it to send weapons and trainers to the Somali warlords battling U.S. forces, an operation directly supervised by al Qaeda's military leader. Scores of trainers flowed to Somalia over the ensuing months, including most of the senior members and weapons training experts of al Qaeda's military committee. These trainers were later heard boasting that their assistance led to the October 1993 shootdown of two U.S. Black Hawk helicopters by members of a Somali militia group and to the subsequent withdrawal of U.S. forces in early 1994.

In November 1995, a car bomb exploded outside a Saudi-U.S. joint facility in Riyadh for training the Saudi National Guard. Five Americans and two officials from India were killed. The Saudi government arrested four perpetrators, who admitted being inspired by Bin Ladin. They were promptly executed. Though nothing proves that Bin Ladin ordered this attack, U.S. intelligence subsequently learned that al Qaeda leaders had decided a year earlier to attack a U.S. target in Saudi Arabia, and had shipped explosives to the peninsula for this purpose. Some of Bin Ladin's associates later took credit.

In June 1996, an enormous truck bomb detonated in the Khobar Towers residential complex in Dhahran, Saudi Arabia, that housed U.S. Air Force personnel. Nineteen Americans were killed, and 372 were wounded. The operation was carried out principally, perhaps exclusively, by Saudi Hezbollah, an organization that had received support from the government of Iran. While the evidence of Iranian involvement is strong, there are also signs that al Qaeda played some role, as yet unknown.

\* \* \*

## Al Qaeda's Renewal in Afghanistan (1996–1998)

[Divided internally and under pressure from both Saudi Arabia and the United States, the Sudanese regime made Sudan an increasingly less welcoming place for Bin Ladin. In May 1996, he moved back to Afghanistan.]

Pakistan was the nation that held the key to his ability to use Afghanistan as a base from which to revive his ambitious enterprise for war against the United States.

From the 1970s onward, religion had become an increasingly powerful force in Pakistani politics. After a coup in 1977, military leaders turned to Islamist groups for support, and fundamentalists became more prominent. South Asia had an indigenous form of Islamic fundamentalism, which had developed in the nineteenth century at a school in the Indian village of Deoband. The influence of the Wahhabi school of Islam had also grown, nurtured by Saudi-funded institutions. Moreover, the fighting in Afghanistan made Pakistan home to an enormous population of Afghan refugees.

Pakistan's rulers found these multitudes of ardent young Afghans a source of potential trouble at home but potentially useful abroad. Those who joined the Taliban movement, espousing a ruthless version of Islamic law, perhaps could bring order in chaotic Afghanistan and make it a cooperative ally. They thus might give Pakistan greater security on one of the several borders where Pakistani military officers hoped for what they called "strategic depth."

\* \* \*

Bin Ladin eventually enjoyed a strong financial position in Afghanistan, thanks to Saudi and other financiers associated with the Golden Chain. Through his relationship with [the Taliban leader] Mullah Omar—and the monetary and other benefits that it brought the Taliban—Bin Ladin was able to circumvent restrictions; Mullah Omar would stand by him even when other Taliban leaders raised objections. The Taliban seemed to open the doors to all who wanted to come to Afghanistan to train in the camps. The alliance with the Taliban provided al Qaeda a sanctuary in which to train and indoctrinate fighters and terrorists, import weapons, forge ties with other jihad groups and leaders, and plot and staff terrorist schemes. While Bin Ladin maintained his own al Qaeda guesthouses and camps for vetting and training recruits, he also provided support to and benefited from the broad infrastructure of such facilities in Afghanistan made available to the global network of Islamist movements. U.S. intelligence estimates put the total number of fighters who underwent instruction in Bin Ladin–supported camps in Afghanistan from 1996 through 9/11 at 10,000 to 20,000.

In addition to training fighters and special operators, this larger network of guesthouses and camps provided a mechanism by which al Qaeda could screen and vet candidates for induction into its own organization. Thousands flowed through the camps, but no more than a few hundred seem to have become al Qaeda members. From the time of its founding, al Qaeda had employed training and indoctrination to identify "worthy" candidates.

Al Qaeda continued meanwhile to collaborate closely with the many Middle Eastern groups—in Egypt, Algeria, Yemen, Lebanon, Morocco,

Tunisia, Somalia, and elsewhere—with which it had been linked when Bin Ladin was in Sudan. It also reinforced its London base and its other offices around Europe. Bin Ladin bolstered his links to extremists in South and Southeast Asia.

The February 1998 fatwa thus seems to have been a kind of public launch of a renewed and stronger al Qaeda, after a year and a half of work. Having rebuilt his fund-raising network, Bin Ladin had again become the rich man of the jihad movement. He had maintained or restored many of his links with terrorists elsewhere in the world. And he had strengthened the internal ties in his own organization.

The inner core of al Qaeda continued to be a hierarchical top-down group with defined positions, tasks, and salaries. Most but not all in this core swore fealty (or *bayat*) to Bin Ladin. Other operatives were committed to Bin Ladin or to his goals and would take assignments for him, but they did not swear bayat and maintained, or tried to maintain, some autonomy. A looser circle of adherents might give money to al Qaeda or train in its camps but remained essentially independent. Nevertheless, they constituted a potential resource for al Qaeda.

Al Qaeda's role in organizing terrorist operations had also changed. Before the move to Afghanistan, it had concentrated on providing funds, training, and weapons for actions carried out by members of allied groups. The attacks on the U.S. embassies in East Africa in the summer of 1998 would take a different form—planned, directed, and executed by al Qaeda, under the direct supervision of Bin Ladin and his chief aides.

\* \* \*

THE EMBASSY BOMBINGS

On the morning of August 7, [1998,] bomb-laden trucks drove into [two U.S.] embassies roughly five minutes apart—about 10:35 A.M. in Nairobi [Kenya] and 10:39 A.M. in Dar es Salaam [Tanzania]. Shortly afterward, a phone call was placed from Baku [Azerbaijan] to London. The previously prepared messages were then faxed to London.

The attack on the U.S. embassy in Nairobi destroyed the embassy and killed 12 Americans and 201 others, almost all Kenyans. About 5,000 people were injured. The attack on the U.S. embassy in Dar es Salaam killed 11 more people, none of them Americans. Interviewed later about the deaths of the Africans, Bin Ladin answered that "when it becomes apparent that it would be impossible to repel these

Americans without assaulting them, even if this involved the killing of Muslims, this is permissible under Islam." Asked if he had indeed masterminded these bombings, Bin Ladin said that the World Islamic Front for jihad against "Jews and Crusaders" had issued a "crystal clear" fatwa. If the instigation for jihad against the Jews and the Americans to liberate the holy places "is considered a crime," he said, "let history be a witness that I am a criminal."

# 3. COUNTERTERRORISM EVOLVES

In chapter 2, we described the growth of a new kind of terrorism, and a new terrorist organization—especially from 1988 to 1998, when Usama Bin Ladin declared war and organized the bombing of two U.S. embassies. In this chapter, we trace the parallel evolution of government efforts to counter terrorism by Islamic extremists against the United States.

We mention many personalities in this report. As in any study of the U.S. government, some of the most important characters are institutions. We will introduce various agencies, and how they adapted to a new kind of terrorism.

## From the Old Terrorism to the New: The First World Trade Center Bombing

At 18 minutes after noon on February 26, 1993, a huge bomb went off beneath the two towers of the World Trade Center. This was not a suicide attack. The terrorists parked a truck bomb with a timing device on Level B-2 of the underground garage, then departed. The ensuing explosion opened a hole seven stories up. Six people died. More than a thousand were injured. An FBI agent at the scene described the relatively low number of fatalities as a miracle.

Four features of this episode have significance for the story of 9/11.

First, the bombing signaled a new terrorist challenge, one whose rage and malice had no limit. Ramzi Yousef, the Sunni extremist who planted the bomb, said later that he had hoped to kill 250,000 people.

Second, the FBI and the Justice Department did excellent work investigating the bombing. Within days, the FBI identified a truck remnant as part of a Ryder rental van reported stolen in Jersey City the day before the bombing.

Mohammed Salameh, who had rented the truck and reported it stolen, kept calling the rental office to get back his $400 deposit. The FBI arrested him there on March 4, 1993. In short order, the Bureau had several [other] plotters in custody. It quickly became clear that Yousef had been a central player in the attack. He had fled to Pakistan immediately after the bombing and would remain at large for nearly two years.

The arrests led the FBI to the Farouq mosque in Brooklyn, where a central figure was Sheikh Omar Abdel Rahman, an extremist Sunni Muslim cleric who had moved to the United States from Egypt in 1990. In speeches and writings, the sightless Rahman, often called the "Blind Sheikh," preached the message of Sayyid Qutb's *Milestones*, characterizing the United States as the oppressor of Muslims world-wide and asserting that it was their religious duty to fight against God's enemies. An FBI informant learned of a plan to bomb major New York landmarks, including the Holland and Lincoln tunnels. Disrupting this "landmarks plot," the FBI in June 1993 arrested Rahman and various confederates.

As a result of the investigations and arrests, the U.S. Attorney for the Southern District of New York prosecuted and convicted multiple individuals for crimes related to the World Trade Center bombing and other plots.

An unfortunate consequence of this superb investigative and prosecutorial effort was that it created an impression that the law enforcement system was well-equipped to cope with terrorism. Neither President Clinton, his principal advisers, the Congress, nor the news media felt prompted, until later, to press the question of whether the procedures that put the Blind Sheikh and Ramzi Yousef behind bars would really protect Americans against the new virus of which these individuals were just the first symptoms.

Third, the successful use of the legal system to address the first World Trade Center bombing had the side effect of obscuring the need to examine the character and extent of the new threat facing the United States.

Fourth, although the bombing heightened awareness of a new terrorist danger, successful prosecutions contributed to widespread underestimation of the threat. The government's attorneys stressed the seriousness of the crimes, and put forward evidence of Yousef's technical ingenuity. Yet the public image that persisted was not of clever Yousef but of stupid Salameh going back again and again to reclaim his $400 truck rental deposit.

## Adaptation — and Nonadaptation — in the Law Enforcement Community

Legal processes were the primary method for responding to these early manifestations of a new type of terrorism. Our overview of U.S. capabilities for dealing with it thus begins with the nation's vast complex of law enforcement agencies.

### THE JUSTICE DEPARTMENT AND THE FBI

At the federal level, much law enforcement activity is concentrated in the Department of Justice. For countering terrorism, the dominant agency under Justice is the Federal Bureau of Investigation. The FBI does not have a general grant of authority but instead works under specific statutory authorizations. Most of its work is done in local offices called field offices. There are 56 of them, each covering a specified geographic area, and each quite separate from all others. Prior to 9/11, the special agent in charge was in general free to set his or her office's priorities and assign personnel accordingly.

The [field] office's priorities were driven by two primary concerns. First, performance in the Bureau was generally measured against statistics such as numbers of arrests, indictments, prosecutions, and convictions. Counterterrorism and counterintelligence work, often involving lengthy intelligence investigations that might never have positive or quantifiable results, was not career-enhancing. Most agents who reached management ranks had little counterterrorism experience. Second, priorities were driven at the local level by the field offices, whose concerns centered on traditional crimes such as white-collar offenses and those pertaining to drugs and gangs. Individual field offices made choices to serve local priorities, not national priorities.

The Bureau also operates under an "office of origin" system. To avoid duplication and possible conflicts, the FBI designates a single office to be in charge of an entire investigation. Because the New York Field Office indicted Bin Ladin prior to the East Africa bombings, it became the office of origin for all Bin Ladin cases. Most of the FBI's institutional knowledge on Bin Ladin and al Qaeda resided there. Field offices other than the specified office of origin were often reluctant to spend much energy on matters over which they had no control and for which they received no credit.

The FBI's domestic intelligence gathering dates from the 1930s. With World War II looming, President Franklin D. Roosevelt ordered

FBI Director J. Edgar Hoover to investigate foreign and foreign-inspired subversion—Communist, Nazi, and Japanese. Hoover added investigation of possible espionage, sabotage, or subversion to the duties of field offices. After the war, the FBI's domestic intelligence activities kept growing.

Decades of encouragement to perform as a domestic intelligence agency abruptly ended in the 1970s. Two years after Hoover's death in 1972, congressional and news media investigations of the Watergate scandals of the Nixon administration expanded into general investigations of foreign and domestic intelligence. They disclosed a covert action program against domestic organizations and, eventually, domestic dissidents. The FBI had spied on a wide range of political figures, especially individuals whom Hoover wanted to discredit (notably the Reverend Martin Luther King, Jr.), and had authorized unlawful wire-taps and surveillance. The shock registered in public opinion polls, where the percentage of Americans declaring a "highly favorable" view of the FBI dropped from 84 percent to 37 percent. The FBI's Domestic Intelligence Division was dissolved.

[In the 1970s, the FBI began to be assigned more responsibility for counterterrorism, but Justice Department guidelines] took account of the reality that suspicion of "terrorism," like suspicion of "subversion," could lead to making individuals targets for investigation more because of their beliefs than because of their acts. [These] guidelines also took account of the reality that potential terrorists were often members of extremist religious organizations and that investigation of terrorism could cross the line separating state and church.

In 1986, Congress authorized the FBI to investigate terrorist attacks against Americans that occur outside the United States. Three years later, it added authority for the FBI to make arrests abroad without consent from the host country.

In 1993, President Clinton chose Louis Freeh as the Director of the Bureau. Freeh, who would remain Director until June 2001, recognized terrorism as a major threat. He increased the number of legal attaché offices abroad, focusing in particular on the Middle East. He also urged agents not to wait for terrorist acts to occur before taking action.

LEGAL CONSTRAINTS ON THE FBI AND "THE WALL"

The FBI had different tools for law enforcement and intelligence. For criminal matters, it could apply for and use traditional criminal warrants. For intelligence matters involving international terrorism, however, the rules were different. [In] 1978 Congress passed the Foreign Intelligence Surveillance Act [FISA]. This law was interpreted by the courts to require that a search be approved only if its "primary purpose" was to obtain foreign intelligence information.

In July 1995, Attorney General [Janet] Reno issued formal procedures [regulating] the manner in which such information could be shared from the intelligence side of the house to the criminal side.

These procedures were almost immediately misunderstood and misapplied. Over time the procedures came to be referred to as "the wall." Agents in the field began to believe—incorrectly—that no FISA information could be shared with agents working on criminal investigations.

This perception evolved into the still more exaggerated belief that the FBI could not share *any* intelligence information with criminal investigators.

OTHER LAW ENFORCEMENT AGENCIES

The Justice Department is much more than the FBI. It also has a U.S. Marshals Service, almost 4,000 strong on 9/11 and especially expert in tracking fugitives, with much local police knowledge. The department's Drug Enforcement Administration had, as of 2001, more than 4,500 agents. The Immigration and Naturalization Service (INS), with its 9,000 Border Patrol agents, 4,500 inspectors, and 2,000 immigration special agents, had perhaps the greatest potential to develop an expanded role in counterterrorism.

The chief vehicle for INS and for state and local participation in law enforcement was the Joint Terrorism Task Force (JTTF), first tried out in New York City in 1980 in response to a spate of incidents involving domestic terrorist organizations. This task force was managed by the New York Field Office of the FBI, and its existence provided an opportunity to exchange information and, as happened after the first World Trade Center bombing, to enlist local officers, as well as other agency representatives, as partners in the FBI investigation. The FBI expanded the number of JTTFs throughout the 1990s, and by 9/11 there were 34. While useful, the JTTFs had limitations. They set priorities in accordance with regional and field office concerns, and most were not fully staffed. Many state and local entities believed they had little to gain from having a full-time representative on a JTTF.

Other federal law enforcement resources, also not seriously enlisted for counterterrorism, were to be found in the Treasury Department [which] housed the Secret Service, the Customs Service, and the Bureau of Alcohol, Tobacco, and Firearms.

Before 9/11, with the exception of one portion of the FBI, very little of the sprawling U.S. law enforcement community was engaged in countering terrorism.

* * *

## ... and in the Intelligence Community

The National Security Act of 1947 created the position of Director of Central Intelligence (DCI). Independent from the departments of Defense, State, Justice, and other policy departments, the DCI heads the U.S. intelligence community and provides intelligence to federal entities.

The sole element of the intelligence community independent from a cabinet agency is the CIA. As an independent agency, it collects, analyzes, and disseminates intelligence from all sources. The CIA's number one customer is the president of the United States, who also has the authority to direct it to conduct covert operations. Although covert actions represent a very small fraction of the Agency's entire budget, these operations have at times been controversial and over time have dominated the public's perception of the CIA.

Intelligence agencies under the Department of Defense account for approximately 80 percent of all U.S. spending for intelligence, including some that supports a national customer base and some that supports specific Defense Department or military service needs. As they are housed in the Defense Department, these agencies are keenly attentive to the military's strategic and tactical requirements.

One of the intelligence agencies in Defense with a national customer base is the National Security Agency [NSA], which intercepts and analyzes foreign communications and breaks codes. The NSA also creates codes and ciphers to protect government information.

The National Security Agency's intercepts of terrorist communications often set off alarms elsewhere in the government. Often, too, its intercepts are conclusive elements in the analyst's jigsaw puzzle. NSA engineers build technical systems to break ciphers and to make sense of today's complex signals environment. Its analysts listen to conversations between foreigners not meant for them. They also perform "traffic analysis"—studying technical communications systems and codes as well as foreign organizational structures, including those of terrorist organizations.

The law requires the NSA to not deliberately collect data on U.S. citizens or on persons in the United States without a warrant based on foreign intelligence requirements. Later in this story, we will learn that while the NSA had the technical capability to report on communications with suspected terrorist facilities in the Middle East, the NSA did not seek warrants to collect communications between individuals in the United States and foreign countries, because it believed that this was an FBI role. It also did not want to be viewed as targeting persons in the United States and possibly violating laws that governed NSA's collection of foreign intelligence.

## THE CIA

The CIA is a descendant of the Office of Strategic Services (OSS), which President Roosevelt created early in World War II after having first thought the FBI might take that role. The father of the OSS was William J. "Wild Bill" Donovan, a Wall Street lawyer. He recruited into the OSS others like himself—well traveled, well connected, well-to-do professional men and women.

## CLANDESTINE AND COVERT ACTION

With this history, the CIA brought to the era of 9/11 many attributes of an elite organization, viewing itself as serving on the nation's front lines to engage America's enemies. Officers in its Clandestine Service, under what became the Directorate of Operations, fanned out into stations abroad. Each chief of station was a very important person in the organization. In this decentralized system, analogous in some ways to the culture of the FBI field offices in the United States, everyone in the Directorate of Operations presumed that it was the job of headquarters to support the field, rather than manage field activities.

In the 1960s, the CIA suffered exposure of its botched effort to land Cuban exiles at the Bay of Pigs. The Vietnam War brought on more criticism. A prominent feature of the Watergate era was investigations of the CIA by committees headed by Frank Church in the Senate and Otis Pike in the House [of Representatives]. They published evidence that the CIA had secretly planned to assassinate Fidel Castro and other foreign leaders. The President had not taken plain responsibility for these judgments. CIA officials had taken most of the blame, saying they had done so in order to preserve the President's "plausible deniability."

During the 1990s, tension sometimes arose between policymakers who wanted the CIA to undertake more aggressive covert action and wary CIA leaders who counseled prudence and making sure that the legal basis and presidential authorization for their actions were undeniably clear.

ANALYSIS

The CIA's Directorate of Intelligence retained some of its original character of a university gone to war. Its men and women tended to judge one another by the quantity and quality of their publications (in this case, classified publications). Apart from their own peers, they looked for approval and guidance to policymakers. During the 1990s and today, particular value is attached to having a contribution included in one of the classified daily "newspapers"—the Senior Executive Intelligence Brief—or, better still, selected for inclusion in the President's Daily Brief.

The CIA had been created to wage the Cold War. Its steady focus on one or two primary adversaries, decade after decade, had at least one positive effect: it created an environment in which managers and analysts could safely invest time and resources in basic research, detailed and reflective. Payoffs might not be immediate. But when they wrote their estimates, even in brief papers, they could draw on a deep base of knowledge.

When the Cold War ended, those investments could not easily be reallocated to new enemies. The cultural effects ran even deeper. In a more fluid international environment with uncertain, changing goals and interests, intelligence managers no longer felt they could afford such a patient, strategic approach to long-term accumulation of intellectual capital. A university culture with its versions of books and articles was giving way to the culture of the newsroom.

\* \* \*

EARLY COUNTERTERRORISM EFFORTS

In the 1970s and 1980s, terrorism had been tied to regional conflicts, mainly in the Middle East. The majority of terrorist groups either were sponsored by governments or, like the Palestine Liberation Organization, were militants trying to create governments.

In the mid-1980s, on the basis of a report from a task force headed by Vice President George H. W. Bush and after terrorist attacks at airports in Rome and Athens, the DCI created a Counterterrorist Center to unify activities across the Directorate of Operations and the Directorate of Intelligence. The Counterterrorist Center had representation from the FBI and other agencies. In the formal table of organization it reported to the DCI, but in fact most of the Center's chiefs belonged to the Clandestine Service and usually looked for guidance to the head of the Directorate of Operations.

The Center stimulated and coordinated collection of information by CIA stations, compiled the results, and passed selected reports to appropriate stations, the Directorate of Intelligence analysts, other parts of the intelligence community, or to policymakers. The Center protected its bureaucratic turf. The Director of Central Intelligence had once had a national intelligence officer for terrorism to coordinate analysis; that office was abolished in the late 1980s and its duties absorbed in part by the Counterterrorist Center. Though analysts assigned to the Center produced a large number of papers, the focus was support to operations. A CIA inspector general's report in 1994 criticized the Center's capacity to provide warning of terrorist attacks.

Subsequent chapters will raise the issue of whether, despite tremendous talent, energy, and dedication, the intelligence community failed to do enough in coping with the challenge from Bin Ladin and al Qaeda. Confronted with such questions, managers in the intelligence community often responded that they had meager resources with which to work.

## . . . and in the State Department and the Defense Department

### THE STATE DEPARTMENT

Until the late 1950s, the [State Department] dominated the processes of advising the president and Congress on U.S. relations with the rest of the world. The State Department retained primacy until the 1960s, when the Kennedy and Johnson administrations turned instead to Robert McNamara's Defense Department, where a mini–state department was created to analyze foreign policy issues. President Richard Nixon then concentrated policy planning and policy coordination in a powerful National Security Council staff, overseen by Henry Kissinger. In later years, individual secretaries of state were important figures, but the department's role continued to erode.

President Reagan's second secretary of state, George Shultz, advocated active U.S. efforts to combat terrorism. Though Shultz elevated the status and visibility of counterterrorism coordination, the department continued to be dominated by regional bureaus for which terrorism was not a first-order concern.

## THE DEPARTMENT OF DEFENSE

The Department of Defense is the behemoth among federal agencies. With an annual budget larger than the gross domestic product of Russia, it is an empire. The Pentagon first became concerned about terrorism as a result of hostage taking in the 1970s. The Army set about creating the Delta Force, one of whose missions was hostage rescue.

The first test for the new force did not go well. It came in April 1980 during the Iranian hostage crisis, when [a rescue] mission [was] aborted [with the] loss of eight aircraft, five airmen, and three marines. Remembered as "Desert One," this failure remained vivid for members of the armed forces.

A decade later, [in Somalia] two Black Hawk helicopters were shot down, 73 Americans were wounded, 18 were killed, and the world's television screens showed images of an American corpse dragged through the streets by exultant Somalis. "Black Hawk down" joined "Desert One" as a symbol [of] the risks of daring exploits without maximum preparation, overwhelming force, and a well-defined mission.

The Department of Defense, like the Department of State, had a coordinator who represented the department on the interagency committee concerned with counterterrorism. By the end of President Clinton's first term, this official had become the assistant secretary of defense for special operations and low-intensity conflict. The experience of the 1980s had suggested to the military establishment that if it were to have a role in counterterrorism, it would be a traditional military role—to act against state sponsors of terrorism. And the military had what seemed an excellent example of how to do it. In 1986, a bomb went off at a disco in Berlin, killing two American soldiers. Intelligence clearly linked the bombing to Libya's Colonel Muammar Qadhafi. President Reagan ordered air strikes against Libya.

Evidence accumulated later, including the 1988 bombing of Pan Am 103, clearly showed that the operation did not curb Qadhafi's interest in terrorism. However, it was seen at the time as a success. The lesson then taken from Libya was that terrorism could be stopped by the use of U.S. air power that inflicted pain on the authors or sponsors of terrorist acts. What remained was the hard question of how deterrence could be effective when the adversary was a loose transnational network.

## . . . and in the White House

Because coping with terrorism was not (and is not) the sole province of any component of the U.S. government, some coordinating mechanism is necessary. When terrorism was not a prominent issue, the State Department could perform this role. When the Iranian hostage crisis developed, this procedure went by the board: National Security Advisor Zbigniew Brzezinski took charge of crisis management. The Reagan administration continued and formalized the practice of having presidential staff coordinate counterterrorism. When President Clinton took office, he decided right away to coordinate counterterrorism from the White House. On January 25, 1993, Mir Amal Kansi, an Islamic extremist from Pakistan, shot and killed two CIA employees at the main highway entrance to CIA headquarters in Virginia. (Kansi drove away and was captured abroad much later.) Only a month afterward came the World Trade Center bombing.

President Clinton's first national security advisor, Anthony Lake, had retained from the Bush administration the staffer who dealt with crime, narcotics, and terrorism (a portfolio often known as "drugs and thugs"), the veteran civil servant Richard Clarke. President Clinton and Lake turned to Clarke to do the staff work for them in coordinating counterterrorism. Before long, he would chair a midlevel interagency committee eventually titled the Counterterrorism Security Group (CSG). We will later tell of Clarke's evolution as adviser on and, in time, manager of the U.S. counterterrorist effort.

When announcing his new national security team after being reelected in 1996, President Clinton mentioned terrorism first in a list of several challenges facing the country. In 1998, after Bin Ladin's fatwa and other alarms, President Clinton accepted a proposal from his national security advisor, Samuel "Sandy" Berger, and gave Clarke a new position as national coordinator for security, infrastructure protection, and counterterrorism. He issued two Presidential Decision Directives, numbers 62 and 63, that laid out ten program areas for counterterrorism and enhanced, at least on paper, Clarke's authority to police these assignments.

Clarke also was awarded a seat on the cabinet-level Principals Committee when it met on his issues—a highly unusual step for a White House staffer. His interagency body, the CSG, ordinarily reported to the Deputies Committee of subcabinet officials, unless Berger asked them to report directly to the principals. [Directive number 63] defined the elements of the nation's critical infrastructure and considered ways to protect it. Taken together, the two directives basically left the Justice Department and the FBI in charge at home and left terrorism abroad to the CIA, the State Department, and other agencies, under Clarke's and Berger's coordinating hands.

\* \* \*

## . . . and in the Congress

Congress as a whole, like the executive branch, adjusted slowly to the rise of transnational terrorism as a threat to national security. In particular, the growing threat and capabilities of Bin Ladin were not understood in Congress. As the most representative branch of the federal government, Congress closely tracks trends in what public opinion and the electorate identify as key issues. In the years before September 11, terrorism seldom registered as important. To the extent that terrorism did break through and engage the attention of the Congress as a whole, it would briefly command attention after a specific incident, and then return to a lower rung on the public policy agenda.

Several points about Congress are worth noting. First, Congress always has a strong orientation toward domestic affairs. It usually takes on foreign policy and national security issues after threats are identified and articulated by the administration.

Second, Congress tends to follow the overall lead of the president on budget issues with respect to national security matters.

Third, Congress did not reorganize itself after the end of the Cold War to address new threats.

Fourth, the oversight function of Congress has diminished over time. [Director of Central Intelligence George] Tenet told us: "We ran from threat to threat to threat. . . . [T]here was not a system in place to say, 'You got to go back and do this and this and this.'"

Fifth, on certain issues, other priorities pointed Congress in a direction that was unhelpful in meeting the threats that were emerging in the months leading up to 9/11. Committees with oversight responsibility for aviation focused overwhelmingly on airport congestion and the economic health of the airlines, not aviation security. Committees with responsibility for the INS focused on the Southwest border, not on terrorists.

Each of these trends contributed to what can only be described as Congress's slowness and inadequacy in treating the issue of terrorism in the years before 9/11. Terrorism was a second- or third-order priority within the committees of Congress responsible for national security.

# 4. RESPONSES TO AL QAEDA'S INITIAL ASSAULTS

## Before the Bombings in Kenya and Tanzania

Although [a] 1995 National Intelligence Estimate had warned of a new type of terrorism, many officials continued to think of terrorists as agents of states (Saudi Hezbollah acting for Iran against Khobar Towers) or as domestic criminals (Timothy McVeigh in Oklahoma City). [The] White House is not a natural locus for program management. Hence, government efforts to cope with terrorism were essentially the work of individual agencies.

Richard Clarke and his interagency Counterterrorism Security Group (CSG) might prod or push agencies to act, [but] what actually happened was usually decided at the State Department, the Pentagon, the CIA, or the Justice Department. The efforts of these agencies were sometimes energetic and sometimes effective. Terrorist plots were disrupted and individual terrorists were captured. But the United States did not, before 9/11, adopt as a clear strategic objective the elimination of al Qaeda.

### EARLY EFFORTS AGAINST BIN LADIN

In 1996, the CIA set up a special unit of a dozen officers to analyze intelligence on and plan operations against Bin Ladin. David Cohen, the head of the CIA's Directorate of Operations, wanted to test the idea of having a "virtual station"—a station based at headquarters but collecting and operating against a subject much as stations in the field focus on a country. Cohen formed his virtual station as a terrorist financial links unit. He recruited a former analyst who was especially knowledgeable about Afghanistan, had noticed a recent stream of reports about Bin Ladin and something called al Qaeda, and suggested to Cohen that the station focus on this one individual. Cohen agreed. Thus was born the Bin Ladin unit.

By 1997, officers in the Bin Ladin unit recognized that Bin Ladin was more than just a financier. They learned that al Qaeda had a military committee that was planning operations against U.S. interests worldwide and was actively trying to obtain nuclear material. Analysts assigned to the station looked at the information it had gathered and "found connections everywhere," including links to the attacks on U.S. troops in Aden and Somalia in 1992 and 1993 and to the Manila air plot in the Philippines in 1994–1995.

The chief of the Bin Ladin station, whom we will call "Mike," saw Bin Ladin's move to Afghanistan as a stroke of luck. Though the CIA had virtually abandoned Afghanistan after the Soviet withdrawal, case officers had reestablished old contacts while tracking down Mir Amal Kansi, the Pakistani gunman who had murdered two CIA employees in January 1993. One of the contacts was a group associated with particular tribes among Afghanistan's ethnic Pashtun community. By the fall of 1997, the Bin Ladin unit had roughed out a plan for these Afghan tribals to capture Bin Ladin and hand him over for trial either in the United States or in an Arab country.

\* \* \*

THE CIA DEVELOPS A CAPTURE PLAN

Initially, the DCI's Counterterrorist Center and its Bin Ladin unit considered a plan to ambush Bin Ladin when he traveled between Kandahar, the Taliban capital where he sometimes stayed the night, and his primary residence at the time, Tarnak Farms. After the Afghan tribals reported that they had tried such an ambush and failed, the Center gave up on it, despite suspicions that the tribals' story might be fiction. Thereafter, the capture plan focused on a nighttime raid on Tarnak Farms.

A compound of about 80 concrete or mud-brick buildings surrounded by a 10-foot wall, Tarnak Farms was located in an isolated desert area on the outskirts of the Kandahar airport. CIA officers were able to map the entire site, identifying the houses that belonged to Bin Ladin's wives and the one where Bin Ladin himself was most likely to sleep. Working with the tribals, they drew up plans for the raid. They ran two complete rehearsals in the United States during the fall of 1997.

\* \* \*

On May 18, [1998,] CIA's managers reviewed a draft Memorandum of Notification (MON), a legal document authorizing the capture operation. A 1986 presidential finding had authorized worldwide covert action against terrorism and probably provided adequate authority. But senior CIA managers may have wanted something on paper to show that they were not acting on their own.

Discussion of this memorandum brought to the surface an unease about paramilitary covert action that had become ingrained, at least among some CIA senior managers. James Pavitt, the assistant head of the Directorate of Operations, expressed concern that people might get killed; it appears he thought the operation had at least a slight flavor of a plan for an assassination. Moreover, he calculated that it would cost several million dollars. He was not prepared to take that money "out of hide," and he did not want to go to all the necessary congressional committees to get special money. Despite Pavitt's misgivings, the CIA leadership cleared the draft memorandum and sent it on to the National Security Council [NSC].

From May 20 to 24, the CIA ran a final, graded rehearsal of the operation, spread over three time zones, even bringing in personnel from the region. The FBI also participated. The rehearsal went well. The Counterterrorist Center [CTC] planned to brief cabinet-level principals and their deputies the following week, giving June 23 as the date for the raid, with Bin Ladin to be brought out of Afghanistan no later than July 23.

On May 20, Director Tenet discussed the high risk of the operation with Berger and his deputies, warning that people might be killed, including Bin Ladin. Success was to be defined as the exfiltration of Bin Ladin out of Afghanistan. A meeting of principals was scheduled for May 29 to decide whether the operation should go ahead.

The decision was made not to go ahead with the operation. "Mike" cabled the field that he had been directed to "stand down on the operation for the time being." He had been told, he wrote, that cabinet-level officials thought the risk of civilian casualties — "collateral damage" — was too high. They were concerned about the tribals' safety, and had worried that "the purpose and nature of the operation would be subject to unavoidable misinterpretation and misrepresentation — and probably recriminations — in the event that Bin Ladin, despite our best intentions and efforts, did not survive."

Impressions vary as to who actually decided not to proceed with the operation. Clarke told us that the CSG saw the plan as flawed. He was said to have described it to a colleague on the NSC staff as "half-assed" and predicted that the principals would not approve it. [The chief of the CTC, whom we call "Jeff,"] thought the decision had been made at the cabinet level. Pavitt thought that it was Berger's doing, though perhaps on Tenet's advice. Tenet told us that given the recommendation of his chief operations officers, he alone had decided to "turn off" the operation. He had simply informed Berger, who had not pushed back. Berger's recollection was similar. He said the plan was never presented to the White House for a decision.

The CIA's senior management clearly did not think the plan would work. But working-level CIA officers were disappointed. Before it was canceled, [Gary] Schroen [CIA chief of station in Pakistan] described it as the "best plan we are going to come up with to capture [Bin Ladin] while he is in Afghanistan and bring him to justice." No capture plan before 9/11 ever again attained the same level of detail and preparation.

At this time, 9/11 was more than three years away. It was the duty of Tenet and the CIA leadership to balance the risks of inaction against jeopardizing the lives of their operatives and agents. And they had reason to worry about failure: millions of dollars down the drain; a shoot-out that could be seen as an assassination; and, if there were repercussions in Pakistan, perhaps a coup. The decisions of the U.S. government in May 1998 were made, as Berger has put it, from the vantage point of the driver looking through a muddy windshield moving forward, not through a clean rearview mirror.

* * *

### Crisis: August 1998

On August 7, 1998, National Security Advisor Berger woke President Clinton with a phone call at 5:35 A.M. to tell him of the almost simultaneous bombings of the U.S. embassies in Nairobi, Kenya, and Dar es Salaam, Tanzania. Suspicion quickly focused on Bin Ladin. Unusually good intelligence, chiefly from the yearlong monitoring of al Qaeda's cell in Nairobi, soon firmly fixed responsibility on him and his associates.

Debate about what to do settled very soon on one option: Tomahawk cruise missiles. [These were 20-foot-long pilotless aircraft, launched from vessels at sea, which could fly at about 550 miles per hour with an 875-mile range while carrying a 1,000-pound warhead.] Months earlier, after cancellation of the covert capture operation, Clarke had prodded the Pentagon to explore possibilities for military action. On June 2, General Hugh Shelton, the chairman of the Joint Chiefs of Staff, had directed General [Anthony] Zinni at Central Command [CENTCOM] to develop a plan, which he had submitted during the first week of July. Zinni's planners proposed firing Tomahawks against eight terrorist camps in Afghanistan, including Bin Ladin's compound at Tarnak Farms. After the embassy attacks, the Pentagon offered this plan to the White House.

The day after the embassy bombings, Tenet brought to a principals meeting intelligence that terrorist leaders were expected to gather at a camp near Khowst, Afghanistan, to plan future attacks. According to Berger, Tenet said that several hundred would attend, including Bin Ladin. The CIA described the area as effectively a military cantonment, away from civilian population centers and overwhelmingly populated by jihadists. Clarke remembered sitting next to Tenet in a White House meeting, asking Tenet "You thinking what I'm thinking?" and his nodding "yes." The principals quickly reached a consensus on attacking the gathering. The strike's purpose was to kill Bin Ladin and his chief lieutenants.

Considerable debate went to the question of whether to strike targets outside of Afghanistan, including two facilities in Sudan. One was a tannery believed to belong to Bin Ladin. The other was al Shifa, a Khartoum pharmaceutical plant, which intelligence reports said was manufacturing a precursor ingredient for nerve gas with Bin Ladin's financial support. The argument for hitting the tannery was that it could hurt Bin Ladin financially. The argument for hitting al Shifa was that it would lessen the chance of Bin Ladin's having nerve gas for a later attack.

Ever since March 1995, American officials had had in the backs of their minds [the Japanese cult] Aum Shinrikyo's release of sarin nerve gas in the Tokyo subway. President Clinton himself had expressed great concern about chemical and biological terrorism in the United States. Bin Ladin had reportedly been heard to speak of wanting a "Hiroshima" and at least 10,000 casualties. The CIA reported that a soil sample from the vicinity of the al Shifa plant had tested positive for EMPTA, a precursor chemical for VX, a nerve gas whose lone use was for mass killing. Two days before the embassy bombings, Clarke's staff wrote that Bin Ladin "has invested in and almost certainly has access to VX produced at a plant in Sudan." Mary McCarthy, the NSC senior director responsible for intelligence programs, initially cautioned Berger that the "bottom line" was that "we will need much better intelligence on this facility before we seriously consider any options." She added that the link between Bin Ladin and al Shifa was "rather uncertain at this point." Berger has told us that he thought about what might happen if the decision went against hitting al Shifa, and nerve gas was used in a New York subway two weeks later.

By the early hours of the morning of August 20, President Clinton and all his principal advisers had agreed to strike Bin Ladin camps in Afghanistan near Khowst, as well as hitting al Shifa. The President took the Sudanese tannery off the target list because he saw little point in killing uninvolved people without doing significant harm to

Bin Ladin. The principal with the most qualms regarding al Shifa was Attorney General Reno. She expressed concern about attacking two Muslim countries at the same time. Looking back, she said that she felt the "premise kept shifting."

Later on August 20, Navy vessels in the Arabian Sea fired their cruise missiles. Though most of them hit their intended targets, neither Bin Ladin nor any other terrorist leader was killed. Berger told us that an after-action review by Director Tenet concluded that the strikes had killed 20–30 people in the camps but probably missed Bin Ladin by a few hours.

The air strikes marked the climax of an intense 48-hour period in which Berger notified congressional leaders, the principals called their foreign counterparts, and President Clinton flew back from his vacation on Martha's Vineyard to address the nation from the Oval Office.

At the time, President Clinton was embroiled in the [Monica] Lewinsky scandal, which continued to consume public attention for the rest of that year and the first months of 1999. As it happened, a popular 1997 movie, *Wag the Dog*, features a president who fakes a war to distract public attention from a domestic scandal. Some Republicans in Congress raised questions about the timing of the strikes. Berger was particularly rankled by an editorial in the *Economist* that said that only the future would tell whether the U.S. missile strikes had "created 10,000 new fanatics where there would have been none."

Much public commentary turned immediately to scalding criticism that the action was too aggressive. The Sudanese denied that al Shifa produced nerve gas, and they allowed journalists to visit what was left of a seemingly harmless facility. President Clinton, Vice President Gore, Berger, Tenet, and Clarke insisted to us that their judgment was right, pointing to the soil sample evidence. No independent evidence has emerged to corroborate the CIA's assessment.

Everyone involved in the decision had, of course, been aware of President Clinton's problems. He told them to ignore them. Berger recalled the President saying to him "that they were going to get crap either way, so they should do the right thing." All his aides testified to us that they based their advice solely on national security considerations. We have found no reason to question their statements.

The failure of the strikes, the "wag the dog" slur, the intense partisanship of the period, and the nature of the al Shifa evidence likely had a cumulative effect on future decisions about the use of force against Bin Ladin. Berger told us that he did not feel any sense of constraint.

The period after the August 1998 embassy bombings was critical in shaping U.S. policy toward Bin Ladin. Although more Americans had been killed in the 1996 Khobar Towers attack, and many more in Beirut in 1983, the overall loss of life rivaled the worst attacks in memory. More ominous, perhaps, was the demonstration of an operational capability to coordinate two nearly simultaneous attacks on U.S. embassies in different countries.

Despite the availability of information that al Qaeda was a global network, in 1998 policymakers knew little about the organization. The reams of new information that the CIA's Bin Ladin unit had been developing since 1996 had not been pulled together and synthesized for the rest of the government. Indeed, analysts in the unit felt that they were viewed as alarmists even within the CIA. A National Intelligence Estimate on terrorism in 1997 had only briefly mentioned Bin Ladin, and no subsequent national estimate would authoritatively evaluate the terrorism danger until after 9/11. Policymakers knew there was a dangerous individual, Usama Bin Ladin, whom they had been trying to capture and bring to trial. Documents at the time referred to Bin Ladin "and his associates" or Bin Ladin and his "network." They did not emphasize the existence of a structured worldwide organization gearing up to train thousands of potential terrorists.

In the critical days and weeks after the August 1998 attacks, senior policymakers in the Clinton administration had to reevaluate the threat posed by Bin Ladin. Was this just a new and especially venomous version of the ordinary terrorist threat America had lived with for decades, or was it radically new, posing a danger beyond any yet experienced?

Even after the embassy attacks, Bin Ladin had been responsible for the deaths of fewer than 50 Americans, most of them overseas. An NSC staffer working for Richard Clarke told us the threat was seen as one that could cause hundreds of casualties, not thousands. Even officials who acknowledge a vital threat intellectually may not be ready to act on such beliefs at great cost or at high risk.

Therefore, the government experts who believed that Bin Ladin and his network posed such a novel danger needed a way to win broad support for their views, or at least spotlight the areas of dispute. The President's Daily Brief and the similar, more widely circulated daily reports for high officials—consisting mainly of brief reports of intelligence "news" without much analysis or context—did not provide such a vehicle. The national intelligence estimate has often played this role, and is sometimes controversial for this very reason. It played no role in judging the threat posed by al Qaeda, either in 1998 or later.

In the late summer and fall of 1998, the U.S. government also was worrying about the deployment of military power in two other ongoing conflicts. After years of war in the Balkans, the United States had finally committed itself to significant military intervention in 1995–1996. Already maintaining a NATO-led peacekeeping force in Bosnia, U.S. officials were beginning to consider major combat operations against Serbia to protect Muslim civilians in Kosovo from ethnic cleansing. Air strikes were threatened in October 1998; a full-scale NATO bombing campaign against Serbia was launched in March 1999.

In addition, the Clinton administration was facing the possibility of major combat operations against Iraq. Since 1996, the UN inspections regime had been increasingly obstructed by Saddam Hussein. The United States was threatening to attack unless unfettered inspections could resume. The Clinton administration eventually launched a large-scale set of air strikes against Iraq, Operation Desert Fox, in December 1998. These military commitments became the context in which the Clinton administration had to consider opening another front of military engagement against a new terrorist threat based in Afghanistan.

A FOLLOW-ON CAMPAIGN?

Clarke hoped the August 1998 missile strikes would mark the beginning of a sustained campaign against Bin Ladin. Clarke was, as he later admitted, "obsessed" with Bin Ladin, and the embassy bombings gave him new scope for pursuing his obsession. Terrorism had moved high up among the President's concerns, and Clarke's position had elevated accordingly. In practice, the CSG often reported not even to the full Principals Committee but instead to the so-called Small Group formed by Berger, consisting only of those principals cleared to know about the most sensitive issues connected with counterterrorism activities concerning Bin Ladin or the Khobar Towers investigation.

For this inner cabinet, Clarke drew up what he called "Political-Military Plan Delenda." The Latin *delenda*, meaning that something "must be destroyed," evoked the famous Roman vow to destroy its rival, Carthage. The overall goal of Clarke's paper was to "immediately eliminate any significant threat to Americans" from the "Bin Ladin network." The paper called for diplomacy to deny Bin Ladin sanctuary; covert action to disrupt terrorist activities, but above all to capture Bin

Ladin and his deputies and bring them to trial; efforts to dry up Bin Ladin's money supply; and preparation for follow-on military action. The status of the document was and remained uncertain. It was never formally adopted by the principals, and participants in the Small Group now have little or no recollection of it. It did, however, guide Clarke's efforts.

The military component of Clarke's plan was its most fully articulated element. He envisioned an ongoing campaign of strikes against Bin Ladin's bases in Afghanistan or elsewhere, whenever target information was ripe. Acknowledging that individual targets might not have much value, he cautioned Berger not to expect ever again to have an assembly of terrorist leaders in his sights. But he argued that rolling attacks might persuade the Taliban to hand over Bin Ladin and, in any case, would show that the action in August was not a "one-off" event. It would show that the United States was committed to a relentless effort to take down Bin Ladin's network.

Members of the Small Group found themselves unpersuaded of the merits of rolling attacks. Defense Secretary William Cohen told us Bin Ladin's training camps were primitive, built with "rope ladders"; General Shelton called them "jungle gym" camps. Neither thought them worthwhile targets for very expensive missiles. President Clinton and Berger also worried about the *Economist*'s point—that attacks that missed Bin Ladin could enhance his stature and win him new recruits. After the United States launched air attacks against Iraq at the end of 1998 and against Serbia in 1999, in each case provoking worldwide criticism, Deputy National Security Advisor James Steinberg added the argument that attacks in Afghanistan offered "little benefit, lots of blowback against [a] bomb-happy U.S."

\* \* \*

## Covert Action

As part of the response to the embassy bombings, President Clinton signed a Memorandum of Notification authorizing the CIA to let its tribal assets use force to capture Bin Ladin and his associates. CIA officers told the tribals that the plan to capture Bin Ladin, which had been "turned off" three months earlier, was back on. The memorandum also authorized the CIA to attack Bin Ladin in other ways. Also, an executive order froze financial holdings that could be linked to Bin Ladin.

\* \* \*

The CIA reported on December 18 [1998] that Bin Ladin might be traveling to Kandahar and could be targeted there with cruise missiles. Vessels with Tomahawk cruise missiles were on station in the Arabian Sea, and could fire within a few hours of receiving target data.

On December 20, intelligence indicated Bin Ladin would be spending the night at the Haji Habash house, part of the governor's residence in Kandahar. The chief of the Bin Ladin unit, "Mike," told us that he promptly briefed Tenet and his deputy, John Gordon. From the field, the CIA's Gary Schroen advised: "Hit him tonight—we may not get another chance." An urgent teleconference of principals was arranged.

The principals considered a cruise missile strike to try to kill Bin Ladin. One issue they discussed was the potential collateral damage— the number of innocent bystanders who would be killed or wounded. General Zinni predicted a number well over 200 and was concerned about damage to a nearby mosque. By the end of the meeting, the principals decided against recommending to the President that he order a strike. A few weeks later, in January 1999, Clarke wrote that the principals had thought the intelligence only half reliable and had worried about killing or injuring perhaps 300 people. Tenet said he remembered doubts about the reliability of the source and concern about hitting the nearby mosque. "Mike" remembered Tenet telling him that the military was concerned that a few hours had passed since the last sighting of Bin Ladin and that this persuaded everyone that the chance of failure was too great.

Some lower-level officials were angry. "Mike" reported to Schroen that he had been unable to sleep after this decision. "I'm sure we'll regret not acting last night," he wrote, criticizing the principals for "worrying that some stray shrapnel might hit the Habash mosque and 'offend' Muslims."

The principals began considering other, more aggressive covert alternatives using the tribals. The current Memorandum of Notification instructed the CIA to capture Bin Ladin and to use lethal force only in self-defense. Work now began on a new memorandum that would give the tribals more latitude. The intention was to say that they could use lethal force if the attempted capture seemed impossible to complete successfully.

Early drafts of this highly sensitive document emphasized that it authorized only a capture operation. The tribals were to be paid only if they captured Bin Ladin, not if they killed him. Officials throughout the government approved this draft. But on December 21, the day after principals decided not to launch the cruise missile strike against Kandahar, the CIA's leaders urged strengthening the language to allow the tribals to be paid whether Bin Ladin was captured *or* killed. Berger and Tenet then worked together to take this line of thought even further.

They finally agreed, as Berger reported to President Clinton, that an extraordinary step was necessary. The new memorandum would allow the killing of Bin Ladin if the CIA and the tribals judged that capture was not feasible (a judgment it already seemed clear they had reached). On Christmas Eve 1998, Berger sent a final draft to President Clinton, with an explanatory memo. The President approved the document.

Because the White House considered this operation highly sensitive, only a tiny number of people knew about this Memorandum of Notification. Berger arranged for the NSC's legal adviser to inform [Secretary of State Madeleine] Albright, Cohen, Shelton, and Reno. None was allowed to keep a copy. Congressional leaders were briefed, as required by law. Attorney General Reno had sent a letter to the President expressing her concern: she warned of possible retaliation, including the targeting of U.S. officials. She did not pose any legal objection. A copy of the final document, along with the carefully crafted instructions that were to be sent to the tribals, was given to Tenet.

A message from Tenet to CIA field agents directed them to communicate to the tribals the instructions authorized by the President: the United States preferred that Bin Ladin and his lieutenants be captured, but if a successful capture operation was not feasible, the tribals were permitted to kill them. The instructions added that the tribals must avoid killing others unnecessarily and must not kill or abuse Bin Ladin or his lieutenants if they surrendered. Finally, the tribals would not be paid if this set of requirements was not met.

Policymakers in the Clinton administration, including the President and his national security advisor, told us that the President's intent regarding covert action against Bin Ladin was clear: he wanted him dead. This intent was never well communicated or understood within the CIA. Tenet told the Commission that except in one specific case (discussed later), the CIA was authorized to kill Bin Ladin only in the context of a capture operation. CIA senior managers, operators, and lawyers confirmed this understanding. "We always talked about how

much easier it would have been to kill him," a former chief of the Bin
Ladin unit said. Given the closely held character of the document
approved in December 1998, and the subsequent return to the earlier
language, it is possible to understand how the former White House
officials and the CIA officials might disagree as to whether the CIA
was ever authorized by the President to kill Bin Ladin.

## Searching for Fresh Options

"BOOTS ON THE GROUND?"

Starting on the day the August 1998 strikes were launched, General
Shelton had issued a planning order to prepare follow-on strikes and
think beyond just using cruise missiles. The initial strikes had been
called Operation Infinite Reach. The follow-on plans were given the
code name Operation Infinite Resolve.

At the time, any actual military action in Afghanistan would have
been carried out by General Zinni's Central Command. This command
was therefore the locus for most military planning. Zinni was even less
enthusiastic than Cohen and Shelton about follow-on cruise missile
strikes. He knew that the Tomahawks did not always hit their targets.
After the August 20 strikes, President Clinton had had to call Pakistani
Prime Minister [Nawaa] Sharif to apologize for a wayward missile that
had killed several people in a Pakistani village. Sharif had been understanding, while commenting on American "overkill."

Shelton and officers in the Pentagon developed plans for using an
AC-130 [helicopter] gunship instead of cruise missile strikes.
Designed specifically for the special forces, the version of the AC-130
known as "Spooky" can fly in fast or from high altitude, undetected by
radar; guided to its zone by extraordinarily complex electronics, it is
capable of rapidly firing precision-guided 25, 40, and 105 mm projec-
tiles. Because this system could target more precisely than a salvo of
cruise missiles, it had a much lower risk of causing collateral damage.

Though Berger and Clarke continued to indicate interest in this
option, the AC-130s were never deployed. [Zinni] told us that he
understood the Special Operations Command had never thought the
intelligence good enough to justify actually moving AC-130s into position. [General Peter] Schoomaker [commander of the Special Operations Command] says, on the contrary, that he thought the AC-130
option feasible.

The most likely explanation for the two generals' differing recollections is that both of them thought serious preparation for any such operations would require a long-term redeployment of Special Operations forces to the Middle East or South Asia. The AC-130s would need bases because the aircraft's unrefueled range was only a little over 2,000 miles. They needed search-and-rescue backup, which would have still less range. Thus an AC-130 deployment had to be embedded in a wider political and military concept involving Pakistan or other neighboring countries to address issues relating to basing and overflight. No one ever put such an initiative on the table. Zinni therefore cautioned about simply ordering up AC-130 deployments for a quick strike; Schoomaker planned for what he saw as a practical strike option; and the underlying issues were not fully engaged.

The same was true for the option of using ground units from the Special Operations Command.

President Clinton relied on the advice of General Shelton, who informed him that without intelligence on Bin Ladin's location, a commando raid's chance of failure was high. Shelton told President Clinton he would go forward with "boots on the ground" if the President ordered him to do so; however, he had to ensure that the President was completely aware of the large logistical problems inherent in a military operation.

The debate looked to some like bold proposals from civilians meeting hypercaution from the military. Clarke saw it this way. Of the military, he said to us, "They were very, very, very reluctant." But from another perspective, poorly informed proposals for bold action were pitted against experienced professional judgment. That was how Secretary of Defense Cohen viewed it. He said to us: "I would have to place my judgment call in terms of, do I believe that the chairman of the Joint Chiefs, former commander of Special Forces command, is in a better position to make a judgment on the feasibility of this than, perhaps, Mr. Clarke?"

Beyond a large-scale political-military commitment to build up a covert or clandestine capability using American personnel on the ground, either military or CIA, there was a still larger option that could have been considered—invading Afghanistan itself. Every official we questioned about the possibility of an invasion of Afghanistan said that it was almost unthinkable, absent a provocation such as 9/11, because of poor prospects for cooperation from Pakistan and other nations and because they believed the public would not support it.

Cruise missiles were and would remain the only military option on the table.

## THE DESERT CAMP, FEBRUARY 1999

Early in 1999, the CIA received reporting that Bin Ladin was spending much of his time at one of several camps in the Afghan desert south of Kandahar. At the beginning of February, Bin Ladin was reportedly located in the vicinity of the Sheikh Ali camp, a desert hunting camp being used by visitors from a Gulf state. Public sources have stated that these visitors were from the United Arab Emirates.

Reporting from the CIA's assets provided a detailed description of the hunting camp, including its size, location, resources, and security, as well as of Bin Ladin's smaller, adjacent camp. Because this was not in an urban area, missiles launched against it would have less risk of causing collateral damage. On February 8, the military began to ready itself for a possible strike.

No strike was launched. By February 12 Bin Ladin had apparently moved on, and the immediate strike plans became moot. According to CIA and Defense officials, policymakers were concerned about the danger that a strike would kill an Emirati prince or other senior officials who might be with Bin Ladin or close by. Clarke told us the strike was called off after consultations with Director Tenet because the intelligence was dubious, and it seemed to Clarke as if the CIA was presenting an option to attack America's best counterterrorism ally in the Gulf. The lead CIA official in the field, Gary Schroen, felt that the intelligence reporting in this case was very reliable; the Bin Ladin unit chief, "Mike," agreed. Schroen believes today that this was a lost opportunity to kill Bin Ladin before 9/11.

## LOOKING FOR NEW PARTNERS

The chief of the Counterterrorist Center, supported by Clarke, pressed for developing a partnership with the Northern Alliance, even though doing so might bring the United States squarely behind one side in Afghanistan's long-running civil war.

The Northern Alliance was dominated by Tajiks and drew its strength mainly from the northern and eastern parts of Afghanistan. In contrast, Taliban members came principally from Afghanistan's most numerous ethnic group, the Pashtuns, who are concentrated in the southern part of the country, extending into the North-West Frontier and Baluchistan provinces of Pakistan.

The alliance's leader was Afghanistan's most renowned military commander, Ahmed Shah Massoud. Reflective and charismatic, he had been one of the true heroes of the war against the Soviets. But his bands had been charged with more than one massacre, and the Northern Alliance was widely thought to finance itself in part through trade in heroin.

In February 1999, Tenet sought President Clinton's authorization to enlist Massoud and his forces as partners. In response to this request, the President signed the Memorandum of Notification whose language he personally altered. The idea, however, was a long shot. Bin Ladin's usual base of activity was near Kandahar, far from the front lines of Taliban operations against the Northern Alliance.

KANDAHAR, MAY 1999

It was in Kandahar that perhaps the last, and most likely the best, opportunity arose for targeting Bin Ladin with cruise missiles before 9/11. In May 1999, CIA assets in Afghanistan reported on Bin Ladin's location in and around Kandahar over the course of five days and nights. The reporting was very detailed and came from several sources. If this intelligence was not "actionable," working-level officials said at the time and today, it was hard for them to imagine how any intelligence on Bin Ladin in Afghanistan would meet the standard. Communications were good, and the cruise missiles were ready. "This was in our strike zone," a senior military officer said. "It was a fat pitch, a home run." He expected the missiles to fly. When the decision came back that they should stand down, not shoot, the officer said, "we all just slumped." He told us he knew of no one at the Pentagon or the CIA who thought it was a bad gamble. Bin Ladin "should have been a dead man" that night, he said.

Working-level CIA officials agreed. While there was a conflicting intelligence report about Bin Ladin's whereabouts, the experts discounted it. At the time, CIA working-level officials were told by their managers that the strikes were not ordered because the military doubted the intelligence and worried about collateral damage. Replying to a frustrated colleague in the field, the Bin Ladin unit chief wrote: "having a chance to get [Bin Ladin] three times in 36 hours and foregoing the chance each time has made me a bit angry. . . . [T]he DCI finds himself alone at the table, with the other princip[als] basically saying 'we'll go along with your decision Mr. Director,' and implicitly saying that the Agency will hang alone if the attack doesn't get Bin Ladin." But the military officer quoted earlier recalled that the Pentagon had been willing to act. He told us that Clarke informed him and others that Tenet assessed the chance of the intelligence being accurate as 50-50. This officer believed that Tenet's assessment was the key to the decision.

Tenet told us he does not remember any details about this episode, except that the intelligence came from a single uncorroborated source and that there was a risk of collateral damage. The story is further complicated by Tenet's absence from the critical principals meeting on this strike (he was apparently out of town); his deputy, John Gordon, was representing the CIA. Gordon recalled having presented the intelligence in a positive light, with appropriate caveats, but stating that this intelligence was about as good as it could get.

Berger remembered only that in all such cases, the call had been Tenet's. Berger felt sure that Tenet was eager to get Bin Ladin. In his view, Tenet did his job responsibly. "George would call and say, 'We just don't have it,'" Berger said.

The decision not to strike in May 1999 may now seem hard to understand. In fairness, we note two points: First, in December 1998, the principals' wariness about ordering a strike appears to have been vindicated: Bin Ladin left his room unexpectedly, and if a strike had been ordered he would not have been hit. Second, the administration, and the CIA in particular, was in the midst of intense scrutiny and criticism in May 1999 because faulty intelligence had just led the United States to mistakenly bomb the Chinese embassy in Belgrade during the NATO war against Serbia. This episode may have made officials more cautious than might otherwise have been the case.

From May 1999 until September 2001, policymakers did not again actively consider a missile strike against Bin Ladin.

In fall 1999, DCI Tenet unveiled the CIA's new Bin Ladin strategy. It was called, simply, "the Plan." The Plan proposed continuing disruption and rendition operations worldwide. It announced a program for hiring and training better officers with counterterrorism skills, recruiting more assets, and trying to penetrate al Qaeda's ranks. The Plan aimed to close gaps in technical intelligence collection (signal and imagery) as well. In addition, the CIA would increase contacts with the Northern Alliance rebels fighting the Taliban.

As 1999 came to a close, the CIA had a new strategic plan in place for capturing Bin Ladin, but no option was rated as having more than a 15 percent chance of achieving that objective.

# 5. AL QAEDA AIMS AT THE AMERICAN HOMELAND

## Terrorist Entrepreneurs

By early 1999, al Qaeda was already a potent adversary of the United States. Bin Ladin and his chief of operations, Abu Hafs al Masri, also known as Mohammed Atef, occupied undisputed leadership positions atop al Qaeda's organizational structure. Within this structure, al Qaeda's worldwide terrorist operations relied heavily on the ideas and work of enterprising and strong-willed field commanders who enjoyed considerable autonomy.

### KHALID SHEIKH MOHAMMED [KSM]

No one exemplifies the model of the terrorist entrepreneur more clearly than Khalid Sheikh Mohammed, the principal architect of the 9/11 attacks. KSM followed a rather tortuous path to his eventual membership in al Qaeda. Highly educated and equally comfortable in a government office or a terrorist safehouse, KSM applied his imagination, technical aptitude, and managerial skills to hatching and planning an extraordinary array of terrorist schemes. These ideas included conventional car bombing, political assassination, aircraft bombing, hijacking, reservoir poisoning, and, ultimately, the use of aircraft as missiles guided by suicide operatives.

Like his nephew Ramzi Yousef (three years KSM's junior), KSM grew up in Kuwait but traces his ethnic lineage to the Baluchistan region straddling Iran and Pakistan. Raised in a religious family, KSM claims to have joined the Muslim Brotherhood at age 16 and to have become enamored of violent jihad at youth camps in the desert. In 1983, following his graduation from secondary school, KSM left Kuwait to enroll at Chowan College, a small Baptist school in Murfreesboro, North Carolina. After a semester at Chowan, KSM transferred to North Carolina Agricultural and Technical State University in Greensboro, which he attended with Yousef's brother, another future al Qaeda member. KSM earned a degree in mechanical engineering in December 1986. Although he apparently did not attract attention for extreme Islamist beliefs or activities while in the United States, KSM plunged into the anti-Soviet Afghan jihad soon after graduating from college.

KSM first came to the attention of U.S. law enforcement as a result of his cameo role in the first World Trade Center bombing. According to KSM, he learned of Ramzi Yousef's intention to launch an attack inside the United States in 1991 or 1992, when Yousef was receiving explosives training in Afghanistan. During the fall of 1992, while Yousef was building the bomb he would use in that attack, KSM and Yousef had numerous telephone conversations during which Yousef discussed his progress and sought additional funding. On November 3, 1992, KSM wired $660 from Qatar to the bank account of Yousef's co-conspirator, Mohammed Salameh. KSM does not appear to have contributed any more substantially to this operation.

Yousef's instant notoriety as the mastermind of the 1993 World Trade Center bombing inspired KSM to become involved in planning attacks against the United States. By his own account, KSM's animus toward the United States stemmed not from his experiences there as a student, but rather from his violent disagreement with U.S. foreign policy favoring Israel. In 1994, KSM accompanied Yousef to the Philippines, and the two of them began planning what is now known as the Manila air or "Bojinka" plot—the intended bombing of 12 U.S. commercial jumbo jets over the Pacific during a two-day span. This marked the first time KSM took part in the actual planning of a terrorist operation. While sharing an apartment in Manila during the summer of 1994, he and Yousef acquired chemicals and other materials necessary to construct bombs and timers. They also cased target flights to Hong Kong and Seoul that would have onward legs to the United States.

KSM left the Philippines in September 1994 and met up with Yousef in Karachi [Pakistan] following their casing flights. During the fall of 1994, Yousef returned to Manila and successfully tested the digital watch timer he had invented, bombing a movie theater and a Philippine Airlines flight en route to Tokyo. The plot unraveled after the Philippine authorities discovered Yousef's bomb-making operation in Manila; but by that time, KSM was safely back at his government job in Qatar. Yousef attempted to follow through on the cargo carriers plan, but he was arrested in Islamabad by Pakistani authorities on February 7, 1995, after an accomplice turned him in.

KSM continued to travel among the worldwide jihadist community after Yousef's arrest, visiting Sudan, Yemen, Malaysia, and Brazil in 1995. No clear evidence connects him to terrorist activities in those locations. While in Sudan, he reportedly failed in his attempt to meet with Bin Ladin. But KSM did see Atef, who gave him a contact in Brazil. In January 1996, well aware that U.S. authorities were chasing him, he left Qatar for good and fled to Afghanistan.

Just as KSM was reestablishing himself in Afghanistan in mid-1996,

Bin Ladin and his colleagues were also completing their migration from Sudan. Through Atef, KSM arranged a meeting with Bin Ladin in Tora Bora, a mountainous redoubt from the Afghan war days. At the meeting, KSM presented the al Qaeda leader with a menu of ideas for terrorist operations. According to KSM, this meeting was the first time he had seen Bin Ladin since 1989. Although they had fought together in 1987, Bin Ladin and KSM did not yet enjoy an especially close working relationship. Indeed, KSM has acknowledged that Bin Ladin likely agreed to meet with him because of the renown of his nephew, Yousef.

At the meeting, KSM briefed Bin Ladin and Atef on the first World Trade Center bombing, the Manila air plot, the cargo carriers plan, and other activities pursued by KSM and his colleagues in the Philippines. KSM also presented a proposal for an operation that would involve training pilots who would crash planes into buildings in the United States. This proposal eventually would become the 9/11 operation.

KSM knew that the successful staging of such an attack would require personnel, money, and logistical support that only an extensive and well-funded organization like al Qaeda could provide. He thought the operation might appeal to Bin Ladin, who had a long record of denouncing the United States.

According to KSM, the 1998 bombings of the U.S. embassies in Nairobi and Dar es Salaam marked a watershed in the evolution of the 9/11 plot. KSM claims these bombings convinced him that Bin Ladin was truly committed to attacking the United States. He continued to make himself useful, collecting news articles and helping other al Qaeda members with their outdated computer equipment. Bin Ladin, apparently at Atef's urging, finally decided to give KSM the green light for the 9/11 operation sometime in late 1998 or early 1999.

\* \* \*

## The "Planes Operation"

Certainly KSM was not alone in contemplating new kinds of terrorist operations. A study reportedly conducted by Atef, while he and Bin Ladin were still in Sudan, concluded that traditional terrorist hijacking operations did not fit the needs of al Qaeda, because such hijackings were used to negotiate the release of prisoners rather than to inflict mass casualties. The study is said to have considered the feasibility of hijacking planes and blowing them up in flight, paralleling the Bojinka concept. Such a study, if it actually existed, yields significant insight into the thinking of al Qaeda's leaders: (1) they rejected hijackings aimed at gaining the release of imprisoned comrades as too complex, because al Qaeda had no friendly countries in which to land a plane and then negotiate; (2) they considered the bombing of commercial flights in midair—as carried out against Pan Am Flight 103 over Lockerbie, Scotland—a promising means to inflict massive casualties; and (3) they did not yet consider using hijacked aircraft as weapons against other targets.

KSM has insisted to his interrogators that he always contemplated hijacking and crashing large commercial aircraft. Indeed, KSM describes a grandiose original plan: a total of ten aircraft to be hijacked, nine of which would crash into targets on both coasts—they included those eventually hit on September 11 plus CIA and FBI headquarters, nuclear power plants, and the tallest buildings in California and the state of Washington. KSM himself was to land the tenth plane at a U.S. airport and, after killing all adult male passengers on board and alerting the media, deliver a speech excoriating U.S. support for Israel, the Philippines, and repressive governments in the Arab world. Beyond KSM's rationalizations about targeting the U.S. economy, this vision gives a better glimpse of his true ambitions. This is theater, a spectacle of destruction with KSM as the self-cast star—the superterrorist.

KSM concedes that this proposal received a lukewarm response from al Qaeda leaders skeptical of its scale and complexity. Although Bin Ladin listened to KSM's proposal, he was not convinced that it was practical. As mentioned earlier, Bin Ladin was receiving numerous ideas for potential operations—KSM's proposal to attack U.S. targets with commercial airplanes was only one of many.

KSM presents himself as an entrepreneur seeking venture capital and people. He simply wanted al Qaeda to supply the money and operatives needed for the attack while retaining his independence. It is easy to question such a statement. Money is one thing; supplying a cadre of trained operatives willing to die is much more. Thus, although KSM contends he would have been just as likely to consider working with any comparable terrorist organization, he gives no indication of what other groups he thought could supply such exceptional commodities.

KSM acknowledges formally joining al Qaeda, in late 1998 or [early] 1999, and states that soon afterward, Bin Ladin also made the decision to support his proposal to attack the United States using commercial airplanes as weapons. Though KSM speculates about how Bin Ladin came to share his preoccupation with attacking America, Bin Ladin in fact had long been an opponent of the United States. KSM thinks that Atef may have persuaded Bin Ladin to approve this specific proposal. Atef's role in the entire operation is unquestionably very significant but tends to fade into the background, in part because Atef himself is not available to describe it. He was killed in November 2001 by an American air strike in Afghanistan.

Bin Ladin summoned KSM to Kandahar in March or April 1999 to tell him that al Qaeda would support his proposal. The plot was now referred to within al Qaeda as the "planes operation."

THE PLAN EVOLVES

Bin Ladin reportedly discussed the planes operation with KSM and Atef in a series of meetings in the spring of 1999 at the al Matar complex near Kandahar. KSM's original concept of using one of the hijacked planes to make a media statement was scrapped, but Bin Ladin considered the basic idea feasible. Bin Ladin, Atef, and KSM developed an initial list of targets. These included the White House, the U.S. Capitol, the Pentagon, and the World Trade Center. According to KSM, Bin Ladin wanted to destroy the White House and the Pentagon, KSM wanted to strike the World Trade Center, and all of them wanted to hit the Capitol. No one else was involved in the initial selection of targets.

Bin Ladin also soon selected four individuals to serve as suicide operatives: Khalid al Mihdhar, Nawaf al Hazmi, Khallad, and Abu Bara al Yemeni. During the al Matar meetings, Bin Ladin told KSM that Mihdhar and Hazmi were so eager to participate in an operation against the United States that they had already obtained U.S. visas. KSM states that they had done so on their own after the suicide of their friend Azzam (Nashiri's cousin) in carrying out the Nairobi bombing. KSM had not met them. His only guidance from Bin Ladin was that the two should eventually go to the United States for pilot training.

In early December 1999, Khallad and Abu Bara arrived in Karachi. Hazmi joined them there a few days later. On his way to Karachi, Hazmi spent a night in Quetta at a safehouse where, according to KSM, an Egyptian named Mohamed Atta simultaneously stayed on his way to Afghanistan for jihad training.

Mihdhar did not attend the training in Karachi with the others. KSM says that he never met with Mihdhar in 1999 but assumed that

Bin Ladin and Atef had briefed Mihdhar on the planes operation and
had excused him from the Karachi training.

The course in Karachi apparently lasted about one or two weeks.
According to KSM, he taught the three operatives basic English
words and phrases. He showed them how to read phone books, inter-
pret airline timetables, use the Internet, use code words in communications, make travel reservations, and rent an apartment. Khallad adds
that the training involved using flight simulator computer games, viewing movies that featured hijackings, and reading flight schedules to
determine which flights would be in the air at the same time in different parts of the world. They used the game software to increase their
familiarity with aircraft models and functions, and to highlight gaps in
cabin security. While in Karachi, they also discussed how to case
flights in Southeast Asia. KSM told them to watch the cabin doors at
takeoff and landing, to observe whether the captain went to the lava-
tory during the flight, and to note whether the flight attendants
brought food into the cockpit. KSM, Khallad, and Hazmi also visited
travel agencies to learn the visa requirements for Asian countries.

## The Hamburg Contingent

Although Bin Ladin, Atef, and KSM initially contemplated using established al Qaeda members to execute the planes operation, the late
1999 arrival in Kandahar of four aspiring jihadists from Germany suddenly presented a more attractive alternative. The Hamburg group
shared the anti-U.S. fervor of the other candidates for the operation,
but added the enormous advantages of fluency in English and familiarity with life in the West, based on years that each member of the
group had spent living in Germany. Not surprisingly, Mohamed Atta,
Ramzi Binalshibh, Marwan al Shehhi, and Ziad Jarrah would all
become key players in the 9/11 conspiracy.

### MOHAMED ATTA

Mohamed Atta was born on September 1, 1968, in Kafr el Sheikh,
Egypt, to a middle-class family headed by his father, an attorney. After
graduating from Cairo University with a degree in architectural engineering in 1990, Atta worked as an urban planner in Cairo for a couple
of years. In the fall of 1991, he asked a German family he had met in
Cairo to help him continue his education in Germany. They suggested
he come to Hamburg and invited him to live with them there, at least
initially. After completing a course in German, Atta traveled to Ger-

many for the first time in July 1992. He resided briefly in Stuttgart and then, in the fall of 1992, moved to Hamburg to live with his host family. After enrolling at the University of Hamburg, he promptly transferred into the city engineering and planning course at the Technical University of Hamburg-Harburg, where he would remain registered as a student until the fall of 1999. He appears to have applied himself fairly seriously to his studies (at least in comparison to his jihadist friends) and actually received his degree shortly before traveling to Afghanistan. In school, Atta came across as very intelligent and reasonably pleasant, with an excellent command of the German language.

When Atta arrived in Germany, he appeared religious, but not fanatically so. This would change, especially as his tendency to assert leadership became increasingly pronounced. According to Binalshibh, as early as 1995 Atta sought to organize a Muslim student association in Hamburg. In the fall of 1997, he joined a working group at the Quds mosque in Hamburg, a group designed to bridge the gap between Muslims and Christians. Atta proved a poor bridge, however, because of his abrasive and increasingly dogmatic personality. But among those who shared his beliefs, Atta stood out as a decisionmaker. Atta's friends during this period remember him as charismatic, intelligent, and persuasive, albeit intolerant of dissent.

In his interactions with other students, Atta voiced virulently anti-Semitic and anti-American opinions, ranging from condemnations of what he described as a global Jewish movement centered in New York City that supposedly controlled the financial world and the media, to polemics against governments of the Arab world. To him, Saddam Hussein was an American stooge set up to give Washington an excuse to intervene in the Middle East. Within his circle, Atta advocated violent jihad. He reportedly asked one individual close to the group if he was "ready to fight for [his] belief" and dismissed him as too weak for jihad when the person declined. On a visit home to Egypt in 1998, Atta met one of his college friends. According to this friend, Atta had changed a great deal, had grown a beard, and had "obviously adopted fundamentalism" by that time.

RAMZI BINALSHIBH

Ramzi Binalshibh was born on May 1, 1972, in Ghayl Bawazir, Yemen. There does not seem to be anything remarkable about his family or early background. A friend who knew Binalshibh in Yemen remembers him as "religious, but not too religious." From 1987 to 1995, Binalshibh worked as a clerk for the International Bank of Yemen. He first attempted to leave Yemen in 1995, when he applied for a U.S. visa. After his application was rejected, he went to Germany and applied for asylum under the name Ramzi Omar, claiming to be a Sudanese citizen seeking asylum. While his asylum petition was pending, Binalshibh lived in Hamburg and associated with individuals from several mosques there. In 1997, after his asylum application was denied, Binalshibh went home to Yemen but returned to Germany shortly thereafter under his true name, this time registering as a student in Hamburg. Binalshibh continually had academic problems, failing tests and cutting classes; he was expelled from one school in September 1998.

According to Binalshibh, he and Atta first met at a mosque in Hamburg in 1995. The two men became close friends and became identified with their shared extremist outlook. Like Atta, by the late 1990s Binalshibh was decrying what he perceived to be a "Jewish world conspiracy." He proclaimed that the highest duty of every Muslim was to pursue jihad, and that the highest honor was to die during the jihad. Despite his rhetoric, however, Binalshibh presented a more amiable figure than the austere Atta, and was known within the community as being sociable, extroverted, polite, and adventuresome.

In 1998, Binalshibh and Atta began sharing an apartment in the Harburg section of Hamburg, together with a young student from the United Arab Emirates [UAE] named Marwan al Shehhi.

## MARWAN AL SHEHHI

Marwan al Shehhi was born on May 9, 1978, in Ras al Khaimah, United Arab Emirates. His father, who died in 1997, was a prayer leader at the local mosque. After graduating from high school in 1995, Shehhi joined the Emirati military and received half a year of basic training before gaining admission to a military scholarship program that would fund his continued study in Germany.

Shehhi first entered Germany in April 1996. After sharing an apartment in Bonn for two months with three other scholarship students, Shehhi moved in with a German family, with whom he resided for several months before moving into his own apartment. During this period, he came across as very religious, praying five times a day. Friends also remember him as convivial and "a regular guy," wearing Western clothes and occasionally renting cars for trips to Berlin, France, and the Netherlands.

As a student, Shehhi was less than a success. Upon completing a course in German, he enrolled at the University of Bonn in a program for technical, mathematical, and scientific studies. In June 1997, he requested a leave from his studies, citing the need to attend to unspecified "problems" in his home country. Although the university denied his request, Shehhi left anyway, and consequently was compelled to repeat the first semester of his studies. In addition to having academic difficulties at this time, Shehhi appeared to become more extreme in the practice of his faith; for example, he specifically avoided restaurants that cooked with or served alcohol. In late 1997, he applied for permission to complete his course work in Hamburg, a request apparently motivated by his desire to join Atta and Binalshibh. Just how and when the three of them first met remains unclear, although they seemed to know each other already when Shehhi relocated to Hamburg in early 1998. Atta and Binalshibh moved into his apartment in April.

The transfer to Hamburg did not help Shehhi's academic progress; he was directed by the scholarship program administrators at the Emirati embassy to repeat his second semester starting in August 1998, but back in Bonn. Shehhi initially flouted this directive, however, and did not reenroll at the University of Bonn until the following January, barely passing his course there. By the end of July 1999, he had returned to Hamburg, applying to study shipbuilding at the Technical University and, more significantly, residing once again with Atta and Binalshibh, in an apartment at 54 Marienstrasse.

After Shehhi moved in with Atta and Binalshibh, his evolution toward Islamic fundamentalism became more pronounced. A fellow Emirati student who came to Hamburg to visit Shehhi noticed he no longer lived as comfortably as before. Shehhi now occupied an old apartment with a roommate, had no television, and wore inexpensive clothes. When asked why he was living so frugally, Shehhi responded that he was living the way the Prophet had lived. Similarly, when someone asked why he and Atta never laughed, Shehhi retorted, "How can you laugh when people are dying in Palestine?"

ZIAD JARRAH

Born on May 11, 1975, in Mazraa, Lebanon, Ziad Jarrah came from an affluent [and a secular Muslim] family and attended private, Christian schools. Like Atta, Binalshibh, and Shehhi, Jarrah aspired to pursue higher education in Germany. In April 1996, he and a cousin enrolled at a junior college in Greifswald, in northeastern Germany. There Jarrah met and became intimate with Aysel Senguen, the daughter of Turkish immigrants, who was preparing to study dentistry.

Even with the benefit of hindsight, Jarrah hardly seems a likely candidate for becoming an Islamic extremist. Far from displaying radical beliefs when he first moved to Germany, he arrived with a reputation for knowing where to find the best discos and beaches in Beirut, and in Greifswald was known to enjoy student parties and drinking beer. Although he continued to share an apartment in Greifswald with his cousin, Jarrah was mostly at Senguen's apartment. Witnesses interviewed by German authorities after 9/11, however, recall that Jarrah started showing signs of radicalization as early as the end of 1996. After returning from a trip home to Lebanon, Jarrah started living more strictly according to the [Qur'an]. He read brochures in Arabic about jihad, held forth to friends on the subject of holy war, and professed disaffection with his previous life and a desire not to leave the world "in a natural way."

In September 1997, Jarrah abruptly switched his intended course of study from dentistry to aircraft engineering—at the Technical University of Hamburg-Harburg. His motivation for this decision remains unclear. The rationale he expressed to Senguen—that he had been interested in aviation since playing with toy airplanes as a child—rings somewhat hollow. In any event, Jarrah appears already to have had Hamburg contacts by this time, some of whom may have played a role in steering him toward Islamic extremism.

Following his move to Hamburg that fall, he began visiting Senguen in Greifswald on weekends, until she moved to the German city of Bochum one year later to enroll in dental school. Around the same time, he began speaking increasingly about religion, and his visits to Senguen became less and less frequent. He began criticizing her for not being religious enough and for dressing too provocatively. He grew a full beard and started praying regularly. He refused to introduce her to his Hamburg friends because, he told her, they were religious Muslims and her refusal to become more observant embarrassed him. At some point in 1999, Jarrah told Senguen that he was planning to wage a jihad because there was no greater honor than to die for Allah. Although Jarrah's transformation generated numerous quarrels, their breakups invariably were followed by reconciliation.

In retrospect, the speed with which Atta, Shehhi, Jarrah, and Binalshibh became core members of the 9/11 plot—with Atta designated its operational leader—is remarkable. They had not yet met with KSM when all this occurred. It is clear, then, that Bin Ladin and Atef were very much in charge of the operation. That these candidates were selected so quickly—before comprehensive testing in the training camps or in operations—demonstrates that Bin Ladin and Atef probably already understood the deficiencies of their initial team, Hazmi and Mihdhar. The new recruits from Germany possessed an ideal combination of technical skill and knowledge that the original 9/11 operatives, veteran fighters though they were, lacked. Bin Ladin and Atef wasted no time in assigning the Hamburg group to the most ambitious operation yet planned by al Qaeda.

Bin Ladin and Atef also plainly judged that Atta was best suited to be the tactical commander of the operation. Such a quick and critical judgment invites speculation about whether they had already taken Atta's measure at some earlier meeting. To be sure, some gaps do appear in the record of Atta's known whereabouts during the preceding years. One such gap is February–March 1998, a period for which there is no evidence of his presence in Germany and when he conceivably could have been in Afghanistan. Yet to date, neither KSM, Binalshibh, nor any other al Qaeda figure interrogated about the 9/11 plot has claimed that Atta or any other member of the Hamburg group traveled to Afghanistan before the trip in late 1999.

After leaving Afghanistan, the four began researching flight schools and aviation training. In early January 2000, Ali Abdul Aziz Ali—a nephew of KSM living in the UAE who would become an important facilitator in the plot—used Shehhi's credit card to order a Boeing 747-400 flight simulator program and a Boeing 767 flight deck video, together with attendant literature; Ali had all these items shipped to his employer's address. Jarrah soon decided that the schools in Germany were not acceptable and that he would have to learn to fly in the United States. Binalshibh also researched flight schools in Europe, and in the Netherlands he met a flight school director who recommended flight schools in the United States because they were less expensive and required shorter training periods.

Before seeking visas to enter the United States, Atta, Shehhi, and Jarrah obtained new passports, each claiming that his old passport had been lost. Presumably they were concerned that the Pakistani visas in their old passports would raise suspicions about possible travel to Afghanistan. Shehhi obtained his visa on January 18, 2000; Atta, on May 18; and Jarrah, on May 25. Binalshibh's visa request was rejected, however, as were his three subsequent applications. Binalshibh proved unable to obtain a visa, a victim of the generalized suspicion that visa applicants from Yemen—especially young men applying in another country (Binalshibh first applied in Berlin)—might join the ranks of undocumented aliens seeking work in the United States.

Bin Ladin and his aides did not need a very large sum to finance their planned attack on America. The 9/11 plotters eventually spent somewhere between $400,000 and $500,000 to plan and conduct their attack. Consistent with the importance of the project, al Qaeda funded the plotters. KSM provided his operatives with nearly all the money they needed to travel to the United States, train, and live. The plotters' tradecraft was not especially sophisticated, but it was good enough. They moved, stored, and spent their money in ordinary ways, easily defeating the detection mechanisms in place at the time. The origin of the funds remains unknown, although we have a general idea of how al Qaeda financed itself during the period leading up to 9/11.

REQUIREMENTS FOR A SUCCESSFUL ATTACK

As some of the core operatives prepared to leave for the United States, al Qaeda's leaders could have reflected on what they needed to be able to do in order to organize and conduct a complex international terrorist operation to inflict catastrophic harm. We believe such a list of requirements would have included

— leaders able to evaluate, approve, and supervise the planning and direction of the operation;
— communications sufficient to enable planning and direction of the operatives and those who would be helping them;
— a personnel system that could recruit candidates, vet them, indoctrinate them, and give them necessary training;
— an intelligence effort to gather required information and form assessments of enemy strengths and weaknesses;
— the ability to move people; and
— the ability to raise and move the necessary money.

The information we have presented about the development of the planes operation shows how, by the spring and summer of 2000, al Qaeda was able to meet these requirements.

By late May 2000, two operatives assigned to the planes operation were already in the United States. Three of the four Hamburg cell members would soon arrive.

## 6. FROM THREAT TO THREAT

After the August 1998 bombings of the American embassies in Kenya and Tanzania, President Bill Clinton and his chief aides explored ways of getting Bin Ladin expelled from Afghanistan or possibly capturing or even killing him. In public, President Clinton spoke repeatedly about the threat of terrorism, referring to terrorist training camps but saying little about Bin Ladin and nothing about al Qaeda. He explained to us that this was deliberate—intended to avoid enhancing Bin Ladin's stature by giving him unnecessary publicity. His speeches focused especially on the danger of nonstate actors and of chemical and biological weapons.

As the millennium approached, the most publicized worries were not about terrorism but about computer breakdowns—the Y2K scare [the possibility that computers would reset themselves to 1900 instead of switching over to 2000, with the result of massively disrupting financial and other systems that tracked data by date]. Some government officials were concerned that terrorists would take advantage of such breakdowns.

## The Millennium Crisis

"BODIES WILL PILE UP IN SACKS"

On November 30, 1999, Jordanian intelligence intercepted a telephone call between Abu Zubaydah, a longtime ally of Bin Ladin, and Khadr Abu Hoshar, a Palestinian extremist. Abu Zubaydah said, "The time for training is over." Suspecting that this was a signal for Abu Hoshar to commence a terrorist operation, Jordanian police arrested Abu Hoshar and 15 others and informed Washington.

One of the 16, Raed Hijazi, had been born in California to Palestinian parents; after spending his childhood in the Middle East, he had returned to northern California, taken refuge in extremist Islamist beliefs, and then made his way to Abu Zubaydah's Khaldan camp in Afghanistan, where he learned the fundamentals of guerrilla warfare.

In late 1998, Hijazi and Abu Hoshar had settled on a plan [to attack locations] likely to be thronged with American and other tourists.

In early 1999, Hijazi and Abu Hoshar contacted Khalil Deek, an American citizen and an associate of Abu Zubaydah who lived in Peshawar, Pakistan, and who, with Afghanistan-based extremists, had created an electronic version of a terrorist manual, the *Encyclopedia of Jihad*. They obtained a CD-ROM of this encyclopedia from Deek. In June, with help from Deek, Abu Hoshar arranged with Abu Zubaydah for Hijazi and three others to go to Afghanistan for added training in handling explosives.

After the arrests of Abu Hoshar and 15 others, the Jordanians tracked Deek to Peshawar, persuaded Pakistan to extradite him, and added him to their catch. Searches in Amman found the rented house and, among other things, 71 drums of acids, several forged Saudi passports, detonators, and Deek's *Encyclopedia*. Six of the accomplices were sentenced to death. In custody, Hijazi's younger brother said that the group's motto had been "The season is coming, and bodies will pile up in sacks."

Then, on December 14, an Algerian jihadist was caught bringing a load of explosives into the United States.

RESSAM'S ARREST

Ahmed Ressam, 23, had illegally immigrated to Canada in 1994 [and] trained in Afghanistan in 1998. Ressam left Afghanistan in early 1999 carrying precursor chemicals for explosives disguised in toiletry bottles, a notebook containing bomb assembly instructions, and $12,000. Back in Canada, he went about procuring weapons, chemicals, and false papers.

On December 14, 1999, Ressam drove his rental car onto the ferry from Victoria, Canada, to Port Angeles, Washington. Ressam planned to drive to Los Angeles and case LAX [Los Angeles International Airport, then] detonate the bomb on or around January 1, 2000.

Late in the afternoon of December 14, Ressam arrived in Port Angeles. He waited for all the other cars to depart the ferry, assuming (incorrectly) that the last car off would draw the least scrutiny. Customs officers assigned to the port, noticing Ressam's nervousness, referred him to secondary inspection. When asked for additional identification, Ressam handed the Customs agent a Price Costco membership card in the same false name as his passport. As that agent began an initial pat-down, Ressam panicked and tried to run away.

Inspectors examining Ressam's rental car found the explosives concealed in the spare tire well. Ressam was placed under arrest.

EMERGENCY COOPERATION

After the disruption of the plot in Amman, it had not escaped notice in Washington that Hijazi had lived in California and driven a cab in Boston and that Deek was a naturalized U.S. citizen who, as Berger reminded President Clinton, had been in touch with extremists in the United States as well as abroad. Before Ressam's arrest, Berger saw no need to raise a public alarm at home—although the FBI put all field offices on alert.

Now, following Ressam's arrest, the FBI asked for an unprecedented number of special wiretaps. Both Berger and Tenet told us that their impression was that more Foreign Intelligence Surveillance Act (FISA) wiretap requests were processed during the millennium alert than ever before.

The Counterterrorism Security Group (CSG) met daily.

There was a mounting sense of public alarm. The earlier Jordanian arrests had been covered in the press, and Ressam's arrest was featured on network evening news broadcasts throughout the Christmas season.

The FBI was more communicative during the millennium crisis than it had ever been. The senior FBI official for counterterrorism, Dale Watson, was a regular member of the CSG, and Clarke had good relations both with him and with some of the FBI agents handling al Qaeda–related investigations, including John O'Neill in New York. As a rule, however, neither Watson nor these agents brought much information to the group. The FBI simply did not produce the kind of intelligence reports that other agencies routinely wrote and disseminated. As law enforcement officers, Bureau agents tended to write up only witness interviews. Written case analysis usually occurred only in memoranda to supervisors requesting authority to initiate or expand an investigation.

But during the millennium alert, with its direct links into the United States from Hijazi, Deek, and Ressam, FBI officials were briefing in person about ongoing investigations, not relying on the dissemination of written reports. After the alert, the FBI returned to its normal practice of withholding written reports and saying little about investigations or witness interviews, taking the position that any information related to pending investigations might be presented to a grand jury and hence could not be disclosed under then prevailing federal law.

The terrorist plots that were broken up at the end of 1999 display the variety of operations that might be attributed, however indirectly, to al Qaeda. The Jordanian cell was a loose affiliate; we now know that it sought approval and training from Afghanistan, and at least one key member swore loyalty to Bin Ladin. But the cell's plans and preparations were autonomous. Ressam's ties to al Qaeda were even looser. Though he had been recruited, trained, and prepared in a network affiliated with the organization and its allies, Ressam's own plans were, nonetheless, essentially independent.

Al Qaeda, and Bin Ladin himself, did have at least one operation of their very own in mind for the millennium period. On January 3, an attempt was made to attack a U.S. warship in Aden, the USS *The Sullivans*. The attempt failed when the small boat, overloaded with explosives, sank. The operatives salvaged their equipment without the attempt becoming known, and they put off their plans for another day.

Al Qaeda's "planes operation" was also coming along. In January 2000, the United States caught a glimpse of its preparations.

A LOST TRAIL IN SOUTHEAST ASIA

In late 1999, the National Security Agency (NSA) analyzed communications associated with a suspected terrorist facility in the Middle East, indicating that several members of "an operational cadre" were planning to travel to Kuala Lumpur in early January 2000. Initially, only the first names of three were known—"Nawaf," "Salem," and "Khalid." NSA analysts surmised correctly that Salem was Nawaf's younger brother.

Though Nawaf's trail was temporarily lost, the CIA soon identified "Khalid" as Khalid al Mihdhar. He was located leaving Yemen and tracked until he arrived in Kuala Lumpur on January 5, 2000. Other Arabs, unidentified at the time, were watched as they gathered with him in the Malaysian capital.

On January 8, the surveillance teams reported that three of the Arabs had suddenly left Kuala Lumpur on a short flight to Bangkok. They identified one as Mihdhar. They later learned that one of his companions was named Alhazmi, although it was not yet known that he was "Nawaf." In Bangkok, CIA officers received the information too late to track the three men as they came in, and the travelers disappeared into the streets of Bangkok.

The Counterterrorist Center (CTC) had briefed the CIA leadership on the gathering in Kuala Lumpur, and the information had been passed on to Berger and the NSC staff and to Director Freeh and others at the FBI. The head of the Bin Ladin unit kept providing updates, unaware at first even that the Arabs had left Kuala Lumpur, let alone that their trail had been lost in Bangkok.

Several weeks later, CIA officers in Kuala Lumpur prodded colleagues in Bangkok for additional information regarding the three travelers. In early March 2000, Bangkok reported that Nawaf al Hazmi, now identified for the first time with his full name, had departed on January 15 on a United Airlines flight to Los Angeles. As for Khalid al Mihdhar, there was no report of his departure even though he had accompanied Hazmi on the United flight to Los Angeles. No one outside of the Counterterrorist Center was told any of this. The CIA did not try to register Mihdhar or Hazmi with the State Department's TIPOFF [terrorist] watchlist—either in January, when word arrived of Mihdhar's visa, or in March, when word came that Hazmi, too, had had a U.S. visa and a ticket to Los Angeles.

None of this information—about Mihdhar's U.S. visa or Hazmi's travel to the United States—went to the FBI, and nothing more was done to track any of the three until January 2001, when the investigation of another bombing, that of the USS *Cole*, reignited interest in Khallad.

### Post-Crisis Reflection: Agenda for 2000

After the millennium alert, elements of the U.S. government reviewed their performance. The CIA's leadership was told that while a number of plots had been disrupted, the millennium might be only the "kick-off" for a period of extended attacks. Clarke wrote Berger on January 11, 2000, that the CIA, the FBI, Justice, and the NSC staff had come to two main conclusions. First, U.S. disruption efforts thus far had "not put too much of a dent" in Bin Ladin's network. If the United States wanted to "roll back" the threat, disruption would have to proceed at "a markedly different tempo." Second, "sleeper cells" and "a variety of terrorist groups" had turned up at home.

The Principals Committee met on March 10, 2000, to review possible new moves. The principals ended up agreeing that the government should take three major steps. First, more money should go to the CIA to accelerate its efforts to "seriously attrit" al Qaeda. Second, there should be a crackdown on foreign terrorist organizations in the United States. Third, immigration law enforcement should be strengthened, and the INS should tighten controls on the Canadian border (including stepping up U.S.-Canada cooperation). The principals endorsed the proposed programs; some, like expanding the number of Joint Terrorism Task Forces, moved forward, and others, like creating a centralized translation unit for domestic intelligence intercepts in Arabic and other languages, did not.

* * *

"AFGHAN EYES"

At some point during this period, President Clinton expressed his frustration with the lack of military options to take out Bin Ladin and the al Qaeda leadership, remarking to General Hugh Shelton, "You know, it would scare the shit out of al-Qaeda if suddenly a bunch of black ninjas rappelled out of helicopters into the middle of their camp."

One option was to use a small, unmanned U.S. Air Force drone called the Predator, which could survey the territory below and send back video footage. In the spring of 2000, Clarke brought in the CIA's assistant director for collection, Charles Allen, to work on a joint CIA-Pentagon effort that Clarke dubbed "Afghan Eyes." After much argument between the CIA and the Defense Department about who should pay for the program, the White House eventually imposed a cost-sharing agreement. The CIA agreed to pay for Predator operations as a 60-day "proof of concept" trial run.

On September 7, the Predator flew for the first time over Afghanistan. When Clarke saw video taken during the trial flight, he described the imagery to Berger as "truly astonishing," and he argued immediately for more flights seeking to find Bin Ladin and target him for cruise missile or air attack.

Ten out of 15 trial missions of the Predator over Afghanistan were rated successful. On the first flight, a Predator saw a security detail around a tall man in a white robe at Bin Ladin's Tarnak Farms compound outside Kandahar. After a second sighting of the "man in white" at the compound on September 28, intelligence community analysts determined that he was probably Bin Ladin.

During at least one trial mission, the Taliban spotted the Predator and scrambled MiG fighters to try, without success, to intercept it. Berger worried that a Predator might be shot down, and warned Clarke that a shootdown would be a "bonanza" for Bin Ladin and the Taliban.

Still, Clarke was optimistic about Predator—as well as progress with disruptions of al Qaeda cells elsewhere. Berger was more cautious, praising the NSC staff's performance but observing that this was no time for complacency. "Unfortunately," he wrote, "the light at the end of the tunnel is another tunnel."

## The Attack on the USS *Cole*

On October 12, 2000, al Qaeda operatives in a small boat laden with explosives attacked a U.S. Navy destroyer, the USS *Cole*. The blast ripped a hole in the side of the *Cole*, killing 17 members of the ship's crew and wounding at least 40.

The plot, we now know, was a full-fledged al Qaeda operation, supervised directly by Bin Ladin. He chose the target and location of the attack, selected the suicide operatives, and provided the money needed to purchase explosives and equipment.

Back in Afghanistan, Bin Ladin anticipated U.S. military retaliation. He ordered the evacuation of al Qaeda's Kandahar airport compound and fled—first to the desert area near Kabul, then to Khowst and Jalalabad, and eventually back to Kandahar. In Kandahar, he rotated between five to six residences, spending one night at each residence. In addition, he sent his senior advisor, Mohammed Atef, to a different part of Kandahar and his deputy, Ayman al Zawahiri, to Kabul so that all three could not be killed in one attack.

There was no American strike. In February 2001, a source reported that an individual whom he identified as the big instructor (probably a reference to Bin Ladin) complained frequently that the United States had not yet attacked. According to the source, Bin Ladin wanted the United States to attack, and if it did not he would launch something bigger.

The attack on the USS *Cole* galvanized al Qaeda's recruitment efforts. Following the attack, Bin Ladin instructed the media committee, then headed by Khalid Sheikh Mohammed, to produce a propaganda video that included a reenactment of the attack along with images of the al Qaeda training camps and training methods; it also highlighted Muslim suffering in Palestine, Kashmir, Indonesia, and Chechnya. Al Qaeda's image was very important to Bin Ladin, and the video was widely disseminated. Portions were aired on Al Jazeera, CNN, and other television outlets. It was also disseminated among many young men in Saudi Arabia and Yemen, and caused many extremists to travel to Afghanistan for training and jihad. Al Qaeda members considered the video an effective tool in their struggle for preeminence among other Islamist and jihadist movements.

\* \* \*

CONSIDERING A RESPONSE

The *Cole* attack prompted renewed consideration of what could be done about al Qaeda. According to Clarke, Berger upbraided DCI Tenet so sharply after the *Cole* attack—repeatedly demanding to know why the United States had to put up with such attacks—that Tenet walked out of a meeting of the principals.

On the diplomatic track, Berger agreed on October 30, 2000, to let the State Department make another approach to Taliban Deputy Foreign Minister Abdul Jalil about expelling Bin Ladin. The national security advisor ordered that the U.S. message "be stern and foreboding." This warning was similar to those issued in 1998 and 1999.

President Clinton told us that before he could launch further attacks on al Qaeda in Afghanistan, or deliver an ultimatum to the Taliban threatening strikes if they did not immediately expel Bin Ladin, the CIA or the FBI had to be sure enough that they would "be willing to stand up in public and say, we believe that he [Bin Ladin] did this." He said he was very frustrated that he could not get a definitive enough answer to do something about the *Cole* attack. Similarly, Berger recalled that the intelligence agencies had strong suspicions, but had reached "no conclusion by the time we left office that it was al Qaeda."

In mid-November, as the evidence of al Qaeda involvement mounted, Berger asked General Shelton to reevaluate military plans to act quickly against Bin Ladin. General Shelton tasked General Tommy Franks, the new commander of CENTCOM, to look again at the options. Shelton wanted to demonstrate that the military was imaginative and knowledgeable enough to move on an array of options, and to show the complexity of the operations. He briefed Berger on the "Infinite Resolve" strike options developed since 1998, which the Joint Staff and CENTCOM had refined during the summer into a list of 13 possibilities or combinations. CENTCOM added a new "phased campaign" concept for wider-ranging strikes, including attacks against the Taliban. For the first time, these strikes envisioned an air campaign against Afghanistan of indefinite duration. Military planners did not include contingency planning for an invasion of Afghanistan.

On December 21, the CIA made another presentation to the Small Group of principals on the investigative team's findings. The CIA's briefing slides said that their "preliminary judgment" was that Bin Ladin's al Qaeda group "supported the attack" on the *Cole*, based on strong circumstantial evidence tying key perpetrators of the attack to al Qaeda.

The slides said that so far the CIA had "no definitive answer on [the] crucial question of outside direction of the attack—how and by whom."

This, President Clinton and Berger told us, was not the conclusion they needed in order to go to war or deliver an ultimatum to the Taliban threatening war. The election and change of power was not the issue, President Clinton added. There was enough time. If the agencies had given him a definitive answer, he said, he would have sought a UN Security Council ultimatum and given the Taliban one, two, or three days before taking further action against both al Qaeda and the Taliban. But he did not think it would be responsible for a president to launch an invasion of another country just based on a "preliminary judgment."

Clarke recalled that the issue never came to a head because the FBI and the CIA never reached a firm conclusion. He thought they were "holding back." He said he did not know why, but his impression was that Tenet and Reno possibly thought the White House "didn't really want to know," since the principals' discussions by November suggested that there was not much White House interest in conducting further military operations against Afghanistan in the administration's last weeks.

## Change and Continuity

On November 7, 2000, American voters went to the polls in what turned out to be one of the closest presidential contests in U.S. history—an election campaign during which there was a notable absence of serious discussion of the al Qaeda threat or terrorism. Election night became a 36-day legal fight. Until the Supreme Court's 5–4 ruling on December 12 and Vice President Al Gore's concession, no one knew whether Gore or his Republican opponent, Texas Governor George W. Bush, would become president in 2001.

The dispute over the election and the 36-day delay cut in half the normal transition period. Given that a presidential election in the United States brings wholesale change in personnel, this loss of time hampered the new administration in identifying, recruiting, clearing, and obtaining Senate confirmation of key appointees.

In December, Bush met with Clinton for a two-hour, one-on-one discussion of national security and foreign policy challenges. Clinton recalled saying to Bush, "I think you will find that by far your biggest threat is Bin Ladin and the al Qaeda." Clinton told us that he also said, "One of the great regrets of my presidency is that I didn't get him [Bin Ladin] for you, because I tried to." Bush told the Commission that he felt sure President Clinton had mentioned terrorism, but did not remember much being said about al Qaeda. Bush recalled that Clinton had emphasized other issues such as North Korea and the Israeli-Palestinian peace process.

In early January, Clarke briefed [National Security Advisor–designate Condoleezza] Rice on terrorism. He gave similar presentations—describing al Qaeda as both an adaptable global network of jihadist organizations and a lethal core terrorist organization—to Vice President–elect Cheney, [Deputy National Security Advisor–designate

Stephen] Hadley, and Secretary of State–designate [Colin] Powell. One line in the briefing slides said that al Qaeda had sleeper cells in more than 40 countries, including the United States. Berger told us that he made a point of dropping in on Clarke's briefing of Rice to emphasize the importance of the issue. Later the same day, Berger met with Rice. He says that he told her the Bush administration would spend more time on terrorism in general and al Qaeda in particular than on anything else. Rice's recollection was that Berger told her she would be surprised at how much more time she was going to spend on terrorism than she expected, but that the bulk of their conversation dealt with the faltering Middle East peace process and North Korea. Clarke said that the new team, having been out of government for eight years, had a steep learning curve to understand al Qaeda and the new transnational terrorist threat.

Rice made an initial decision to hold over both Clarke and his entire counterterrorism staff, a decision that she called rare for a new administration. She decided also that Clarke should retain the title of national counterterrorism coordinator, although he would no longer be a de facto member of the Principals Committee on his issues. The decision to keep Clarke, Rice said, was "not uncontroversial," since he was known as someone who "broke china," but she and Hadley wanted an experienced crisis manager. No one else from Berger's staff had Clarke's detailed knowledge of the levers of government.

Clarke was disappointed at what he perceived as a demotion. He also worried that reporting through the Deputies Committee would slow decisionmaking on counterterrorism.

The result, amid all the changes accompanying the transition, was significant continuity in counterterrorism policy. Clarke and his Counterterrorism Security Group would continue to manage coordination. Tenet remained Director of Central Intelligence and kept the same chief subordinates. Shelton remained chairman of the Joint Chiefs, with the Joint Staff largely the same. At the FBI, Director [Louis] Freeh and Assistant Director for Counterterrorism Dale Watson remained. Working-level counterterrorism officials at the State Department and the Pentagon stayed on, as is typically the case. The changes were at the cabinet and subcabinet level and in the CSG's reporting arrangements.

The procedures of the Bush administration were to be at once more formal and less formal than its predecessor's. President Clinton, a voracious reader, received his daily intelligence briefings in writing. He often scrawled questions and comments in the margins, eliciting written responses. The new president, by contrast, reinstated the practice of face-to-face briefings from the DCI. President Bush and Tenet met in the Oval Office at 8:00 A.M., with Vice President Cheney, Rice, and [White House Chief of Staff Andrew] Card usually also present. The President and the DCI both told us that these daily sessions provided a useful opportunity for exchanges on intelligence issues.

The President talked with Rice every day, and she in turn talked by phone at least daily with Powell and [Secretary of Defense Donald] Rumsfeld. As a result, the President often felt less need for formal meetings. If, however, he decided that an event or an issue called for action, Rice would typically call on Hadley to have the Deputies Committee develop and review options. The President said that this process often tried his patience but that he understood the necessity for coordination.

EARLY DECISIONS

Within the first few days after Bush's inauguration, Clarke approached Rice in an effort to get her—and the new President—to give terrorism very high priority and to act on the agenda that he had pushed during the last few months of the previous administration. After Rice requested that all senior staff identify desirable major policy reviews or initiatives, Clarke submitted an elaborate memorandum on January 25, 2001. He attached to it his 1998 Delenda Plan and the December 2000 strategy paper. "We *urgently* need . . . a Principals level review on the *al Qida* network," Clarke wrote.

He wanted the Principals Committee to decide whether al Qaeda was "a first order threat" or a more modest worry being overblown by "chicken little" alarmists.

The national security advisor did not respond directly to Clarke's memorandum. No Principals Committee meeting on al Qaeda was held until September 4, 2001 (although the Principals Committee met frequently on other subjects, such as the Middle East peace process, Russia, and the Persian Gulf). But Rice and Hadley began to address the issues Clarke had listed. What to do or say about the *Cole* had been an obvious question since inauguration day.

Rice told us that there was never a formal, recorded decision not to retaliate specifically for the *Cole* attack. Exchanges with the President, between the President and Tenet, and between herself and Powell and Rumsfeld had produced a consensus that "tit-for-tat" responses were likely to be counterproductive. This had been the case, she thought, with the cruise missile strikes of August 1998. Hadley said that in the end, the administration's real response to the *Cole* would be a new, more aggressive strategy against al Qaeda.

STARTING A REVIEW

Rice and others recalled the President saying, "I'm tired of swatting at flies." The President reportedly also said, "I'm tired of playing defense. I want to play offense. I want to take the fight to the terrorists." President Bush explained to us that he had become impatient. He apparently had heard proposals for rolling back al Qaeda but felt that catching terrorists one by one or even cell by cell was not an approach likely to succeed in the long run. At the same time, he said, he understood that policy had to be developed slowly so that diplomacy and financial and military measures could mesh with one another.

## The New Administration's Approach

The Bush administration in its first months faced many problems other than terrorism. They included the collapse of the Middle East peace process and, in April, a crisis over a U.S. "spy plane" brought down in Chinese territory. The new administration also focused heavily on Russia, a new nuclear strategy that allowed missile defenses, Europe, Mexico, and the Persian Gulf.

In the spring, reporting on terrorism surged dramatically. These increasingly alarming reports, briefed to the President and top officials, became part of the context in which the new administration weighed its options for policy on al Qaeda.

Except for a few reports that the CSG considered and apparently judged to be unreliable, none of these pointed specifically to possible al Qaeda action inside the United States—although the CSG continued to be concerned about the domestic threat. The mosaic of threat intelligence came from the Counterterrorist Center, which collected only abroad. Its reports were not supplemented by reports from the FBI.

On May 29, at Tenet's request, Rice and Tenet converted their usual weekly meeting into a broader discussion on al Qaeda; participants included Clarke, CTC chief Cofer Black, and "Richard," a group chief with authority over the Bin Ladin unit. Rice asked about "taking the offensive" and whether any approach could be made to influence Bin Ladin or the Taliban. A wide-ranging discussion then ensued about "breaking the back" of Bin Ladin's organization.

The CIA official, "Richard," told us that Rice "got it." He said she agreed with his conclusions about what needed to be done, although he complained to us that the policy process did not follow through quickly enough.

Rice and Hadley asked Clarke and his staff to draw up the new presidential directive. On June 7, Hadley circulated the first draft, describing it as "an admittedly ambitious" program for confronting al Qaeda. The goal was to "eliminate the al Qida network of terrorist groups as a threat to the United States and to friendly governments." It called for a multiyear effort involving diplomacy, covert action, economic measures, law enforcement, public diplomacy, and if necessary military efforts.

Rice viewed this draft directive as the embodiment of a comprehensive new strategy employing all instruments of national power to eliminate the al Qaeda threat. Clarke, however, regarded the new draft as essentially similar to the proposal he had developed in December 2000 and put forward to the new administration in January 2001. In May or June, Clarke asked to be moved from his counterterrorism portfolio to a new set of responsibilities for cybersecurity. He told us that he was frustrated with his role and with an administration that he considered not "serious about al Qaeda." If Clarke was frustrated, he never expressed it to her, Rice told us.

* * *

SEPTEMBER 2001

The Principals Committee had its first meeting on al Qaeda on September 4. On the day of the meeting, Clarke sent Rice an impassioned personal note. He criticized U.S. counterterrorism efforts past and present. The "real question" before the principals, he wrote, was "are we serious about dealing with the al Qida threat? . . . Is al Qida a big deal? . . . *Decision makers should imagine themselves on a future day when the CSG has not succeeded in stopping al Qida attacks and hundreds of Americans lay dead in several countries, including the US,*" Clarke wrote. "What would those decision makers wish that they had done earlier? That future day could happen at any time."

Clarke then turned to the *Cole*. "*The fact that the USS Cole was attacked during the last Administration does not absolve us of responding for the attack,*" he wrote. "Many in al Qida and the Taliban may have drawn the wrong lesson from the Cole: that they can kill Americans without there being a US response, without there being a price. . . . One might have thought that with a $250m hole in a destroyer and 17 dead sailors, the Pentagon might have wanted to respond. Instead, they have often talked about the fact that there is 'nothing worth hitting in Afghanistan' and said 'the cruise missiles cost more than the jungle gyms and mud huts' at terrorist camps." Clarke could not understand *"why we continue to allow the existence of large scale al Qida bases where we know people are being trained to kill Americans."*

Turning to the CIA, Clarke warned that its bureaucracy, which was "masterful at passive aggressive behavior," would resist funding the new national security presidential directive, leaving it a "hollow shell of words without deeds." The CIA would insist its other priorities were more important. Invoking President Bush's own language, Clarke wrote, *"You are left with a modest effort to swat flies,* to try to prevent specific al Qida attacks by using [intelligence] to detect them and friendly governments' police and intelligence officers to stop them. *You are left waiting for the big attack,* with lots of casualties, after which some major US retaliation will be in order."

Rice told us she took Clarke's memo as a warning not to get dragged down by bureaucratic inertia. While his arguments have force, we also take Clarke's jeremiad as something more. After nine years on the NSC staff and more than three years as the president's national coordinator, he had often failed to persuade these agencies to adopt his views, or to persuade his superiors to set an agenda of the sort he wanted or that the whole government could support.

At the September 4 meeting, the principals approved the draft presidential directive with little discussion. Rice told us that she had, at some point, told President Bush that she and his other advisers thought it would take three years or so for their al Qaeda strategy to work.

On September 10, Hadley gathered the deputies to finalize their three-phase, multiyear plan to pressure and perhaps ultimately topple the Taliban leadership. Funding still needed to be located. The military component remained unclear. Pakistan remained uncooperative. The domestic policy institutions were largely uninvolved. But the pieces were coming together for an integrated policy dealing with al Qaeda, the Taliban, and Pakistan.

## 7. THE ATTACK LOOMS

### First Arrivals in California

In chapter 5 we described the Southeast Asia travels of Nawaf al Hazmi, Khalid al Mihdhar, and others in January 2000 on the first part of the "planes operation." In that chapter we also described how Mihdhar was spotted in Kuala Lumpur early in January 2000, along with associates who were not identified, and then was lost to sight when the group passed through Bangkok. On January 15, Hazmi and Mihdhar arrived in Los Angeles. They spent about two weeks there before moving on to San Diego.

Why Hazmi and Mihdhar came to California, we do not know for certain. Khalid Sheikh Mohammed (KSM), the organizer of the planes operation, explains that California was a convenient point of entry from Asia and had the added benefit of being far away from the intended target area.

Hazmi and Mihdhar were ill-prepared for a mission in the United States. Their only qualifications for this plot were their devotion to Usama Bin Ladin, their veteran service, and their ability to get valid U.S. visas. Neither had spent any substantial time in the West, and neither spoke much, if any, English. [Though] KSM denies that al Qaeda had any agents in Southern California, we believe it is unlikely that Hazmi and Mihdhar would have come to the United States without arranging to receive assistance from one or more individuals informed in advance of their arrival.

Although the evidence is thin as to specific motivations, our overall impression is that soon after arriving in California, Hazmi and Mihdhar sought out and found a group of young and ideologically like-minded Muslims with roots in Yemen and Saudi Arabia. The al Qaeda operatives lived openly in San Diego under their true names, listing Hazmi in the telephone directory. They managed to avoid attracting much attention.

Hazmi and Mihdhar came to the United States to learn English, take flying lessons, and become pilots as quickly as possible. They turned out, however, to have no aptitude for English. Even with help and tutoring from bilingual friends, Hazmi and Mihdhar's efforts to learn proved futile. This lack of language skills in turn became an insurmountable barrier to learning how to fly.

Mihdhar's mind seems to have been with his family back in Yemen, as evidenced by calls he made from the apartment telephone. When news of the birth of his first child arrived, he could stand life in California no longer. In late May and early June of 2000, he arranged his return to Yemen. According to KSM, Mihdhar foresaw no problem in coming back to the United States since he had not overstayed his visa.

By the fall of 2000, Hazmi no longer even pretended to study English or take flying lessons. Aware that his co-conspirators in Afghanistan and Pakistan would be sending him a new colleague shortly, he bided his time and worked for a few weeks at a gas station in La Mesa where some of his friends were employed. On one occasion, Hazmi told a fellow employee that he was planning to find a better job, and let slip a prediction that he would become famous.

## The 9/11 Pilots in the United States

In the early summer of 2000, the Hamburg group arrived in the United States to begin flight training. Marwan al Shehhi came on May 29, arriving in Newark on a flight from Brussels. He went to New York City and waited there for Mohamed Atta to join him. On June 2, Atta traveled to the Czech Republic by bus from Germany and then flew from Prague to Newark the next day. According to Ramzi Binalshibh, Atta did not meet with anyone in Prague; he simply believed it would contribute to operational security to fly out of Prague rather than Hamburg, the departure point for much of his previous international travel.

Atta and Shehhi had not settled on where they would obtain their flight training. In contrast, Ziad Jarrah had already arranged to attend the Florida Flight Training Center (FFTC) in Venice, Florida. Jarrah arrived in Newark on June 27 and then flew to Venice. He immediately began the private pilot program at FFTC, intending to get a multi-engine license. Jarrah moved in with some of the flight instructors affiliated with his school and bought a car.

Binalshibh could not obtain a U.S. visa. Unable to participate directly in the operation, Binalshibh instead took on the role of coordinating between KSM and the operatives in the United States. Apart from sending a total of about $10,000 in wire transfers to Atta and Shehhi during the summer of 2000, one of Binalshibh's first tasks in his new role as plot coordinator was to assist another possible pilot, Zacarias Moussaoui.

In the fall of 2000, KSM had sent Moussaoui to Malaysia for flight training, but Moussaoui did not find a school he liked. He worked instead on other terrorist schemes, such as buying four tons of ammonium nitrate for bombs to be planted on cargo planes flying to the United States. When KSM found out, he recalled Moussaoui back to Pakistan and directed him to go to the United States for flight training. In early October, Moussaoui went to London. From London, Moussaoui sent inquiries to the Airman Flight School in Norman, Oklahoma.

Confronting training or travel problems with Hazmi, Mihdhar, Binalshibh, and Moussaoui, al Qaeda was looking for another possible pilot candidate. A new recruit with just the right background conveniently presented himself in Afghanistan.

## THE FOURTH PILOT: HANI HANJOUR

Hani Hanjour, from Ta'if, Saudi Arabia, first came to the United States in 1991 to study at the Center for English as a Second Language at the University of Arizona. He seems to have been a rigorously observant Muslim. According to his older brother, Hani Hanjour went to Afghanistan for the first time in the late 1980s, as a teenager, to participate in the jihad and, because the Soviets had already withdrawn, worked for a relief agency there.

In 1996, Hanjour returned to the United States to pursue flight training. He checked out flight schools in Florida, California, and Arizona; returned to Florida[;] and then went back to Arizona and began his flight training there in earnest. After about three months, Hanjour was able to obtain his private pilot's license. Several more months of training yielded him a commercial pilot certificate, issued by the Federal Aviation Administration (FAA) in April 1999.

By the spring of 2000, Hanjour was back in Afghanistan. According to KSM, Hanjour was sent to him in Karachi for inclusion in the plot after Hanjour was identified in al Qaeda's al Faruq camp as a trained pilot, on the basis of background information he had provided. Hanjour had been at a camp in Afghanistan for a few weeks when Bin Ladin or Atef apparently realized that he was a trained pilot; he was told to report to KSM, who then trained Hanjour for a few days in the use of code words.

On December 8, Hanjour joined Nawaf al Hazmi in San Diego.

Hazmi and Hanjour left San Diego almost immediately and drove to Arizona. Settling in Mesa, Hanjour began refresher training at his old school, Arizona Aviation. He wanted to train on multi-engine planes, but had difficulties because his English was not good enough. The instructor advised him to discontinue but Hanjour said he could not go home without completing the training. In early 2001, he started training on a Boeing 737 simulator at Pan Am International Flight Academy in Mesa. An instructor there found his work well below standard and discouraged him from continuing. Again, Hanjour persevered; he completed the initial training by the end of March 2001. At that point, Hanjour and Hazmi vacated their apartment and started driving east. By as early as April 4, Hanjour and Hazmi had arrived in Falls Church, Virginia.

The three pilots in Florida continued with their training. Atta and

Shehhi earned their instrument certificates from the FAA in November. In mid-December 2000, they passed their commercial pilot tests and received their licenses. They then began training to fly large jets on a flight simulator. At about the same time, Jarrah began simulator training, also in Florida but at a different center. By the end of 2000, less than six months after their arrival, the three pilots on the East Coast were simulating flights on large jets.

* * *

## Assembling the Teams

During the summer and early autumn of 2000, Bin Ladin and senior al Qaeda leaders in Afghanistan started selecting the muscle hijackers — the operatives who would storm the cockpits and control the passengers. Despite the phrase widely used to describe them, the so-called muscle hijackers were not at all physically imposing; most were between 5'5" and 5'7" in height.

Twelve of the 13 muscle hijackers (excluding Nawaf al Hazmi and Mihdhar) came from Saudi Arabia. [They] came from a variety of educational and societal backgrounds. All were between 20 and 28 years old; most were unemployed with no more than a high school education and were unmarried.

* * *

Having acquired U.S. visas in Saudi Arabia, the muscle hijackers returned to Afghanistan for special training in late 2000 to early 2001. The training reportedly was conducted at the al Matar complex by Abu Turab al Jordani, one of only a handful of al Qaeda operatives who, according to KSM, was aware of the full details of the planned planes operation. Abu Turab taught the operatives how to conduct hijackings, disarm air marshals, and handle explosives. He also trained them in bodybuilding and provided them with a few basic English words and phrases.

According to KSM, Abu Turab even had the trainees butcher a sheep and a camel with a knife to prepare to use knives during the hijackings. The recruits learned to focus on storming the cockpit at the earliest opportunity when the doors first opened, and to worry about seizing control over the rest of the plane later. The operatives were taught about other kinds of attack as well, such as truck bombing, so that they would not be able to disclose the exact nature of their operation if they were caught. According to KSM, the muscle [hijackers] did not learn the full details—including the plan to hijack planes and fly them into buildings—before reaching the United States.

The last muscle hijacker to arrive was Khalid al Mihdhar. As mentioned earlier, he had abandoned Hazmi in San Diego in June 2000 and returned to his family in Yemen. Mihdhar reportedly stayed in Yemen for about a month before Khallad persuaded him to return to Afghanistan. Mihdhar complained about life in the United States. He met with KSM, who remained annoyed at his decision to go AWOL. But KSM's desire to drop him from the operation yielded to Bin Ladin's insistence to keep him.

On July 4, 2001, Mihdhar left Saudi Arabia to return to the United States, arriving at John F. Kennedy International Airport in New York. He then joined the group of hijackers in Paterson [New Jersey], reuniting with Nawaf al Hazmi after more than a year. With two months remaining, all 19 hijackers were in the United States and ready to take the final steps toward carrying out the attacks.

\* \* \*

Binalshibh had spent much of the spring of 2001 in Afghanistan and Pakistan, helping move the muscle hijackers as they passed through Karachi. In late May, Binalshibh reported directly to Bin Ladin at an al Qaeda facility known as "Compound Six" near Kandahar.

Bin Ladin told Binalshibh to instruct Atta and the others to focus on their security and that of the operation, and to advise Atta to proceed as planned with the targets discussed before Atta left Afghanistan in early 2000—the World Trade Center, the Pentagon, the White House, and the Capitol. According to Binalshibh, Bin Ladin said he preferred the White House over the Capitol, asking Binalshibh to confirm that Atta understood this preference.

In early July, Atta called Binalshibh to suggest meeting in Madrid, for reasons Binalshibh claims not to know. He says he preferred Berlin, but that he and Atta knew too many people in Germany and feared being spotted together. Unable to buy a ticket to Madrid at the height of the tourist season, Binalshibh booked a seat on a flight to Reus, near Barcelona, the next day. Atta was already en route to Madrid, so Binalshibh phoned Shehhi in the United States to inform him of the change in itinerary.

Atta arrived in Madrid on July 8. He spent the night in a hotel and made three calls from his room, most likely to coordinate with Binal-shibh. The next day, Atta rented a car and drove to Reus to pick up Binalshibh; the two then drove to the nearby town of Cambrils. Hotel records show Atta renting rooms in the same area until July 19, when he returned his rental car in Madrid and flew back to Fort Lauderdale. On July 16, Binalshibh returned to Hamburg, using a ticket Atta had purchased for him earlier that day. According to Binalshibh, they did not meet with anyone else while in Spain.

As to targets, Atta understood Bin Ladin's interest in striking the White House. Atta said he thought this target too difficult, but had tasked Hazmi and Hanjour to evaluate its feasibility and was awaiting their answer. Atta said that those two operatives had rented small air-craft and flown reconnaissance flights near the Pentagon. Atta ex-plained that Hanjour was assigned to attack the Pentagon, Jarrah the Capitol, and that both Atta and Shehhi would hit the World Trade Cen-ter. If any pilot could not reach his intended target, he was to crash the plane. If Atta could not strike the World Trade Center, he planned to crash his aircraft directly into the streets of New York. Atta told Binalshibh that each pilot had volunteered for his assigned target, and that the assignments were subject to change.

Binalshibh claims that during their time in Spain, he and Atta also discussed how the hijackings would be executed. Atta said he, Shehhi, and Jarrah had encountered no problems carrying box cutters on cross-country surveillance flights. The best time to storm the cockpit would be about 10–15 minutes after takeoff, when the cockpit doors typically were opened for the first time. Atta did not believe they would need any other weapons. He had no firm contingency plan in case the cockpit door was locked. While he mentioned general ideas such as using a hostage or claiming to have a bomb, he was confident the cockpit doors would be opened and did not consider breaking them down a viable idea. Atta told Binalshibh he wanted to select planes departing on long flights because they would be full of fuel, and that he wanted to hijack Boeing aircraft because he believed them eas-ier to fly than Airbus aircraft, which he understood had an autopilot feature that did not allow them to be crashed into the ground.

Finally, Atta confirmed that the muscle hijackers had arrived in the United States without incident. They would be divided into teams according to their English-speaking ability. That way they could assist each other before the operation and each team would be able to com-mand the passengers in English. According to Binalshibh, Atta com-plained that some of the hijackers wanted to contact their families to say goodbye, something he had forbidden. Before Binalshibh left Spain, he gave Atta eight necklaces and eight bracelets that Atta had asked him to buy when he was recently in Bangkok, believing that if the hijackers were clean shaven and well dressed, others would think them wealthy Saudis and give them less notice.

Moussaoui had been taking flight lessons at the Airman Flight School in Norman, Oklahoma, since February but stopped in late May. Although at that point he had only about 50 hours of flight time and no solo flights to his credit, Moussaoui began making inquiries about flight materials and simulator training for Boeing 747s. On July 10, he put down a $1,500 deposit for flight simulator training at Pan Am International Flight Academy in Eagan, Minnesota, and by the end of the month, he had received a simulator schedule to train from August 13 through August 20. Moussaoui also purchased two knives and inquired of two manufacturers of GPS equipment whether their products could be converted for aeronautical use—activities that closely resembled those of the 9/11 hijackers during their final preparations for the attacks.

On August 10, shortly after getting the money from Binalshibh, Moussaoui left Oklahoma with a friend and drove to Minnesota. Three days later, Moussaoui paid the $6,800 balance owed for his flight simulator training at Pan Am in cash and began his training. His conduct, however, raised the suspicions of his flight instructor. It was unusual for a student with so little training to be learning to fly large jets without any intention of obtaining a pilot's license or other goal. On August 16, once the instructor reported his suspicion to the authorities, Moussaoui was arrested by the INS on immigration charges.

KSM denies ever considering Moussaoui for the planes operation. Instead he claims that Moussaoui was slated to participate in a "second wave" of attacks. KSM also states that Moussaoui had no contact with Atta, and we are unaware of evidence contradicting this assertion.

Yet KSM has also stated that by the summer of 2001, he was too busy with the planes operation to continue planning for any second-wave attacks. Moreover, he admits that only three potential pilots were ever recruited for the alleged second wave, Moussaoui plus two others who, by midsummer of 2001, had backed out of the plot. We therefore believe that the effort to push Moussaoui forward in August 2001 lends credence to the suspicion that he was being primed as a possible pilot in the immediate planes operation.

Binalshibh says he assumed Moussaoui was to take his place as another pilot in the 9/11 operation. Recounting a post-9/11 discussion with KSM in Kandahar, Binalshibh claims KSM mentioned Moussaoui as being part of the 9/11 operation. Although KSM never referred to Moussaoui by name, Binalshibh understood he was speaking of the operative to whom Binalshibh had wired money. Binalshibh says KSM did not approve of Moussaoui but believes KSM did not remove him from the operation only because Moussaoui had been selected and assigned by Bin Ladin himself.

KSM did not hear about Moussaoui's arrest until after September 11. According to Binalshibh, had Bin Ladin and KSM learned prior to 9/11 that Moussaoui had been detained, they might have canceled the operation. When Binalshibh discussed Moussaoui's arrest with KSM after September 11, KSM congratulated himself on not having Moussaoui contact the other operatives, which would have compromised the operation. Moussaoui had been in contact with Binalshibh, of course, but this was not discovered until after 9/11.

*  *  *

DISSENT WITHIN THE AL QAEDA LEADERSHIP

While tactical preparations for the attack were nearing completion, the entire operation was being questioned at the top, as al Qaeda and the Taliban argued over strategy for 2001. Our focus has naturally been on the specifics of the planes operation. But from the perspective of Bin Ladin and Atef, this operation was only one, admittedly key, element of their unfolding plans for the year. Living in Afghanistan, interacting constantly with the Taliban, the al Qaeda leaders would never lose sight of the situation in that country.

Although Bin Ladin's top priority apparently was to attack the United States, others had a different view. The Taliban leaders put their main emphasis on the year's military offensive against the Northern Alliance, an offensive that ordinarily would begin in the late spring or summer. They certainly hoped that this year's offensive would finally finish off their old enemies, driving them from Afghanistan. From the Taliban's perspective, an attack against the United States might be counterproductive. It might draw the Americans into the war against them, just when final victory seemed within their grasp.

The story of dissension within al Qaeda regarding the 9/11 attacks is probably incomplete. The information on which the account is based comes from sources who were not privy to the full scope of al

Qaeda and Taliban planning. Bin Ladin and Atef, however, probably would have known, at least, that

— The general Taliban offensive against the Northern Alliance would rely on al Qaeda military support.

— Another significant al Qaeda operation was making progress during the summer—a plot to assassinate the Northern Alliance leader, Ahmed Shah Massoud. The operatives, disguised as journalists, were in Massoud's camp and prepared to kill him sometime in August. Their appointment to see him was delayed.

But on September 9, the Massoud assassination took place. The delayed Taliban offensive against the Northern Alliance was apparently coordinated to begin as soon as he was killed, and it got under way on September 10.

As they deliberated earlier in the year, Bin Ladin and Atef would likely have remembered that Mullah Omar was dependent on them for the Massoud assassination and for vital support in the Taliban military operations. KSM remembers Atef telling him that al Qaeda had an agreement with the Taliban to eliminate Massoud, after which the Taliban would begin an offensive to take over Afghanistan. Atef hoped Massoud's death would also appease the Taliban when the 9/11 attacks happened.

MOVING TO DEPARTURE POSITIONS

In the days just before 9/11, the hijackers returned leftover funds to al Qaeda and assembled in their departure cities. They sent the excess funds by wire transfer to the UAE, about $26,000 altogether.

The hijackers targeting American Airlines Flight 77, to depart from Dulles, migrated from New Jersey to Laurel, Maryland, about 20 miles from Washington, D.C. They stayed in a motel during the first week in September and spent time working out at a gym. On the final night before the attacks, they lodged at a hotel in Herndon, Virginia, close to the airport.

Further north, the hijackers targeting United Airlines Flight 93, to depart from Newark, gathered in that city from their base in Florida on September 7. Just after midnight on September 8–9, Jarrah received a speeding ticket in Maryland as he headed north on I-95. He joined the rest of his team at their hotel.

Atta was still busy coordinating the teams. On September 7, he flew from Fort Lauderdale to Baltimore, presumably to meet with the Flight 77 team in Laurel. On September 9, he flew from Baltimore to Boston. By then, Shehhi had arrived there, and Atta was seen with him at his hotel. The next day, Atta picked up Omari at another hotel, and the two drove to Portland, Maine, for reasons that remain unknown. In the early morning hours of September 11, they boarded a commuter flight to Boston to connect to American Airlines Flight 11. The two spent their last night pursuing ordinary activities: making ATM withdrawals, eating pizza, and shopping at a convenience store. Their three fellow hijackers for Flight 11 stayed together in a hotel in Newton, Massachusetts, just outside of Boston.

Shehhi and his team targeting United Airlines Flight 175 from Logan Airport spent their last hours at two Boston hotels. The plan that started with a proposal by KSM in 1996 had evolved to overcome numerous obstacles. Now 19 men waited in nondescript hotel rooms to board four flights the next morning.

# 8. "THE SYSTEM WAS BLINKING RED"

## The Summer of Threat

As 2001 began, counterterrorism officials were receiving frequent but fragmentary reports about threats. Indeed, there appeared to be possible threats almost everywhere the United States had interests—including at home.

In the spring of 2001, the level of reporting on terrorist threats and planned attacks increased dramatically to its highest level since the millennium alert.

Threat reports surged in June and July, reaching an even higher peak of urgency. The summer threats seemed to be focused on Saudi Arabia, Israel, Bahrain, Kuwait, Yemen, and possibly Rome, but the danger could be anywhere—including a possible attack on the G-8 summit in Genoa [where President Bush would be meeting with leaders from Britain, Canada, France, Germany, Italy, Japan, and Russia to discuss international economic issues].

On June 21, near the height of the threat reporting, U.S. Central Command raised the force protection condition level for U.S. troops in six countries to the highest possible level, Delta. The U.S. Fifth Fleet moved out of its port in Bahrain, and a U.S. Marine Corps exercise in Jordan was halted. U.S. embassies in the Persian Gulf conducted an emergency security review, and the embassy in Yemen was closed.

The CSG kept up the terrorism alert posture on a "rolling 24 hour basis."

Disruption operations against al Qaeda–affiliated cells were launched involving 20 countries. Several terrorist operatives were detained by foreign governments, possibly disrupting operations in the Gulf and Italy and perhaps averting attacks against two or three U.S. embassies. Clarke and others told us of a particular concern about possible attacks on the Fourth of July. After it passed uneventfully, the CSG decided to maintain the alert.

In late July, because of threats, Italy closed the airspace over Genoa and mounted antiaircraft batteries at the Genoa airport during the G-8 summit, which President Bush attended.

At home, the CSG arranged for the CIA to brief intelligence and security officials from several domestic agencies. On July 5, representatives from the Immigration and Naturalization Service (INS), the FAA, the Coast Guard, the Secret Service, Customs, the CIA, and the FBI met with Clarke to discuss the current threat. Attendees report that they were told not to disseminate the threat information they received at the meeting. They interpreted this direction to mean that although they could brief their superiors, they could not send out advisories to the field. An NSC official recalls a somewhat different emphasis, saying that attendees were asked to take the information back to their home agencies and "do what you can" with it, subject to classification and distribution restrictions. A representative from the INS asked for a summary of the information that she could share with field offices. She never received one.

That same day, the CIA briefed Attorney General Ashcroft on the al Qaeda threat, warning that a significant terrorist attack was imminent. Ashcroft was told that preparations for multiple attacks were in late stages or already complete and that little additional warning could be expected. The briefing addressed only threats outside the United States.

The next day, the CIA representative told the CSG that al Qaeda members believed the upcoming attack would be "spectacular," qualitatively different from anything they had done to date.

Tenet told us that in his world "the system was blinking red." By late July, Tenet said, it could not "get any worse." Not everyone was convinced. Some asked whether all these threats might just be deception. Hadley told Tenet in July that Deputy Secretary of Defense Paul Wolfowitz questioned the reporting. Perhaps Bin Ladin was trying to study U.S. reactions. Tenet replied that he had already addressed the

Defense Department's questions on this point; the reporting was convincing.

On July 27, Clarke informed Rice and Hadley that the spike in intelligence about a near-term al Qaeda attack had stopped. He urged keeping readiness high during the August vacation period, warning that another report suggested an attack had just been postponed for a few months "but will still happen."

On August 1, the FBI issued an advisory that in light of the increased volume of threat reporting and the upcoming anniversary of the East Africa embassy bombings, increased attention should be paid to security planning. It noted that although most of the reporting indicated a potential for attacks on U.S. interests abroad, the possibility of an attack in the United States could not be discounted.

On August 3, the intelligence community issued an advisory concluding that the threat of impending al Qaeda attacks would likely continue indefinitely. Citing threats in the Arabian Peninsula, Jordan, Israel, and Europe, the advisory suggested that al Qaeda was lying in wait and searching for gaps in security before moving forward with the planned attacks.

During the spring and summer of 2001, President Bush had on several occasions asked his briefers whether any of the threats pointed to the United States. Reflecting on these questions, the CIA decided to write a briefing article summarizing its understanding of this danger. Two CIA analysts involved in preparing this briefing article believed it represented an opportunity to communicate their view that the threat of a Bin Ladin attack in the United States remained both current and serious. The result was an article in the August 6 Presidential Daily Brief [PDB] titled "Bin Ladin Determined to Strike in US." It was the 36th PDB item briefed so far that year that related to Bin Ladin or al Qaeda, and the first devoted to the possibility of an attack in the United States.

The President told us the August 6 report was historical in nature. President Bush said the article told him that al Qaeda was dangerous, which he said he had known since he had become President. The President said Bin Ladin had long been talking about his desire to attack America. He recalled some operational data on the FBI, and remembered thinking it was heartening that 70 investigations were under way.

He did not recall discussing the August 6 report with the Attorney General or whether Rice had done so. He said that if his advisers had told him there was a cell in the United States, they would have moved to take care of it. That never happened.

Hadley told us that before 9/11, he and Rice did not feel they had the job of coordinating domestic agencies. They felt that Clarke and the CSG (part of the NSC) were the NSC's bridge between foreign and domestic threats.

There was a clear disparity in the levels of response to foreign versus domestic threats. Numerous actions were taken overseas to disrupt possible attacks—enlisting foreign partners to upset terrorist plans, closing embassies, moving military assets out of the way of possible harm. Far less was done domestically—in part, surely, because to the extent that specifics did exist, they pertained to threats overseas. As noted earlier, a threat against the embassy in Yemen quickly resulted in its closing. Possible domestic threats were more vague. When reports did not specify where the attacks were to take place, officials presumed that they would again be overseas, though they did not rule out a target in the United States. Each of the FBI threat advisories made this point.

In sum, the domestic agencies never mobilized in response to the threat. They did not have direction, and did not have a plan to institute. The borders were not hardened. Transportation systems were not fortified. Electronic surveillance was not targeted against a domestic threat. State and local law enforcement were not marshaled to augment the FBI's efforts. The public was not warned.

The terrorists exploited deep institutional failings within our government. The question is whether extra vigilance might have turned up an opportunity to disrupt the plot. As seen in chapter 7, al Qaeda's operatives made mistakes.

* * *

ZACARIAS MOUSSAOUI

On August 15, 2001, the Minneapolis FBI Field Office initiated an intelligence investigation on Zacarias Moussaoui. Moussaoui stood out because, with little knowledge of flying, he wanted to learn how to "take off and land" a Boeing 747.

The FBI agent who handled the case in conjunction with the INS representative on the Minneapolis Joint Terrorism Task Force suspected that Moussaoui might be planning to hijack a plane. Minneapolis and FBI headquarters debated whether Moussaoui should be arrested immediately or surveilled to obtain additional information. Because it was not clear whether Moussaoui could be imprisoned, the FBI case agent decided the most important thing was to prevent Moussaoui from obtaining any further training that he could use to carry out a potential attack.

As a French national who had overstayed his visa, Moussaoui could be detained immediately. The INS arrested Moussaoui on the immigration violation. A deportation order was signed on August 17, 2001.

The agents in Minnesota were concerned that the U.S. Attorney's Office in Minneapolis would find insufficient probable cause of a crime to obtain a criminal warrant to search Moussaoui's laptop computer. Agents at FBI headquarters believed there was insufficient probable cause. Minneapolis therefore sought a special warrant under the Foreign Intelligence Surveillance Act [FISA] to conduct the search.

To do so, however, the FBI needed to demonstrate probable cause that Moussaoui was an agent of a foreign power, a demonstration that was not required to obtain a criminal warrant but was a statutory requirement for a FISA warrant. The case agent did not have sufficient information to connect Moussaoui to a "foreign power," so he reached out for help, in the United States and overseas.

The FBI legal attaché's office in Paris provided information that made a connection between Moussaoui and a rebel leader in Chechnya, Ibn al Khattab. This set off a spirited debate between the Minneapolis Field Office, FBI headquarters, and the CIA as to whether the Chechen rebels and Khattab were sufficiently associated with a terrorist organization to constitute a "foreign power" for purposes of the FISA statute. FBI headquarters did not believe this was good enough, and its National Security Law Unit declined to submit a FISA application.

On August 28, the CIA sent a request for information to the British government. The FBI office in London raised the matter briefly with British officials as an aside, after a meeting about a more urgent matter on September 3. The case was not handled by the British as a priority amid a large number of other terrorist-related inquiries.

On September 4, the FBI sent a teletype to the CIA, the FAA, the Customs Service, the State Department, the INS, and the Secret Service summarizing the known facts regarding Moussaoui. It did not report the case agent's personal assessment that Moussaoui planned to hijack an airplane. It did contain the FAA's comment that it was not unusual for Middle Easterners to attend flight training schools in the United States.

Although the Minneapolis agents wanted to tell the FAA from the beginning about Moussaoui, FBI headquarters instructed Minneapolis that it could not share the more complete report the case agent had prepared for the FAA. The Minneapolis supervisor sent the case agent in person to the local FAA office to fill in what he thought were gaps in the FBI headquarters teletype. No FAA actions seem to have been taken in response.

There was substantial disagreement between Minneapolis agents and FBI headquarters as to what Moussaoui was planning to do. In one conversation between a Minneapolis supervisor and a headquarters agent, the latter complained that Minneapolis's FISA request was couched in a manner intended to get people "spun up." The supervisor replied that was precisely his intent. He said he was "trying to keep someone from taking a plane and crashing into the World Trade Center." The headquarters agent replied that this was not going to happen and that they did not know if Moussaoui was a terrorist.

There is no evidence that either FBI Acting Director [Thomas] Pickard or Assistant Director for Counterterrorism Dale Watson was briefed on the Moussaoui case prior to 9/11. Michael Rolince, the FBI assistant director heading the Bureau's International Terrorism Operations Section (ITOS), recalled being told about Moussaoui in two passing hallway conversations but only in the context that he might be receiving telephone calls from Minneapolis complaining about how headquarters was handling the matter. He never received such a call. Although the acting special agent in charge of Minneapolis called the ITOS supervisors to discuss the Moussaoui case on August 27, he declined to go up the chain of command at FBI headquarters and call Rolince.

On August 23, DCI Tenet was briefed about the Moussaoui case in a briefing titled "Islamic Extremist Learns to Fly." Tenet was also told that Moussaoui wanted to learn to fly a 747, paid for his training in cash, was interested to learn the doors do not open in flight, and wanted to fly a simulated flight from London to New York. He was told that the FBI had arrested Moussaoui because of a visa overstay and that the CIA was working the case with the FBI. Tenet told us that no connection to al Qaeda was apparent to him at the time. Seeing it as an FBI case, he did not discuss the matter with anyone at the White House or the FBI. No connection was made between Moussaoui's presence in the United States and the threat reporting during the summer of 2001.

On September 11, after the attacks, the FBI office in London renewed their appeal for information about Moussaoui. On September 13, the British government received new, sensitive intelligence that

Moussaoui had attended an al Qaeda training camp in Afghanistan. It passed this intelligence to the United States on the same day.

The FBI also learned after 9/11 that the millennium terrorist Ressam, who by 2001 was cooperating with investigators, recognized Moussaoui as someone who had been in the Afghan camps. As mentioned above, before 9/11 the FBI agents in Minneapolis had failed to persuade supervisors at headquarters that there was enough evidence to seek a FISA warrant to search Moussaoui's computer hard drive and belongings. Either the British information or the Ressam identification would have broken the logjam.

A maximum U.S. effort to investigate Moussaoui conceivably could have unearthed his connections to Binalshibh. Those connections might have brought investigators to the core of the 9/11 plot. The Binalshibh connection was recognized shortly after 9/11, though it was not an easy trail to find. Discovering it would have required quick and very substantial cooperation from the German government, which might well have been difficult to obtain.

However, publicity about Moussaoui's arrest and a possible hijacking threat might have derailed the plot. With time, the search for Mihdhar and Hazmi and the investigation of Moussaoui might also have led to a breakthrough that would have disrupted the plot.

TIME RUNS OUT

As Tenet told us, "the system was blinking red" during the summer of 2001. Officials were alerted across the world. Many were doing everything they possibly could to respond to the threats.

Yet no one working on these late leads in the summer of 2001 connected the case in his or her in-box to the threat reports agitating senior officials and being briefed to the President. Thus, these individual cases did not become national priorities. As [a] CIA supervisor [we will call] "John" told us, no one looked at the bigger picture; no analytic work foresaw the lightning that could connect the thundercloud to the ground.

We see little evidence that the progress of the plot was disturbed by any government action. The U.S. government was unable to capitalize on mistakes made by al Qaeda. Time ran out.

# 9. HEROISM AND HORROR

Emergency response is a product of preparedness. On the morning of September 11, 2001, the last best hope for the community of people working in or visiting the World Trade Center [WTC] rested not with national policymakers but with private firms and local public servants, especially the first responders: fire, police, emergency medical service, and building safety professionals.

\* \* \*

Like the national defense effort described in chapter 1, the emergency response to the attacks on 9/11 was necessarily improvised. In New York, the FDNY [New York City Fire Department], the NYPD [New York City Police Department], the PAPD [Port Authority Police Department], WTC employees, and the building occupants themselves did their best to cope with the effects of an unimaginable catastrophe—unfolding furiously over a mere 102 minutes—for which they were unprepared in terms of both training and mindset. As a result of the efforts of first responders, assistance from each other, and their own good instincts and goodwill, the vast majority of civilians below the impact zone were able to evacuate the towers.

The National Institute of Standards and Technology has provided a preliminary estimation that between 16,400 and 18,800 civilians were in the WTC complex as of 8:46 A.M. on September 11. At most 2,152 individuals died at the WTC complex who were not (1) fire or police first responders, (2) security or fire safety personnel of the WTC or individual companies, (3) volunteer civilians who ran to the WTC after the planes' impact to help others, or (4) on the two planes that crashed into the Twin Towers. Out of this total number of fatalities, we can account for the workplace location of 2,052 individuals, or 95.35 percent. Of this number, 1,942 or 94.64 percent either worked or were supposed to attend a meeting at or above the respective impact zones of the Twin Towers; only 110, or 5.36 percent of those who died, worked below the impact zone. While a given person's office location at the WTC does not definitively indicate where that individual died that morning or whether he or she could have evacuated, these data strongly suggest that the evacuation was a success for civilians below the impact zone.

Several factors influenced the evacuation on September 11. It was aided greatly by changes made by the Port Authority in response to the 1993 bombing and by the training of both Port Authority personnel and civilians after that time. Stairwells remained lit near unaffected floors; some tenants relied on procedures learned in fire drills to help them to safety; others were guided down the stairs by fire safety officials based in the lobby. Because of damage caused by the impact of the planes, the capability of the sophisticated building systems may have been impaired. Rudimentary improvements, however, such as the addition of glow strips to the handrails and stairs, were credited by some as the reason for their survival. The general evacuation time for the towers dropped from more than four hours in 1993 to under one hour on September 11 for most civilians who were not trapped or physically incapable of enduring a long descent.

First responders also played a significant role in the success of the evacuation. Some specific rescues are quantifiable, such as an FDNY company's rescue of civilians trapped on the 22d floor of the North Tower, or the success of FDNY, PAPD, and NYPD personnel in carrying nonambulatory civilians out of both the North and South Towers. In other instances, intangibles combined to reduce what could have been a much higher death total. It is impossible to measure how many more civilians would have died but for the determination of many members of the FDNY, PAPD, and NYPD to continue assisting civilians after the South Tower collapsed. But the positive impact of the first responders on the evacuation came at a tremendous cost of first responder lives lost.

Civilians at or above the impact zone in the North Tower had the smallest hope of survival. Once the plane struck, they were prevented from descending because of damage to or impassable conditions in the building's three stairwells.

The NYPD's 911 operators and FDNY dispatch were not adequately integrated into the emergency response. In several ways, the 911 system was not ready to cope with a major disaster. These operators and dispatchers were one of the only sources of information for individuals at and above the impact zone of the towers. The FDNY ordered both towers fully evacuated by 8:57, but this guidance was not conveyed to 911 operators and FDNY dispatchers, who for the next hour often continued to advise civilians not to self-evacuate, regardless of whether they were above or below the impact zones.

In July 2001, Mayor [Rudolph] Giuliani updated a directive titled "Direction and Control of Emergencies in the City of New York." The directive designated, for different types of emergencies, an appropriate agency as "Incident Commander"; it would be "responsible for the management of the City's response to the emergency."

To some degree, the Mayor's directive for incident command was followed on 9/11. It was clear that the lead response agency was the FDNY, and that the other responding local, federal, bistate, and state agencies acted in a supporting role. There was a tacit understanding that FDNY personnel would have primary responsibility for evacuating civilians who were above the ground floors of the Twin Towers, while NYPD and PAPD personnel would be in charge of evacuating civilians from the WTC complex once they reached ground level. The NYPD also greatly assisted responding FDNY units by clearing emergency lanes to the WTC.

In addition, coordination occurred at high levels of command. For example, the Mayor and Police Commissioner consulted with the Chief of the Department of the FDNY at approximately 9:20. There were other instances of coordination at operational levels, and information was shared on an ad hoc basis.

It is also clear, however, that the response operations lacked the kind of integrated communications and unified command contemplated in the directive. These problems existed both within and among individual responding agencies.

Though almost no one at 9:50 on September 11 was contemplating an imminent total collapse of the Twin Towers, many first responders and civilians were contemplating the possibility of imminent additional terrorist attacks throughout New York City. Had any such attacks occurred, the FDNY's response would have been severely compromised by the concentration of so many of its off-duty personnel, particularly its elite personnel, at the WTC.

The NYPD experienced comparatively fewer internal command and control and communications issues. Because the department has a history of mobilizing thousands of officers for major events requiring crowd control, its technical radio capability and major incident protocols were more easily adapted to an incident of the magnitude of 9/11. In addition, its mission that day lay largely outside the towers themselves. The vast majority of NYPD personnel were staged outside, assisting with crowd control and evacuation and securing other sites in the city.

### Emergency Response at the Pentagon

If it had happened on any other day, the disaster at the Pentagon would be remembered as a singular challenge and an extraordinary national story. Yet the calamity at the World Trade Center that same morning included catastrophic damage 1,000 feet above the ground that instantly imperiled tens of thousands of people. The two experiences are not comparable. Nonetheless, broader lessons in integrating multiagency response efforts are apparent when we analyze the response at the Pentagon.

The emergency response at the Pentagon represented a mix of local, state, and federal jurisdictions and was generally effective. It overcame the inherent complications of a response across jurisdictions because the Incident Command System, a formalized management structure for emergency response, was in place in the National Capital Region on 9/11.

Because of the nature of the event—a plane crash, fire, and partial building collapse—the Arlington County Fire Department served as incident commander. Different agencies had different roles.

While no emergency response is flawless, the response to the 9/11 terrorist attack on the Pentagon was mainly a success for three reasons: first, the strong professional relationships and trust established among emergency responders; second, the adoption of the Incident Command System; and third, the pursuit of a regional approach to response. Many fire and police agencies that responded had extensive prior experience working together on regional events and training exercises.

Several factors facilitated the response to this incident, and distinguish it from the far more difficult task in New York. There was a single incident, and it was not 1,000 feet above ground. The incident site was relatively easy to secure and contain, and there were no other buildings in the immediate area. There was no collateral damage beyond the Pentagon.

\* \* \*

The lesson of 9/11 for civilians and first responders can be stated simply: in the new age of terror, they—we—are the primary targets. The losses America suffered that day demonstrated both the gravity of the terrorist threat and the commensurate need to prepare ourselves to meet it.

## 10. WARTIME

While the plan at the elementary school [in Florida] had been to return to Washington, by the time Air Force One was airborne at 9:55 A.M. the Secret Service, the President's advisers, and Vice President Cheney were strongly advising against it. President Bush reluctantly acceded to this advice and, at about 10:10, Air Force One changed course and began heading due west. The immediate objective was to find a safe location—not too far away—where the President could land and speak to the American people. The Secret Service was also interested in refueling the aircraft and paring down the size of the traveling party. The President's military aide, an Air Force officer, quickly researched the options and, sometime around 10:20, identified Barksdale Air Force Base [in Louisiana] as an appropriate interim destination.

The President completed his statement, which for security reasons was taped and not broadcast live, and the traveling party returned to Air Force One. The next destination was discussed: once again the Secret Service recommended against returning to Washington, and the Vice President agreed. Offutt Air Force Base in Nebraska was chosen because of its elaborate command and control facilities, and because it could accommodate overnight lodging for 50 persons. The Secret Service wanted a place where the President could spend several days, if necessary.

Air Force One arrived at Offutt at 2:50 P.M. At about 3:15, President Bush met with his principal advisers through a secure video teleconference. Rice said President Bush began the meeting with the words, "We're at war," and that Director of Central Intelligence George Tenet said the agency was still assessing who was responsible, but the early signs all pointed to al Qaeda.

In the late afternoon, the President overruled his aides' continuing reluctance to have him return to Washington and ordered Air Force One back to Andrews Air Force Base. He was flown by helicopter back to the White House, passing over the still-smoldering Pentagon. At 8:30 that evening, President Bush addressed the nation from the White House. After emphasizing that the first priority was to help the injured and protect against any further attacks, he said: "We will make no distinction between the terrorists who committed these acts and those who harbor them." No American, he said, "will ever forget this day."

Following his speech, President Bush met again with his National Security Council (NSC), expanded to include Secretary of Transportation Norman Mineta and Joseph Allbaugh, the director of the Federal Emergency Management Agency. Secretary of State Colin Powell, who had returned from Peru after hearing of the attacks, joined the discussion. They reviewed the day's events.

**Immediate Responses at Home**

As the urgent domestic issues accumulated, White House Deputy Chief of Staff Joshua Bolten chaired a temporary "domestic consequences" group. The agenda in those first days began with problems of how to help victims and stanch the flowing losses to the American economy, such as

— Organizing federal emergency assistance. One question was what kind of public health advice to give about the air quality in Lower Manhattan in the vicinity of the fallen buildings.
— Compensating victims. They evaluated legislative options, eventually setting up a federal compensation fund and defining the powers of a special master to run it.
— Determining federal assistance. On September 13, President Bush promised to provide $20 billion for New York City, in addition to the $20 billion his budget director had already guessed might be needed for the country as a whole.
— Restoring civil aviation. On the morning of September 13, the national airspace reopened for use by airports that met newly improvised security standards.
— Reopening the financial markets. After extraordinary emergency efforts involving the White House, the Treasury Department, and the Securities and Exchange Commission, aided by unprecedented cooperation among the usually competitive firms of the financial industry, the markets reopened on Monday, September 17.
— Deciding when and how to return border and port security to more normal operations.
— Evaluating legislative proposals to bail out the airline industry and cap its liability.

The very process of reviewing these issues underscored the absence of an effective government organization dedicated to assessing vulnerabilities and handling problems of protection and preparedness. Though a number of agencies had some part of the task, none had security as its primary mission.

By September 14, Vice President Cheney had decided to recommend, at least as a first step, a new White House entity to coordinate all the relevant agencies rather than tackle the challenge of combining them in a new department. This new White House entity would be a homeland security adviser and Homeland Security Council—paralleling the National Security Council system. Vice President Cheney reviewed the proposal with President Bush and other advisers. President Bush announced the new post and its first occupant—Pennsylvania governor Tom Ridge—in his address to a joint session of Congress on September 20.

Beginning on September 11, Immigration and Naturalization Service [INS] agents working in cooperation with the FBI began arresting individuals for immigration violations whom they encountered while following up leads in the FBI's investigation of the 9/11 attacks. Eventually, 768 aliens were arrested as "special interest" detainees. Some (such as Zacarias Moussaoui) were actually in INS custody before 9/11; most were arrested after. Attorney General John Ashcroft told us that he saw his job in directing this effort as "risk minimization," both to find out who had committed the attacks and to prevent a subsequent attack. Ashcroft ordered all special interest immigration hearings closed to the public, family members, and press; directed government attorneys to seek denial of bond until such time as they were "cleared" of terrorist connections by the FBI and other agencies; and ordered the identity of the detainees kept secret. INS attorneys charged with prosecuting the immigration violations had trouble getting information about the detainees and any terrorist connections; in the chaos after the attacks, it was very difficult to reach law enforcement officials, who were following up on other leads. The clearance process approved by the Justice Department was time-consuming, lasting an average of about 80 days.

We have assessed this effort to detain aliens of "special interest." The detainees were lawfully held on immigration charges. Records indicate that 531 were deported, 162 were released on bond, 24 received some kind of immigration benefits, 12 had their proceedings terminated, and 8—one of whom was Moussaoui—were remanded to the custody of the U.S. Marshals Service. The inspector general of the Justice Department found significant problems in the way the 9/11 detainees were treated. In response to a request about the counterterrorism benefits of the 9/11 detainee program, the Justice Department cited six individuals on the special interest detainee list, noting that two (including Moussaoui) were linked directly to a terrorist organization and that it had obtained new leads helpful to the investigation of the 9/11 terrorist attacks. A senior al Qaeda detainee has stated that U.S. government efforts after the 9/11 attacks to monitor the American homeland, including review of Muslims' immigration files and deportation of nonpermanent residents, forced al Qaeda to operate less freely in the United States.

The government's ability to collect intelligence inside the United States, and the sharing of such information between the intelligence and law enforcement communities, was not a priority before 9/11. Guidelines on this subject issued in August 2001 by Deputy Attorney

General Larry Thompson essentially recapitulated prior guidance. However, the attacks of 9/11 changed everything. Less than one week after September 11, an early version of what was to become the Patriot Act (officially, the USA PATRIOT Act) began to take shape. A central provision of the proposal was the removal of "the wall" on information sharing between the intelligence and law enforcement communities (discussed in chapter 3). Ashcroft told us he was determined to take every conceivable action, within the limits of the Constitution, to identify potential terrorists and deter additional attacks. The administration developed a proposal that eventually passed both houses of Congress by large majorities and was signed into law on October 26.

## Planning for War

By late in the evening of September 11, the President had addressed the nation on the terrible events of the day. Vice President Cheney described the President's mood as somber. The long day was not yet over. When the larger meeting that included his domestic department heads broke up, President Bush chaired a smaller meeting of top advisers, a group he would later call his "war council." This group usually included Vice President Cheney, Secretary of State Powell, Secretary of Defense Donald Rumsfeld, General Hugh Shelton, Vice Chairman of the Joint Chiefs (later to become chairman) General Myers, DCI Tenet, Attorney General Ashcroft, and FBI Director Robert Mueller. From the White House staff, National Security Advisor Condoleezza Rice and Chief of Staff Card were part of the core group, often joined by their deputies, Stephen Hadley and Joshua Bolten.

In this restricted National Security Council meeting, the President said it was a time for self-defense. The United States would punish not just the perpetrators of the attacks, but also those who harbored them. Secretary Powell said the United States had to make it clear to Pakistan, Afghanistan, and the Arab states that the time to act was now. He said we would need to build a coalition. The President noted that the attacks provided a great opportunity to engage Russia and China. Secretary Rumsfeld urged the President and the principals to think broadly about who might have harbored the attackers, including Iraq, Afghanistan, Libya, Sudan, and Iran. He wondered aloud how much evidence the United States would need in order to deal with these countries, pointing out that major strikes could take up to 60 days to assemble.

President Bush chaired two more meetings of the NSC on September 12. In the first meeting, he stressed that the United States was at war with a new and different kind of enemy. The President tasked principals to go beyond their pre-9/11 work and develop a strategy to eliminate terrorists and punish those who support them. As they worked on defining the goals and objectives of the upcoming campaign, they considered a paper that went beyond al Qaeda to propose the "elimination of terrorism as a threat to our way of life," an aim that would include pursuing other international terrorist organizations in the Middle East.

Rice chaired a Principals Committee meeting on September 13 in the Situation Room to refine how the fight against al Qaeda would be conducted. The principals agreed that the overall message should be that anyone supporting al Qaeda would risk harm. The United States would need to integrate diplomacy, financial measures, intelligence, and military actions into an overarching strategy. The principals also focused on Pakistan and what it could do to turn the Taliban against al Qaeda. They concluded that if Pakistan decided not to help the United States, it too would be at risk.

The same day, Deputy Secretary of State Richard Armitage met with the Pakistani ambassador to the United States, Maleeha Lodhi, and the visiting head of Pakistan's military intelligence service, Mahmud Ahmed. That afternoon, Secretary of State Powell announced at the beginning of an NSC meeting that Pakistani President [Pervez] Musharraf had agreed to every U.S. request for support in the war on terrorism.

At the September 13 NSC meeting, when Secretary Powell described Pakistan's reply, President Bush led a discussion of an appropriate ultimatum to the Taliban. He also ordered Secretary Rumsfeld to develop a military plan against the Taliban. The President wanted the United States to strike the Taliban, step back, wait to see if they got the message, and hit them hard if they did not. He made clear that the military should focus on targets that would influence the Taliban's behavior.

The State Department proposed delivering an ultimatum to the Taliban: produce Bin Ladin and his deputies and shut down al Qaeda camps within 24 to 48 hours, or the United States will use all necessary means to destroy the terrorist infrastructure. The State Department did not expect the Taliban to comply. Therefore, State and Defense would plan to build an international coalition to go into Afghanistan. Both departments would consult with NATO and other allies and request intelligence, basing, and other support from countries, according to their capabilities and resources. Finally, the plan detailed a public U.S. stance: America would use all its resources to eliminate terrorism as a threat, punish those responsible for the 9/11 attacks, hold states and other actors responsible for providing sanctuary to terrorists, work with a coalition to eliminate terrorist groups and networks, and avoid malice toward any people, religion, or culture.

President Bush recalled that he quickly realized that the administration would have to invade Afghanistan with ground troops. But the early briefings to the President and Secretary Rumsfeld on military options were disappointing. Tommy Franks, the commanding general of Central Command (CENTCOM), told us that the President was dissatisfied. The U.S. military, Franks said, did not have an off-the-shelf plan to eliminate the al Qaeda threat in Afghanistan. The existing Infinite Resolve options did not, in his view, amount to such a plan.

All these diplomatic and military plans were reviewed over the weekend of September 15–16, as President Bush convened his war council at Camp David.

Tenet described a plan for collecting intelligence and mounting covert operations. He proposed inserting CIA teams into Afghanistan to work with Afghan warlords who would join the fight against al Qaeda. These CIA teams would act jointly with the military's Special Operations units. President Bush later praised this proposal, saying it had been a turning point in his thinking. General Shelton briefed the principals on the preliminary plan for Afghanistan that the military had put together. It drew on the Infinite Resolve "phased campaign" plan the Pentagon had begun developing in November 2000 as an addition to the strike options it had been refining since 1998. But Shelton added a new element—the possible significant use of ground forces—and that is where President Bush reportedly focused his attention.

After hearing from his senior advisers, President Bush discussed with Rice the contents of the directives he would issue to set all the plans into motion. Rice prepared a paper that President Bush then considered with principals on Monday morning, September 17. "The purpose of this meeting," he recalled saying, "is to assign tasks for the first wave of the war against terrorism. It starts today."

The pre-9/11 draft presidential directive on al Qaeda evolved into a new directive, National Security Presidential Directive 9, now titled "Defeating the Terrorist Threat to the United States." The directive would now extend to a global war on terrorism, not just on al Qaeda. It also incorporated the President's determination not to distinguish between terrorists and those who harbor them. It included a determination to use military force if necessary to end al Qaeda's sanctuary in Afghanistan. The new directive—formally signed on October 25, after the fighting in Afghanistan had already begun—included new material followed by annexes discussing each targeted terrorist group. The old draft directive on al Qaeda became, in effect, the first annex. The United States would strive to eliminate all terrorist networks, dry up their financial support, and prevent them from acquiring weapons of mass destruction. The goal was the "elimination of terrorism as a threat to our way of life."

### "Phase Two" and the Question of Iraq

President Bush had wondered immediately after the attack whether Saddam Hussein's regime might have had a hand in it. Iraq had been an enemy of the United States for 11 years, and was the only place in the world where the United States was engaged in ongoing combat operations. As a former pilot, the President was struck by the apparent sophistication of the operation and some of the piloting, especially Hanjour's high-speed dive into the Pentagon. He told us he recalled Iraqi support for Palestinian suicide terrorists as well. Speculating about other possible states that could be involved, the President told us he also thought about Iran.

Clarke has written that on the evening of September 12, President Bush told him and some of his staff to explore possible Iraqi links to 9/11. "See if Saddam did this," Clarke recalls the President telling them. "See if he's linked in any way." While he believed the details of Clarke's account to be incorrect, President Bush acknowledged that he might well have spoken to Clarke at some point, asking him about Iraq.

Responding to a presidential tasking, Clarke's office sent a memo to Rice on September 18, titled "Survey of Intelligence Information on Any Iraq Involvement in the September 11 Attacks." Rice's chief staffer on Afghanistan, Zalmay Khalilzad, concurred in its conclusion that only some anecdotal evidence linked Iraq to al Qaeda. The memo found no "compelling case" that Iraq had either planned or perpetrated the attacks. It pointed out that Bin Ladin resented the secularism of Saddam Hussein's regime. Finally, the memo said, there was no confirmed reporting on Saddam cooperating with Bin Ladin on unconventional weapons.

On the afternoon of 9/11, according to contemporaneous notes, Secretary Rumsfeld instructed General Myers to obtain quickly as much information as possible. The notes indicate that he also told Myers that he was not simply interested in striking empty training sites. He thought the U.S. response should consider a wide range of options and possibilities. The secretary said his instinct was to hit Saddam Hussein at the same time—not only Bin Ladin. Secretary Rumsfeld later explained that at the time, he had been considering either one of them, or perhaps someone else, as the responsible party.

According to Rice, the issue of what, if anything, to do about Iraq was really engaged at Camp David. Briefing papers on Iraq, along with many others, were in briefing materials for the participants. Rice told us the administration was concerned that Iraq would take advantage of the 9/11 attacks. She recalled that in the first Camp David session chaired by the President, Rumsfeld asked what the administration should do about Iraq. Deputy Secretary Wolfowitz made the case for striking Iraq during "this round" of the war on terrorism.

A Defense Department paper for the Camp David briefing book on the strategic concept for the war on terrorism specified three priority targets for initial action: al Qaeda, the Taliban, and Iraq. It argued that of the three, al Qaeda and Iraq posed a strategic threat to the United States. Iraq's long-standing involvement in terrorism was cited, along with its interest in weapons of mass destruction.

Secretary Powell recalled that Wolfowitz—not Rumsfeld—argued that Iraq was ultimately the source of the terrorist problem and should therefore be attacked. Powell said that Wolfowitz was not able to justify his belief that Iraq was behind 9/11. "Paul was always of the view that Iraq was a problem that had to be dealt with," Powell told us. "And he saw this as one way of using this event as a way to deal with the Iraq problem." Powell said that President Bush did not give Wolfowitz's argument "much weight." Though continuing to worry about Iraq in the following week, Powell said, President Bush saw Afghanistan as the priority.

President Bush told Bob Woodward [of the *Washington Post*] that the decision not to invade Iraq was made at the morning session on September 15. Iraq was not even on the table during the September 15 afternoon session, which dealt solely with Afghanistan. Rice said that when President Bush called her on Sunday, September 16, he said the focus would be on Afghanistan, although he still wanted plans for Iraq should the country take some action or the administration eventually determine that it had been involved in the 9/11 attacks.

At the September 17 NSC meeting, there was some further discussion of "phase two" of the war on terrorism. President Bush ordered the Defense Department to be ready to deal with Iraq if Baghdad acted against U.S. interests, with plans to include possibly occupying Iraqi oil fields.

Within the Pentagon, Deputy Secretary Wolfowitz continued to press the case for dealing with Iraq. Writing to Rumsfeld on September 17 in a memo headlined "Preventing More Events," he argued that if there was even a 10 percent chance that Saddam Hussein was behind the 9/11 attack, maximum priority should be placed on eliminating that threat. Wolfowitz contended that the odds were "far more" than 1 in 10, citing Saddam's praise for the attack, his long record of involvement in terrorism, and theories that Ramzi Yousef was an Iraqi agent and Iraq was behind the 1993 attack on the World Trade Center. The next day, Wolfowitz renewed the argument, writing to Rumsfeld about the interest of Yousef's co-conspirator in the 1995 Manila air plot in crashing an explosives-laden plane into CIA headquarters, and about information from a foreign government regarding Iraqis' involvement in the attempted hijacking of a Gulf Air flight. Given this background, he wondered why so little thought had been devoted to the danger of suicide pilots, seeing a "failure of imagination" and a mind-set that dismissed possibilities.

On September 20, President Bush met with British Prime Minister Tony Blair, and the two leaders discussed the global conflict ahead. When Blair asked about Iraq, the President replied that Iraq was not the immediate problem. Some members of his administration, he commented, had expressed a different view, but he was the one responsible for making the decisions.

Having issued directives to guide his administration's preparations for war, on Thursday, September 20, President Bush addressed the nation before a joint session of Congress. "Tonight," he said, "we are a country awakened to danger." The President blamed al Qaeda for 9/11 and the 1998 embassy bombings and, for the first time, declared that al Qaeda was "responsible for bombing the USS *Cole*." He reiterated the ultimatum that had already been conveyed privately. "The Taliban must act, and act immediately," he said. "They will hand over the terrorists, or they will share in their fate." The President added that America's quarrel was not with Islam: "The enemy of America is not our many Muslim friends; it is not our many Arab friends. Our enemy is a radical network of terrorists, and every government that supports them." Other regimes faced hard choices, he pointed out: "Every nation, in every region, now has a decision to make: Either you are with us, or you are with the terrorists."

President Bush argued that the new war went beyond Bin Ladin. "Our war on terror begins with al Qaeda, but it does not end there,"

he said. "It will not end until every terrorist group of global reach has
been found, stopped, and defeated." The President had a message for
the Pentagon: "The hour is coming when America will act, and you
will make us proud." He also had a message for those outside the
United States. "This is civilization's fight," he said. "We ask every
nation to join us."

President Bush approved military plans to attack Afghanistan in
meetings with Central Command's General Franks and other advisers
on September 21 and October 2. Originally titled "Infinite Justice," the
operation's code word was changed—to avoid [offending] the sensi-
bilities of Muslims who associate the power of infinite justice with God
alone—to the operational name still used for operations in Afghanistan: "Enduring Freedom."

In December 2001, Afghan forces, with limited U.S. support,
engaged al Qaeda elements in a cave complex called Tora Bora. In
March 2002, the largest engagement of the war was fought, in the
mountainous Shah-i-Kot area south of Gardez, against a large force of
al Qaeda jihadists. The three-week battle was substantially successful,
and almost all remaining al Qaeda forces took refuge in Pakistan's
equally mountainous and lightly governed frontier provinces.

Within about two months of the start of combat operations, several
hundred CIA operatives and Special Forces soldiers, backed by the
striking power of U.S. aircraft and a much larger infrastructure of
intelligence and support efforts, had combined with Afghan militias
and a small number of other coalition soldiers to destroy the Taliban
regime and disrupt al Qaeda. They had killed or captured about a
quarter of the enemy's known leaders. Mohammed Atef, al Qaeda's
military commander and a principal figure in the 9/11 plot, had been
killed by a U.S. air strike. According to a senior CIA officer who
helped devise the overall strategy, the CIA provided intelligence, experience, cash, covert action capabilities, and entrée to tribal allies. In
turn, the U.S. military offered combat expertise, firepower, logistics,
and communications. With these initial victories won by the middle of
2002, the global conflict against Islamist terrorism became a different
kind of struggle.

# 11. FORESIGHT—AND HINDSIGHT

In composing this narrative, we have tried to remember that we write
with the benefit and the handicap of hindsight. Hindsight can sometimes see the past clearly—with 20/20 vision. But the path of what

happened is so brightly lit that it places everything else more deeply into shadow. Commenting on Pearl Harbor, Roberta Wohlstetter found it "much easier *after* the event to sort the relevant from the irrelevant signals. After the event, of course, a signal is always crystal clear; we can now see what disaster it was signaling since the disaster has occurred. But before the event it is obscure and pregnant with conflicting meanings."

As time passes, more documents become available, and the bare facts of what happened become still clearer. Yet the picture of *how* those things happened becomes harder to reimagine, as that past world, with its preoccupations and uncertainty, recedes and the remaining memories of it become colored by what happened and what was written about it later. With that caution in mind, we asked ourselves, before we judged others, whether the insights that seem apparent now would really have been meaningful at the time, given the limits of what people then could reasonably have known or done.

We believe the 9/11 attacks revealed four kinds of failures: in imagination, policy, capabilities, and management.

## Imagination

HISTORICAL PERSPECTIVE

The 9/11 attack was an event of surpassing disproportion. America had suffered surprise attacks before—Pearl Harbor is one well-known case, the 1950 Chinese attack in Korea another. But these were attacks by major powers.

While by no means as threatening as Japan's act of war, the 9/11 attack was in some ways more devastating. It was carried out by a tiny group of people, not enough to man a full platoon. Measured on a governmental scale, the resources behind it were trivial. The group itself was dispatched by an organization based in one of the poorest, most remote, and least industrialized countries on earth. This organization recruited a mixture of young fanatics and highly educated zealots who could not find suitable places in their home societies or were driven from them.

To understand these events, we attempted to reconstruct some of the context of the 1990s. Americans celebrated the end of the Cold War with a mixture of relief and satisfaction. The people of the United States hoped to enjoy a peace dividend, as U.S. spending on national security was cut following the end of the Soviet military threat.

The United States emerged into the post–Cold War world as the globe's preeminent military power. America stood out as an object for admiration, envy, and blame. This created a kind of cultural asymmetry. To us, Afghanistan seemed very far away. To members of al Qaeda, America seemed very close. In a sense, they were more globalized than we were.

## UNDERSTANDING THE DANGER

If the government's leaders understood the gravity of the threat they faced and understood at the same time that their policies to eliminate it were not likely to succeed any time soon, then history's judgment will be harsh. Did they understand the gravity of the threat?

Before 9/11, al Qaeda and its affiliates had killed fewer than 50 Americans, including the East Africa embassy bombings and the *Cole* attack. The U.S. government took the threat seriously, but not in the sense of mustering anything like the kind of effort that would be gathered to confront an enemy of the first, second, or even third rank. Bin Ladin, al Qaeda, or even terrorism was not an important topic in the 2000 presidential campaign. Congress and the media called little attention to it.

A National Intelligence Estimate distributed in July 1995 predicted future terrorist attacks against the United States—and *in* the United States. It warned that this danger would increase over the next several years. It specified as particular points of vulnerability the White House, the Capitol, symbols of capitalism such as Wall Street, critical infrastructure such as power grids, areas where people congregate such as sports arenas, and civil aviation generally. It warned that the 1993 World Trade Center bombing had been intended to kill a lot of people, not to achieve any more traditional political goal.

This 1995 estimate described the greatest danger as "transient groupings of individuals" that lacked "strong organization but rather are loose affiliations." They operate "outside traditional circles but have access to a worldwide network of training facilities and safe-havens." This was an excellent summary of the emerging danger, based on what was then known.

In 1996–1997, the intelligence community received new information making clear that Bin Ladin headed his own terrorist group, with its own targeting agenda and operational commanders. Also revealed was the previously unknown involvement of Bin Ladin's organization in the 1992 attack on a Yemeni hotel quartering U.S. military personnel, the 1993 shootdown of U.S. Army Black Hawk helicopters in Somalia, and quite possibly the 1995 Riyadh bombing of the American training mission to the Saudi National Guard.

The 1997 update of the 1995 estimate did not discuss the new intelligence. It did state that the terrorist danger depicted in 1995 would persist. In the update's summary of key points, the only reference to Bin Ladin was this sentence: "Iran and its surrogates, as well as terrorist financier Usama Bin Ladin and his followers, have stepped up their threats and surveillance of US facilities abroad in what also may be a portent of possible additional attacks in the United States." Bin Ladin was mentioned in only two other sentences in the six-page report. The al Qaeda organization was not mentioned. The 1997 update was the last national estimate on the terrorism danger completed before 9/11.

Whatever the weaknesses in the CIA's portraiture, both Presidents Bill Clinton and George Bush and their top advisers told us they got the picture—they understood Bin Ladin was a danger. But given the character and pace of their policy efforts, we do not believe they fully understood just how many people al Qaeda might kill, and how soon it might do it. At some level that is hard to define, we believe the threat had not yet become compelling.

It is hard now to recapture the conventional wisdom before 9/11. For example, a *New York Times* article in April 1999 sought to debunk claims that Bin Ladin was a terrorist leader, with the headline "U.S. Hard Put to Find Proof Bin Laden Directed Attacks." The head of analysis at the CTC until 1999 discounted the alarms about a catastrophic threat as relating only to the danger of chemical, biological, or nuclear attack—and he downplayed even that, writing several months before 9/11: "It would be a mistake to redefine counterterrorism as a task of dealing with 'catastrophic,' 'grand,' or 'super' terrorism, when in fact these labels do not represent most of the terrorism that the United States is likely to face or most of the costs that terrorism imposes on U.S. interests."

By 2001 the government still needed a decision at the highest level as to whether al Qaeda was or was not "a first order threat," Richard Clarke wrote in his first memo to Condoleezza Rice on January 25, 2001. In his blistering protest about foot-dragging in the Pentagon and at the CIA, sent to Rice just a week before 9/11, he repeated that the "real question" for the principals was "are we serious about dealing with the al Qida threat? . . . Is al Qida a big deal?"

One school of thought, Clarke wrote in this September 4 note, implicitly argued that the terrorist network was a nuisance that killed a score of Americans every 18–24 months. If that view was credited, then current policies might be proportionate. Another school saw al

Qaeda as the "point of the spear of radical Islam." But no one forced the argument into the open by calling for a national estimate or a broader discussion of the threat. The issue was never joined as a collective debate by the U.S. government, including the Congress, before 9/11.

We return to the issue of proportion—and imagination. Even Clarke's note challenging Rice to imagine the day after an attack posits a strike that kills "hundreds" of Americans. He did not write "thousands."

INSTITUTIONALIZING IMAGINATION:
THE CASE OF AIRCRAFT AS WEAPONS

Imagination is not a gift usually associated with bureaucracies. For example, before Pearl Harbor the U.S. government had excellent intelligence that a Japanese attack was coming, especially after peace talks stalemated at the end of November 1941. These were days, one historian notes, of "excruciating uncertainty." The most likely targets were judged to be in Southeast Asia. An attack was coming, "but officials were at a loss to know where the blow would fall or what more might be done to prevent it." In retrospect, available intercepts pointed to Japanese examination of Hawaii as a possible target. But, another historian observes, "in the face of a clear warning, alert measures bowed to routine."

It is therefore crucial to find a way of routinizing, even bureaucratizing, the exercise of imagination. Doing so requires more than finding an expert who can imagine that aircraft could be used as weapons. Indeed, since al Qaeda and other groups had already used suicide vehicles, namely truck bombs, the leap to the use of other vehicles such as boats (the *Cole* attack) or planes is not far-fetched.

Yet these scenarios were slow to work their way into the thinking of aviation security experts.

In his testimony, Clarke commented that he thought that warning about the possibility of a suicide hijacking would have been just one more speculative theory among many, hard to spot since the volume of warnings of "al Qaeda threats and other terrorist threats, was in the tens of thousands—probably hundreds of thousands." Yet the possibility was imaginable, and imagined. In early August 1999, the FAA's Civil Aviation Security intelligence office summarized the Bin Ladin hijacking threat. After a solid recitation of all the information available on this topic, the paper identified a few principal scenarios, one of which was a "suicide hijacking operation." The FAA analysts judged such an operation unlikely, because "it does not offer an opportunity for dialogue to achieve the key goal of obtaining captive extremists. . . . A suicide hijacking is assessed to be an option of last resort."

Analysts could have shed some light on what kind of "opportunity for dialogue" al Qaeda desired. The CIA did not write any analytical assessments of possible hijacking scenarios.

Since the Pearl Harbor attack of 1941, the intelligence community has devoted generations of effort to understanding the problem of forestalling a surprise attack. Rigorous analytic methods were developed, focused in particular on the Soviet Union, and several leading practitioners within the intelligence community discussed them with us. These methods have been articulated in many ways, but almost all seem to have at least four elements in common: (1) think about how surprise attacks might be launched; (2) identify telltale indicators connected to the most dangerous possibilities; (3) where feasible, collect intelligence on these indicators; and (4) adopt defenses to deflect the most dangerous possibilities or at least trigger an earlier warning.

With the important exception of analysis of al Qaeda efforts in chemical, biological, radiological, and nuclear weapons, we did not find evidence that the methods to avoid surprise attack that had been so laboriously developed over the years were regularly applied.

Considering what was not done suggests possible ways to institutionalize imagination. To return to the four elements of analysis just mentioned:

1. The CTC did not analyze how an aircraft, hijacked or explosives-laden, might be used as a weapon. It did not perform this kind of analysis from the enemy's perspective ("red team" analysis), even though suicide terrorism had become a principal tactic of Middle Eastern terrorists. If it had done so, we believe such an analysis would soon have spotlighted a critical constraint for the terrorists—finding a suicide operative able to fly large jet aircraft. They had never done so before 9/11.
2. The CTC did not develop a set of telltale indicators for this method of attack. For example, one such indicator might be the discovery of possible terrorists pursuing flight training to fly large jet aircraft, or seeking to buy advanced flight simulators.
3. The CTC did not propose, and the intelligence community collection management process did not set, requirements to monitor such telltale indicators. Therefore the warning system was not looking for information such as the July 2001 FBI

report of potential terrorist interest in various kinds of aircraft training in Arizona, or the August 2001 arrest of Zacarias Moussaoui because of his suspicious behavior in a Minnesota flight school. In late August, the Moussaoui arrest was briefed to the DCI and other top CIA officials under the heading "Islamic Extremist Learns to Fly." Because the system was not tuned to comprehend the potential significance of this information, the news had no effect on warning.

4. Neither the intelligence community nor aviation security experts analyzed systemic defenses within an aircraft or against terrorist controlled aircraft, suicidal or otherwise. The many threat reports mentioning aircraft were passed to the FAA. While that agency continued to react to specific, credible threats, it did not try to perform the broader warning functions we describe here. No one in the government was taking on that role for domestic vulnerabilities.

Richard Clarke told us that he was concerned about the danger posed by aircraft in the context of protecting the Atlanta Olympics of 1996, the White House complex, and the 2001 G-8 summit in Genoa. But he attributed his awareness more to Tom Clancy novels than to warnings from the intelligence community. He did not, or could not, press the government to work on the systemic issues of how to strengthen the layered security defenses to protect aircraft against hijackings or put the adequacy of air defenses against suicide hijackers on the national policy agenda.

The methods for detecting and then warning of surprise attack that the U.S. government had so painstakingly developed in the decades after Pearl Harbor did not fail; instead, they were not really tried. They were not employed to analyze the enemy that, as the twentieth century closed, was most likely to launch a surprise attack directly against the United States.

## Policy

The road to 9/11 again illustrates how the large, unwieldy U.S. government tended to underestimate a threat that grew ever greater. The terrorism fostered by Bin Ladin and al Qaeda was different from anything the government had faced before. The existing mechanisms for handling terrorist acts had been trial and punishment for acts committed by individuals; sanction, reprisal, deterrence, or war for acts by hostile governments. The actions of al Qaeda fit neither category. Its crimes were on a scale approaching acts of war, but they were committed by a loose, far-flung, nebulous conspiracy with no territories or citizens or assets that could be readily threatened, overwhelmed, or destroyed.

Early in 2001, DCI Tenet and Deputy Director for Operations James Pavitt gave an intelligence briefing to President-elect Bush, Vice President–elect Cheney, and Rice; it included the topic of al Qaeda. Pavitt recalled conveying that Bin Ladin was one of the gravest threats to the country.

Bush asked whether killing Bin Ladin would end the problem. Pavitt said he and the DCI had answered that killing Bin Ladin would have an impact, but would not stop the threat. The CIA later provided more formal assessments to the White House reiterating that conclusion. It added that in the long term, the only way to deal with the threat was to end al Qaeda's ability to use Afghanistan as a sanctuary for its operations.

Perhaps the most incisive of the advisors on terrorism to the new administration was the holdover Richard Clarke. Yet he admits that his policy advice, even if it had been accepted immediately and turned into action, would not have prevented 9/11.

We must then ask when the U.S. government had reasonable opportunities to mobilize the country for major action against al Qaeda and its Afghan sanctuary. The main opportunities came after the new information the U.S. government received in 1996–1997, after the embassy bombings of August 1998, after the discoveries of the Jordanian and Ressam plots in late 1999, and after the attack on the USS *Cole* in October 2000.

The U.S. policy response to al Qaeda before 9/11 was essentially defined following the embassy bombings of August 1998. We described those decisions in chapter 4. It is worth noting that they were made by the Clinton administration under extremely difficult domestic political circumstances. Opponents were seeking the President's impeachment. In addition, in 1998–[19]99 President Clinton was preparing the government for possible war against Serbia, and he had authorized major air strikes against Iraq.

The tragedy of the embassy bombings provided an opportunity for a full examination, across the government, of the national security threat that Bin Ladin posed. Such an examination could have made clear to all that issues were at stake that were much larger than the domestic politics of the moment. But the major policy agencies of the government did not meet the threat.

Policymakers turned principally to the CIA and covert action to implement policy. Before 9/11, no agency had more responsibility— or did more—to attack al Qaeda, working day and night, than the CIA. But there were limits to what the CIA was able to achieve in its energetic worldwide efforts to disrupt terrorist activities or use prox- ies to try to capture or kill Bin Ladin and his lieutenants. As early as mid-1997, one CIA officer wrote to his supervisor: "All we're doing is holding the ring until the cavalry gets here."

Military measures failed or were not applied. Before 9/11 the Department of Defense was not given the mission of ending al Qaeda's sanctuary in Afghanistan.

Officials in both the Clinton and Bush administrations regarded a full U.S. invasion of Afghanistan as practically inconceivable before 9/11. It was never the subject of formal interagency deliberation.

Lesser forms of intervention could also have been considered. One would have been the deployment of U.S. military or intelligence per- sonnel, or special strike forces, to Afghanistan itself or nearby— openly, clandestinely (secretly), or covertly (with their connection to the United States hidden). Then the United States would no longer have been dependent on proxies to gather actionable intelligence. However, it would have needed to secure basing and overflight sup- port from neighboring countries. A significant political, military, and intelligence effort would have been required, extending over months and perhaps years, with associated costs and risks. Given how hard it has proved to locate Bin Ladin even today when there are substantial ground forces in Afghanistan, its odds of success are hard to calculate. We have found no indication that President Clinton was offered such an intermediate choice, or that this option was given any more consid- eration than the idea of invasion.

These policy challenges are linked to the problem of imagination we have already discussed. Since we believe that both President Clin- ton and President Bush were genuinely concerned about the danger posed by al Qaeda, approaches involving more direct intervention against the sanctuary in Afghanistan apparently must have seemed— if they were considered at all—to be disproportionate to the threat.

Insight for the future is thus not easy to apply in practice. It is hard- est to mount a major effort while a problem still seems minor. Once the danger has fully materialized, evident to all, mobilizing action is easier—but it then may be too late.

Another possibility, short of putting U.S. personnel on the ground, was to issue a blunt ultimatum to the Taliban, backed by a readiness to at least launch an indefinite air campaign to disable that regime's limited military capabilities and tip the balance in Afghanistan's ongoing civil war. The United States had warned the Taliban that they would be held accountable for further attacks by Bin Ladin. The warning had been given in 1998, again in late 1999, once more in the fall of 2000, and again in the summer of 2001. Delivering it repeatedly did not make it more effective.

As evidence of al Qaeda's responsibility for the *Cole* attack came in during November 2000, National Security Advisor Samuel Berger asked the Pentagon to develop a plan for a sustained air campaign against the Taliban. Clarke developed a paper laying out a formal, specific ultimatum. But Clarke's plan apparently did not advance to formal consideration by the Small Group of principals. We have found no indication that the idea was briefed to the new administration or that Clarke passed his paper to them, although the same team of career officials spanned both administrations.

After 9/11, President Bush announced that al Qaeda was responsible for the attack on the USS *Cole*. Before 9/11, neither president took any action. Bin Ladin's inference may well have been that attacks, at least at the level of the *Cole*, were risk free.

## Capabilities

Earlier chapters describe in detail the actions decided on by the Clinton and Bush administrations. Each president considered or authorized covert actions. After the August 1998 missile strikes in Afghanistan, naval vessels remained on station in or near the region, prepared to fire cruise missiles. General Hugh Shelton developed as many as 13 different strike options, and did not recommend any of them. The most extended debate on counterterrorism in the Bush administration before 9/11 had to do with missions for the unmanned Predator [aircraft]—whether to use it just to locate Bin Ladin or to wait until it was armed with a missile, so that it could find him and also attack him. Looking back, we are struck with the narrow and unimaginative menu of options for action offered to both President Clinton and President Bush.

Before 9/11, the United States tried to solve the al Qaeda problem with the same government institutions and capabilities it had used in the last stages of the Cold War and its immediate aftermath. These capabilities were insufficient, but little was done to expand or reform them.

The high price of keeping counterterrorism policy within the restricted circle of the Counterterrorism Security Group and the highest-level principals was nowhere more apparent than in the military establishment. The vice director of operations on the Joint Staff commented to us that intelligence and planning documents relating to al Qaeda arrived in a ziplock red package and that many flag and general officers never had the clearances to see its contents.

At no point before 9/11 was the Department of Defense fully engaged in the mission of countering al Qaeda, though this was perhaps the most dangerous foreign enemy then threatening the United States. The Clinton administration effectively relied on the CIA to take the lead in preparing long-term offensive plans against an enemy sanctuary. The Bush administration adopted this approach, although its emerging new strategy envisioned some yet undefined further role for the military in addressing the problem. Within Defense, both Secretary Cohen and Secretary Donald Rumsfeld gave their principal attention to other challenges.

America's homeland defenders faced outward. NORAD [North American Air Defense Command] itself was barely able to retain any alert bases. Its planning scenarios occasionally considered the danger of hijacked aircraft being guided to American targets, but only aircraft that were coming from overseas.

The most serious weaknesses in agency capabilities were in the domestic arena. The major pre-9/11 effort to strengthen domestic agency capabilities came in 2000, as part of a millennium after-action review. President Clinton and his principal advisers paid considerable attention then to border security problems, but were not able to bring about significant improvements before leaving office. The NSC-led interagency process did not effectively bring along the leadership of the Justice and Transportation departments in an agenda for institutional change.

The FBI did not have the capability to link the collective knowledge of agents in the field to national priorities. The acting director of the FBI did not learn of his Bureau's hunt for two possible al Qaeda operatives in the United States or about his Bureau's arrest of an Islamic extremist taking flight training until September 11. The director of central intelligence knew about the FBI's Moussaoui investigation weeks before word of it made its way even to the FBI's own assistant director for counterterrorism.

The FAA's capabilities to take aggressive, anticipatory security measures were especially weak. Any serious policy examination of a suicide hijacking scenario, critiquing each of the layers of the security system, could have suggested changes to fix glaring vulnerabilities— expanding no-fly lists, searching passengers identified by the screening system, deploying Federal Air Marshals domestically, hardening cockpit doors, alerting air crew to a different kind of hijacking than what they had been trained to expect, or adjusting the training of controllers and managers in the FAA and NORAD.

Government agencies also sometimes display a tendency to match capabilities to mission by defining away the hardest part of their job. They are often passive, accepting what are viewed as givens, including that efforts to identify and fix glaring vulnerabilities to dangerous threats would be too costly, too controversial, or too disruptive.

## Management

OPERATIONAL MANAGEMENT

Earlier in this report we detailed various missed opportunities to thwart the 9/11 plot. Information was not shared, sometimes inadvertently or because of legal misunderstandings. Analysis was not pooled. Effective operations were not launched. Often the handoffs of information were lost across the divide separating the foreign and domestic agencies of the government.

However the specific problems are labeled, we believe they are symptoms of the government's broader inability to adapt how it manages problems to the new challenges of the twenty-first century. The agencies are like a set of specialists in a hospital, each ordering tests, looking for symptoms, and prescribing medications. What is missing is the attending physician who makes sure they work as a team.

Consider, for example, the case of Mihdhar, Hazmi, and their January 2000 trip to Kuala Lumpur, detailed in chapter 6. In late 1999, the National Security Agency (NSA) analyzed communications associated with a man named Khalid, a man named Nawaf, and a man named Salem.

The NSA did not think its job was to research these identities. It saw itself as an agency to support intelligence consumers, such as

[the] CIA. The NSA tried to respond energetically to any request made. But it waited to be asked.

If [the] NSA had been asked to try to identify these people, the agency would have started by checking its own database [and] would promptly have discovered who Nawaf was, that his full name might be Nawaf al Hazmi.

With the name "Nawaf al Hazmi," a manager could then have asked the State Department also to check that name. State would promptly have found its own record on Nawaf al Hazmi, showing that he too had been issued a visa to visit the United States. Officials would have learned that the visa had been issued at the same place—Jeddah—and on almost the same day as the one given to Khalid al Mihdhar.

When the travelers left Kuala Lumpur for Bangkok, local officials were able to identify one of the travelers as Khalid al Mihdhar. After the flight left, they learned that one of his companions had the name Alhazmi. But the officials did not know what that name meant.

In early March 2000, Bangkok reported that Nawaf al Hazmi, now identified for the first time with his full name, had departed on January 15 on a United Airlines flight to Los Angeles. Since the CIA did not appreciate the significance of that name or notice the cable, we have found no evidence that this information was sent to the FBI.

From the details of this case, one can see how hard it is for the intelligence community to assemble enough of the puzzle pieces gathered by different agencies to make some sense of them and then develop a fully informed joint plan.

Who had the job of managing the case to make sure these things were done? One answer is that everyone had the job. The CIA's deputy director for operations, James Pavitt, stressed to us that the responsibility resided with all involved. Above all he emphasized the primacy of the field. The field had the lead in managing operations. The job of headquarters, he stressed, was to support the field, and do so without delay. If the field asked for information or other support, the job of headquarters was to get it—right away.

This is a traditional perspective on operations and, traditionally, it has had great merit. It reminded us of the FBI's pre-9/11 emphasis on the primacy of its field offices. When asked about how this traditional structure would adapt to the challenge of managing a transnational case, one that hopped from place to place as this one did, the deputy director argued that all involved were responsible for making it work. Pavitt underscored the responsibility of the particular field location where the suspects were being tracked at any given time. On the other hand, he also said that the Counterterrorist Center was supposed to manage all the moving parts, while what happened on the ground was the responsibility of managers in the field.

Headquarters never really took responsibility for the successful management of this case. Hence the managers at CIA headquarters did not realize that omissions in planning had occurred, and they scarcely knew that the case had fallen apart.

The details of this case illuminate real management challenges, past and future. The U.S. government must find a way of pooling intelligence and using it to guide the planning of and assignment of responsibilities for *joint operations* involving organizations as disparate as the CIA, the FBI, the State Department, the military, and the agencies involved in homeland security.

INSTITUTIONAL MANAGEMENT

Beyond those day-to-day tasks of bridging the foreign-domestic divide and matching intelligence with plans, the challenges include broader management issues pertaining to how the top leaders of the government set priorities and allocate resources. Once again it is useful to illustrate the problem by examining the CIA, since before 9/11 this agency's role was so central in the government's counterterrorism efforts.

On December 4, 1998, DCI Tenet issued a directive to several CIA officials and his deputy for community management, stating: "We are at war. I want no resources or people spared in this effort, either inside CIA or the Community." The memorandum had little overall effect on mobilizing the CIA or the intelligence community.

The memo was addressed only to CIA officials and the deputy for community management, Joan Dempsey. She faxed the memo to the heads of the major intelligence agencies after removing covert action sections. Only a handful of people received it. The NSA director at the time, Lieutenant General Kenneth Minihan, believed the memo applied only to the CIA and not the NSA, because no one had informed him of any NSA shortcomings. For their part, CIA officials thought the memorandum was intended for the rest of the intelligence community, given that they were already doing all they could and believed that the rest of the community needed to pull its weight.

The episode indicates some of the limitations of the DCI's authority over the direction and priorities of the intelligence community, especially its elements within the Department of Defense. The DCI has to direct agencies without controlling them. He does not receive an appropriation for their activities, and therefore does not control their purse strings. He has little insight into how they spend their resources.

Lacking a management strategy for the war on terrorism or ways to see how funds were being spent across the community, DCI Tenet and his aides found it difficult to develop an overall intelligence community budget for a war on terrorism.

Responsibility for domestic intelligence gathering on terrorism was vested solely in the FBI, yet during almost all of the Clinton administration the relationship between the FBI Director and the President was nearly nonexistent. The FBI Director would not communicate directly with the President. His key personnel shared very little information with the National Security Council and the rest of the national security community. As a consequence, one of the critical working relationships in the counterterrorism effort was broken.

THE MILLENNIUM EXCEPTION

Before concluding our narrative, we offer a reminder, and an explanation, of the one period in which the government as a whole seemed to be acting in concert to deal with terrorism—the last weeks of December 1999 preceding the millennium.

In the period between December 1999 and early January 2000, information about terrorism flowed widely and abundantly. The flow from the FBI was particularly remarkable because the FBI at other times shared almost no information. That from the intelligence community was also remarkable, because some of it reached officials— local airport managers and local police departments—who had not seen such information before and would not see it again before 9/11. And the terrorist threat, in the United States even more than abroad, engaged the frequent attention of high officials in the executive branch and leaders in both houses of Congress.

Why was this so? Most obviously, it was because everyone was already on edge with the millennium and possible computer programming glitches ("Y2K") that might obliterate records, shut down power and communication lines, or otherwise disrupt daily life. Then, Jordanian authorities arrested 16 al Qaeda terrorists planning a number of bombings in that country. Those in custody included two U.S. citizens. Soon after, an alert Customs agent caught Ahmed Ressam bringing explosives across the Canadian border with the apparent intention of blowing up Los Angeles airport. He was found to have confederates on both sides of the border.

These were not events whispered about in highly classified intelligence dailies or FBI interview memos. The information was in all major newspapers and highlighted in network television news. Though the Jordanian arrests only made page 13 of the *New York Times,* they were featured on every evening newscast. The arrest of Ressam was on front pages, and the original story and its follow-ups dominated television news for a week. FBI field offices around the country were swamped by calls from concerned citizens. Representatives of the Justice Department, the FAA, local police departments, and major airports had microphones in their faces whenever they showed themselves.

After the millennium alert, the government relaxed. Counterterrorism went back to being a secret preserve for segments of the FBI, the Counterterrorist Center, and the Counterterrorism Security Group. But the experience showed that the government was capable of mobilizing itself for an alert against terrorism. While one factor was the preexistence of widespread concern about Y2K, another, at least equally important, was simply shared information. Everyone knew not only of an abstract threat but of at least one terrorist who had been arrested *in the United States.* Terrorism had a face—that of Ahmed Ressam—and Americans from Vermont to southern California went on the watch for his like.

In the summer of 2001, DCI Tenet, the Counterterrorist Center, and the Counterterrorism Security Group did their utmost to sound a loud alarm, its basis being intelligence indicating that al Qaeda planned something big. But the millennium phenomenon was not repeated. FBI field offices apparently saw no abnormal terrorist activity, and headquarters was not shaking them up.

Between May 2001 and September 11, there was very little in newspapers or on television to heighten anyone's concern about terrorism. Front-page stories touching on the subject dealt with the windup of trials dealing with the East Africa embassy bombings and Ressam. All this reportage looked backward, describing problems satisfactorily resolved. Back-page notices told of tightened security at embassies and military installations abroad and government cautions against travel to the Arabian Peninsula. All the rest was secret.

## 12. WHAT TO DO? A GLOBAL STRATEGY

We propose a strategy with three dimensions: (1) attack terrorists and their organizations, (2) prevent the continued growth of Islamist terrorism, and (3) protect against and prepare for terrorist attacks.

## ATTACK TERRORISTS AND THEIR ORGANIZATIONS

— Root out sanctuaries.

## PREVENT THE CONTINUED GROWTH OF ISLAMIST TERRORISM

— Define the message and stand as an example of moral leadership in the world.
— Where Muslim governments, even those who are friends, do not offer opportunity, respect the rule of law, or tolerate differences, then the United States needs to stand for a better future.
— Communicate and defend American ideals in the Islamic world, through much stronger public diplomacy.
— Offer an agenda of opportunity that includes support for public education and economic openness.
— Develop a comprehensive coalition strategy against Islamist terrorism, using a flexible contact group of leading coalition governments and fashioning a common coalition approach.

## PROTECT AGAINST AND PREPARE FOR TERRORIST ATTACKS

— Target terrorist travel, an intelligence and security strategy that the 9/11 story showed could be at least as powerful as the effort devoted to terrorist finance.
— Address problems of screening people with biometric identifiers across agencies and governments.
— Develop strategies for neglected parts of our transportation security system.
— Determine, with leadership from the President, guidelines for gathering and sharing information in the new security systems that integrate safeguards for privacy and other essential liberties.
— Underscore that as government power necessarily expands in certain ways, the burden of retaining such powers remains on the executive to demonstrate the value of such powers and ensure adequate supervision of how they are used, including a new board to oversee the implementation of the guidelines needed for gathering and sharing information in these new security systems.
— Base federal funding for emergency preparedness solely on risks and vulnerabilities, putting New York City and Washington, D.C., at the top of the current list. Such assistance should not remain a program for general revenue sharing or pork-barrel spending.

## 13. HOW TO DO IT? A DIFFERENT WAY OF ORGANIZING GOVERNMENT

The strategy we have recommended is elaborate, even as presented here very briefly. To implement it will require a government better organized than the one that exists today, with its national security institutions designed half a century ago to win the Cold War. We call for unity of effort in five areas, beginning with unity of effort on the challenge of counterterrorism itself:

— unifying strategic intelligence and operational planning against Islamist terrorists across the foreign-domestic divide with a National Counterterrorism Center;
— unifying the intelligence community with a new National Intelligence Director;
— unifying the many participants in the counterterrorism effort and their knowledge in a network-based information sharing system that transcends traditional governmental boundaries;
— unifying and strengthening congressional oversight to improve quality and accountability; and
— strengthening the FBI and homeland defenders.

\* \* \*

We look forward to a national debate on the merits of what we have recommended, and we will participate vigorously in that debate.

# PART THREE

# Related Documents

# 1

## *Declarations by Usama Bin Ladin*

### *August 23, 1996; May 10, 1997; February 23, 1998*

*Chapter 2 of* The 9/11 Commission Report *tells of Usama Bin Ladin's call to Muslims to kill all Americans. The following statements indicate the evolution of his position and also suggest how he couched his message differently for various audiences. The 1996 declaration was addressed chiefly to potential recruits; the 1997 CNN interview and the 1998 fatwa were obviously meant for a wider audience. The question of just how Bin Ladin imagined that audience merits discussion. Did he expect a response from the U.S. government? from governments in Muslim lands? from rich Muslim fundamentalists? from anyone else?*

## From *Declaration of War against the Americans Occupying the Land of the Two Holy Places*

### *August 23, 1996*

... [T]he people of Islam ... suffered from aggression, iniquity and injustice imposed on them by the Zionist-Crusaders'* alliance and their collaborators; to the extent that the Muslims' blood became the cheapest and their wealth as loot in the hands of their enemies. Their blood was spilled in Palestine and Iraq. ... Massacres in Tajikistan, Burma, Kashmir ... Philippines ... Somalia, Eritrea, and Chechnya and in Bosnia-Herzegovina took place, massacres that send shivers in the body and shake the conscience.

The latest and greatest of these aggressions, incurred by the Muslims since the death of the Prophet ... is the occupation of the land of the two Holy Places [Saudi Arabia]. ...

---

*Supporters of Israel, including the United States.

---

http://www.pbs.org/newshour/terrorism/international/fatwa_1966.html.

Our youths believe in paradise after death. They believe that taking part in fighting will not bring their day nearer; and staying behind will not postpone their day either. . . .

These youths believe in what has been told by Allah and His messenger (Allah's Blessings and Salutations may be on him) about the greatness of the reward for the Mujahideen and Martyrs; Allah, the most exalted said: and—so far—those who are slain in the way of Allah, He will by no means allow their deeds to perish. He will guide them and improve their condition, and cause them to enter the garden—paradise. . . .

Those youths know that their rewards in fighting you, the USA, is [sic] double than their rewards in fighting some one else not from the people of the book. They have no intention except to enter paradise by killing you.

My Muslim Brothers of the World: Your brothers in Palestine and in the land of the two Holy Places are calling upon your help and asking you to take part in fighting against the enemy—your enemy and their enemy—the Americans and the Israelis. . . .

## From *CNN Interview by Peter Arnett*

### *May 10, 1997*

We declared jihad against the U.S. government, because the U.S. government is unjust, criminal and tyrannical. . . . And we believe the U.S. is directly responsible for those who were killed in Palestine, Lebanon, and Iraq. . . .

As for what you asked, whether the jihad is directed against U.S. soldiers, the civilians in the land of the Two Holy Places, or against the civilians in America, we have focused our declaration on striking at the soldiers in the country of the Two Holy Places. . . .

[As for future plans,] you'll see them and hear about them in the media, God willing.

www.anusha.com/osamaint.htm.

## From *World Islamic Front Statement,*
## *"Jihad against Jews and Crusaders"*
### *February 23, 1998*

The Arabian Peninsula has never—since Allah made it flat, created its desert, and encircled it with seas—been stormed by any forces like the crusader armies spreading in it like locusts, eating its riches and wiping out its plantations. All this is happening at a time in which nations are attacking Muslims like people fighting over a plate of food. In the light of the grave situation and the lack of support, we and you are obliged to discuss current events, and we should all agree on how to settle the matter.

No one argues today about three facts that are known to everyone; we will list them, in order to remind everyone:

First, for over seven years the United States has been occupying the lands of Islam in the holiest of places, the Arabian Peninsula, plundering its riches, dictating to its rulers, humiliating its people, terrorizing its neighbors, and turning its bases in the Peninsula into a spearhead through which to fight the neighboring Muslim peoples.

If some people have in the past argued about the fact of the occupation, all the people of the Peninsula have now acknowledged it. The best proof of this is the Americans' continuing aggression against the Iraqi people using the Peninsula as a staging post, even though all its rulers are against their territories being used to that end, but they are helpless.

Second, despite the great devastation inflicted on the Iraqi people by the crusader-Zionist alliance, and despite the huge number of those killed, which has exceeded 1 million . . . despite all this, the Americans are once again trying to repeat the horrific massacres, as though they are not content with the protracted blockade imposed after the ferocious war or the fragmentation and devastation.

So here they come to annihilate what is left of this people and to humiliate their Muslim neighbors.

Third, if the Americans' aims behind these wars are religious and economic, the aim is also to serve the Jews' petty state and divert attention from its occupation of Jerusalem and murder of Muslims there. The best proof of this is their eagerness to destroy Iraq, the strongest neighboring Arab state, and their endeavor to fragment all the states of the region such as Iraq, Saudi Arabia, Egypt, and Sudan into paper statelets and through their disunion and weakness to guarantee Israel's survival and the continuation of the brutal crusade occupation of the Peninsula.

All these crimes and sins committed by the Americans are a clear declaration of war on Allah, his messenger, and Muslims. And ulema* have throughout Islamic history unanimously agreed that the jihad is an individual duty if the enemy destroys the Muslim countries. . . .

On that basis, and in compliance with Allah's order, we issue the following fatwa to all Muslims:

The ruling to kill the Americans and their allies—civilians and military—is an individual duty for every Muslim who can do it in any country in which it is possible to do it, in order to liberate the al-Aqsa Mosque [Jerusalem] and the holy mosque [Mecca] from their grip, and in order for their armies to move out of all the lands of Islam, defeated and unable to threaten any Muslim. . . .

We—with Allah's help—call on every Muslim who believes in Allah and wishes to be rewarded to comply with Allah's order to kill the Americans and plunder their money wherever and whenever they find it. We also call on Muslim ulema, leaders, youths, and soldiers to launch the raid on Satan's U.S. troops and the devil's supporters allying with them, and to displace those who are behind them so that they may learn a lesson.

Issued by Usama Bin-Ladin, Ayman al-Zawahiri and Abu-Yasir Rifa'i Ahmad Taha (both of Egyptian Islamic Jihad), Shaykh Mir Hamzah (of the Jamiat-ul-Ulema-e-Pakistan), and Fazlur Rahman (of the Jihad Movement in Bangladesh)

---

*Mullahs; Muslim religious leaders.

# 2

# From *The President's Daily Brief*
## *December 4, 1998, and August 6, 2001*

*The 9/11 Commission's demand for access to the President's Daily Brief (PDB) caused a major dispute with the Bush administration. Although the White House eventually retreated from its initial refusal to allow any access at all, the compromise arrangement limited full access to Chair Thomas Kean; Vice Chair Lee Hamilton; one commissioner, Jamie Gorelick; and the Commission's executive director, Philip Zelikow. The Democratic commissioners asked particularly about a rumored August 2001 PDB item that had warned of possible al Qaeda attacks inside the United States. When National Security Advisor Condoleezza Rice finally gave public testimony before the Commission, she agreed to declassify the item with a few excisions for security reasons. Some Republican commissioners pressed for declassification of a reported Clinton administration PDB item showing that a comparable warning had gone to President Bush's Democratic predecessor. That item also was declassified with excisions. The two texts serve as examples of intelligence reportage to the White House and help to show why high officials so often complain of such reportage on the ground that it is informative but not "actionable."*

*Both of these PDBs appeared in the original report. Brackets indicate edits made by the CIA. The individuals named in the first paragraph of the 1998 PDB had been convicted and imprisoned for involvement in the World Trade Center bombing of 1993 and other plots. The Gama'at al-Islamiyya was an Egyptian radical Islamist group founded by Sheikh Omar Abdel Rahman (Shaykt 'Umar 'Abd al-Rahman), "the Blind Sheikh."*

*The 9/11 Commission Report*, 128–29, 260–62.

## Subject: Bin Ladin Preparing
## to Hijack US Aircraft and Other Attacks
### December 4, 1998

1. Reporting [—] suggests Bin Ladin and his allies are preparing for attacks in the US, including an aircraft hijacking to obtain the release of Shaykh 'Umar 'Abd al-Rahman, Ramzi Yousef, and Muhammad Sadiq 'Awda. One source quoted a senior member of the Gama'at al-Islamiyya (IG) saying that, as of late October, the IG had completed planning for an operation in the US on behalf of Bin Ladin, but that the operation was on hold. A senior Bin Ladin operative from Saudi Arabia was to visit IG counterparts in the US soon thereafter to discuss options—perhaps including an aircraft hijacking.

— IG leader Islambuli in late September was planning to hijack a US airliner during the "next couple of weeks" to free 'Abd al-Rahman and the other prisoners, according to what may be a different source.
— The same source late last month said that Bin Ladin might implement plans to hijack US aircraft before the beginning of Ramadan on 20 December and that two members of the operational team had evaded security checks during a recent trial run at an unidentified New York airport. [—]

2. Some members of the Bin Ladin network have received hijack training, according to various sources, but no group directly tied to Bin Ladin's al-Qa'ida organization has ever carried out an aircraft hijacking. Bin Ladin could be weighing other types of operations against US aircraft. According to [—] the IG in October obtained SA-7 missiles and intended to move them from Yemen into Saudi Arabia to shoot down an Egyptian plane or, if unsuccessful, a US military or civilian aircraft.

— A [—] in October told us that unspecified "extremist elements" in Yemen had acquired SA-7s. [—]

3. [—] indicate the Bin Ladin organization or its allies are moving closer to implementing anti-US attacks at unspecified locations, but we do not know whether they are related to attacks on aircraft. A Bin Ladin associate in Sudan late last month told a colleague in Kandahar that he had shipped a group of containers to Afghanistan. Bin Ladin

associates also talked about the movement of containers to Afghanistan before the East Africa bombings.

— In other [—] Bin Ladin associates last month discussed picking up a package in Malaysia. One told his colleague in Malaysia that "they" were in the "ninth month [of pregnancy]."
— An alleged Bin Ladin supporter in Yemen late last month remarked to his mother that he planned to work in "commerce" from abroad and said his impending "marriage," which would take place soon, would be a "surprise." "Commerce" and "marriage" often are codewords for terrorist attacks. [—]

## Subject: Bin Ladin Determined to Strike in US

### August 6, 2001

*Clandestine, foreign government, and media reports indicate Bin Ladin since 1997 has wanted to conduct terrorist attacks in the US.* Bin Ladin implied in US television interviews in 1997 and 1998 that his followers would follow the example of World Trade Center bomber Ramzi Yousef and "bring the fighting to America."

After US missile strikes on his base in Afghanistan in 1998, Bin Ladin told followers he wanted to retaliate in Washington, according to a [—] service.

An Egyptian Islamic Jihad (EIJ) operative told an [—] service at the same time that Bin Ladin was planning to exploit the operative's access to the US to mount a terrorist strike.

*The millennium plotting in Canada in 1999 may have been part of Bin Ladin's first serious attempt to implement a terrorist strike in the US.* Convicted plotter Ahmed Ressam has told the FBI that he conceived the idea to attack Los Angeles International Airport himself, but that Bin Ladin lieutenant Abu Zubaydah encouraged him and helped facilitate the operation. Ressam also said that in 1998 Abu Zubaydah was planning his own US attack.

Ressam says Bin Ladin was aware of the Los Angeles operation.

*Although Bin Ladin has not succeeded, his attacks against the US Embassies in Kenya and Tanzania in 1998 demonstrate that he prepares operations years in advance and is not deterred by setbacks.* Bin Ladin associates surveilled our Embassies in Nairobi and Dar es Salaam as early as 1993, and some members of the Nairobi cell planning the bombings were arrested and deported in 1997.

*Al-Qa'ida [sic] members—including some who are US citizens—have resided in or traveled to the US for years, and the group apparently maintains a support structure that could aid attacks.* Two al-Qua'da [sic] members found guilty in the conspiracy to bomb our embassies in East Africa were US citizens, and a senior EIJ member lived in California in the mid-1990s.

A clandestine source said in 1998 that a Bin Ladin cell in New York was recruiting Muslim-American youth for attacks.

*We have not been able to corroborate some of the more sensational threat reporting, such as that from a [—] service in 1998 saying that Bin Ladin wanted to hijack a US aircraft to gain the release of "Blind Shaykh" 'Umar 'Abd al-Rahman and other US-held extremists.*

Nevertheless, FBI information since that time indicates patterns of suspicious activity in this country consistent with preparations for hijackings or other types of attacks, including recent surveillance of federal buildings in New York.

The FBI is conducting approximately 70 full field investigations throughout the US that it considers Bin Ladin-related. CIA and the FBI are investigating a call to our Embassy in the UAE in May saying that a group of Bin Ladin supporters was in the US planning attacks with explosives.

## 3

## THE 9/11 COMMISSION

# Final Report on
# 9/11 Commission Recommendations
### December 5, 2005

*By statute, the 9/11 Commission ceased to exist soon after releasing its report. At that time, the ten commissioners formed the privately funded Public Discourse Project to encourage continued discussion of its recommendations. This project held a number of public meetings and issued statements. Before shutting down the project at the end of 2005, the commissioners unanimously issued the following report card on the results of their recommendations.*

## PART I: HOMELAND SECURITY, EMERGENCY PREPAREDNESS AND RESPONSE

RECOMMENDATION                                    GRADE

**Emergency Preparedness and Response**

*Provide adequate radio spectrum for*       **F** (**C** *if bill passes*)
*first responders*

The pending Fiscal Year 2006 budget reconciliation bill would compel the return of the analog TV broadcast (700 Mhz) spectrum, and reserve some for public safety purposes. Both the House and Senate bills contain a 2009 handover date—too distant given the urgency of the threat. A 2007 handover date would make the American people safer sooner.

http://www.9-11pdp.org/.

*Establish a unified Incident Command*     **C**
*System [ICS]*
Although there is awareness of and some training in the ICS, hurricane Katrina demonstrated the absence of full compliance during a multi-jurisdictional/statewide catastrophe—and its resulting costs.

*Allocate homeland security funds based*     **F (A** *if House*
*on risk*                                         *provision passes)*
Congress has still not changed the underlying statutory authority for homeland security grants, or benchmarks to insure that funds are used wisely. As a result, homeland security funds continue to be distributed without regard for risk, vulnerability, or the consequences of an attack, diluting the national security benefits of this important program.

*Critical infrastructure risks and*     **D**
*vulnerabilities assessment*
A draft National Infrastructure Protection Plan (November 2005) spells out a methodology and process for critical infrastructure assessments. No risk and vulnerability assessments actually made; no national priorities established; no recommendations made on allocation of scarce resources. All key decisions are at least a year away. It is time that we stop talking about setting priorities, and actually set some.

*Private sector preparedness*     **C**
National preparedness standards are only beginning to find their way into private sector business practices. Private sector preparedness needs to be a higher priority for DHS [Department of Homeland Security] and for American businesses.


**Transportation Security**

*National Strategy for Transportation Security*     **C–**
DHS has transmitted its National Strategy for Transportation Security to the Congress. While the strategy reportedly outlines broad objectives, this first version lacks the necessary detail to make it an effective management tool.

*Improve airline passenger pre-screening*     **F**
Few improvements have been made to the existing passenger screening system since right after 9/11. The completion of the testing phase of TSA's [Transportation Security Administration's] pre-screening program for airline passengers has been delayed. A new system, utilizing

all names on the consolidated terrorist watch list, is therefore not yet in operation.

*Improve airline screening checkpoints to*     **C**
*detect explosives*
While more advanced screening technology is being developed, Congress needs to provide the funding for, and TSA needs to move as expeditiously as possible with, the appropriate installation of explosives detection trace portals at more of the nation's commercial airports.

*Checked bag and cargo screening*     **D**
Improvements here have not been made a priority by the Congress or the administration. Progress on implementation of in-line screening has been slow. The main impediment is inadequate funding.

## Border Security

*Better terrorist travel strategy*     **Incomplete**
The first Terrorist Travel Strategy is in development, due to be delivered by December 17, 2005 as required by PL 108-458.

*Comprehensive screening system*     **C**
We still do not have a comprehensive screening system. Although agencies are moving ahead on individual screening projects, there is lack of progress on coordination between agencies. DHS' new Screening Coordination Office still needs to establish and implement goals for resolving differences in biometric and traveler systems, credentialing and identification standards.

*Biometric entry-exit screening system*     **B**
The US-VISIT system is running at 115 airports and 15 seaports, and is performing secondary screening at the 50 busiest land borders. But border screening systems are not yet employed at all land borders, nor are these systems interoperable. The exit component of the US-VISIT system has not been widely deployed.

*International collaboration on borders and*     **D**
*document security*
There has been some good collaboration between US-VISIT and Interpol, but little progress elsewhere. There has been no systematic diplomatic effort to share terrorist watch lists, nor has Congress taken a leadership role in passport security.

*Standardize secure identifications*          **B–**
The REAL ID Act has established by statute standards for state-issued IDs acceptable for federal purposes, though states' compliance needs to be closely monitored. New standards for issuing birth certificates (required by law by December 17, 2005) are delayed until at least spring 2006, probably longer. Without movement on the birth certificate issue, state-issued IDs are still not secure.

## PART II: REFORMING THE INSTITUTIONS OF GOVERNMENT

| RECOMMENDATION | GRADE |
| --- | --- |

### The Intelligence Community

*Director of National Intelligence [DNI]*          **B**
The framework for the DNI and his authorities are in place. Now his challenge is to exercise his authorities boldly to smash stovepipes, drive reform, and create a unity of effort—and act soon. He must avoid layering of the bureaucracy and focus on transformation of the Intelligence Community. The success of this office will require decisive leadership from the DNI and the president, and active oversight by the Congress.

*National Counterterrorism Center [NCTC]*          **B**
Shared analysis and evaluation of threat information is in progress; joint operational planning is beginning. But the NCTC does not yet have sufficient resources or personnel to fulfill its intelligence and planning role.

*Create FBI national security workforce*          **C**
Progress is being made—but it is too slow. The FBI's shift to a counterterrorism posture is far from institutionalized, and significant deficiencies remain. Reforms are at risk from inertia and complacency; they must be accelerated, or they will fail. Unless there is improvement in a reasonable period of time, Congress will have to look at alternatives.

*New missions for CIA Director*          **Incomplete**
Reforms are underway at the CIA, especially of human intelligence operations. But their outcome is yet to be seen. If the CIA is to remain an effective arm of national power, Congress and CIA leadership need

to be committed to accelerating the pace of reforms, and must address morale and personnel issues.

*Incentives for information sharing*  **D**
Changes in incentives, in favor of information sharing, have been minimal. The office of the program manager for information sharing is still a start-up, and is not getting the support it needs from the highest levels of government. There remain many complaints about lack of information sharing between federal authorities and state and local level officials.

*Government-wide information sharing*  **D**
Designating individuals to be in charge of information sharing is not enough. They need resources, active presidential backing, policies and procedures in place that compel sharing, and systems of performance evaluation that appraise personnel on how they carry out information sharing.

*Homeland airspace defense*  **B–**
Situational awareness and sharing of information has improved. But it is not routine or comprehensive, no single agency currently leads the interagency response to airspace violations, and there is no overarching plan to secure airspace outside the National Capital region.

## Civil Liberties and Executive Power

*Balance between security and civil liberties*  **B**
The debate surrounding reauthorization of the PATRIOT Act has been strong, and concern for civil liberties has been at the heart of it. Robust and continuing oversight, both within the Executive and by the Congress, will be essential.

*Privacy and Civil Liberties Oversight Board*  **D**
We see little urgency in the creation of this Board. The President nominated a Chair and Vice Chair in June 2005, and sent their names to the Senate in late September. To date, the Senate has not confirmed them. Funding is insufficient, no meetings have been held, no staff named, no work plan outlined, no work begun, no office established.

*Guidelines for government sharing of*  **D**
*personal information*
The Privacy and Civil Liberties Oversight Board has not yet begun its work. The DNI just named a Civil Liberties Protection Officer (November 2005).

## Congressional and Administrative Reform

*Intelligence oversight reform* **D**

The House and Senate have taken limited positive steps, including the creation of oversight subcommittees. However, the ability of the intelligence committees to perform oversight of the intelligence agencies and account for their performance is still undermined by the power of the Defense Appropriations subcommittees and Armed Services committees.

*Homeland Security committees* **B**

The House and Senate have taken positive steps, but Secretary [Michael] Chertoff and his team still report to too many bosses. The House and Senate homeland security committees should have exclusive jurisdiction over all counterterrorism functions of the Department of Homeland Security.

*Declassify overall intelligence budget* **F**

No action has been taken. The Congress cannot do robust intelligence oversight when funding for intelligence programs is buried within the defense budget. Declassifying the overall intelligence budget would allow for a separate annual intelligence appropriations bill, so that the Congress can judge better how intelligence funds are being spent.

*Standardize security clearances* **B**

The President put the Office of Management and Budget (OMB) in charge of standardizing security clearances. OMB issued a plan to improve the personnel security clearance process in November 2005. The Deputy Director of OMB is committed to its success. All the hard work is ahead.

# PART III: FOREIGN POLICY, PUBLIC DIPLOMACY, AND NONPROLIFERATION

| RECOMMENDATION | GRADE |
| --- | --- |

## Nonproliferation

*Maximum effort by U.S. government to secure* **D**
*WMD [weapons of mass destruction]*

Countering the greatest threat to America's security is still not the top national security priority of the President and the Congress.

## Foreign Policy

*Long-term commitment to Afghanistan* **B**
Progress has been made, but attacks by Taliban and other extremists continue and the drug situation has worsened. The U.S. and its partners must commit to a long-term economic plan in order to ensure the country's stability.

*Support Pakistan against extremists* **C+**
U.S. assistance to Pakistan has not moved sufficiently beyond security assistance to include significant funding for education efforts. Musharraf has made efforts to take on the threat from extremism, but has not shut down extremist-linked madrassas or terrorist camps. Taliban forces still pass freely across the Pakistan-Afghanistan border and operate in Pakistani tribal areas.

*Support reform in Saudi Arabia* **D**
Saudi authorities have taken initial steps but need to do much more to regulate charities and control the flow of funds to extremist groups, and to promote tolerance and moderation. A U.S.-Saudi strategic dialogue to address topics including reform and exchange programs has just started; there are no results to report.

*Identify and prioritize terrorist sanctuaries* **B**
Strategies have been articulated to address and eliminate terrorist sanctuaries, but they do not include a useful metric to gauge progress. There is little sign of long-term efforts in place to reduce the conditions that allow the formation of terrorist sanctuaries.

*Coalition strategy against Islamist terrorism* **C**
Components of a common strategy are evident on a bilateral basis, and multilateral policies exist in some areas. But no permanent contact group of leading governments has yet been established to coordinate a coalition counterterrorism strategy.

*Coalition standards for terrorist detention* **F**
The U.S. has not engaged in a common coalition approach to developing standards for detention and prosecution of captured terrorists. Indeed, U.S. treatment of detainees has elicited broad criticism, and makes it harder to build the necessary alliances to cooperate effectively with partners in a global war on terror.

*Economic policies* **B+**
There has been measurable progress in reaching agreements on economic reform in the Middle East, including a free trade agreement

with Bahrain and the likely admission of Saudi Arabia to the WTO [World Trade Organization] before long. However, it is too early to judge whether these agreements will lead to genuine economic reform.

*Vigorous effort against terrorist financing*    **A–**
The U.S. has won the support of key countries in tackling terrorism finance—though there is still much to do in the Gulf States and in South Asia. The government has made significant strides in using terrorism finance as an intelligence tool. However, the State Department and Treasury Department are engaged in unhelpful turf battles, and the overall effort lacks leadership.

## Public Diplomacy

*Define the U.S. message*    **C**
Despite efforts to offer a vision for U.S. leadership in the world based on the expansion of democratic governance, public opinion approval ratings for the U.S. throughout the Middle East remain at or near historic lows. Public diplomacy initiatives need to communicate our values, way of life, and vision for the world without lecturing or condescension.

*International broadcasting*    **B**
Budgets for international broadcasting to the Arab and Muslim world and U.S.-sponsored broadcasting hours have increased dramatically, and audience shares are growing. But we need to move beyond audience size, expose listeners to new ideas and accurate information about the U.S. and its policies, and measure the impact and influence of these ideas.

*Scholarship, exchange, and library programs*    **D**
Funding for educational and cultural exchange programs has increased. But more American libraries (Pakistan, for example) are closing rather than opening. The number of young people coming to study in the U.S. from the Middle East continues to decline (down 2% this year, following declines of 9% and 10% in the previous two years).

*Support secular education in Muslim countries*    **D**
An International Youth Opportunity Fund has been authorized, but has received no funding; secular education programs have been initiated across the Arab world, but are not integrated into a broader counterterrorism strategy. The U.S. has no overarching strategy for educational assistance, and the current level of education reform funding is inadequate.

# A 9/11 Chronology (1978–2005)

**1978–**
**1979** A revolution in Iran unseats the U.S.–backed Shah and substitutes an Islamic republic.

**1979** Soviet armed forces invade Afghanistan to reinstall a Communist regime.

**1988–**
**1989** The Soviet government accepts defeat and withdraws from Afghanistan.

**1989–**
**1991** Usama Bin Ladin (UBL) and others form al Qaeda.

**1990** Saddam Hussein, the dictator of Iraq, sends military forces into oil-rich Kuwait.

**1991** Under President George H. W. Bush, the United States leads a UN-endorsed military campaign that drives the Iraqis out of Kuwait (the Persian Gulf War).

**1992** Islamic extremists bomb a hotel in Aden, Yemen, where U.S. troops are in transit to Somalia in support of a UN humanitarian aid mission.

**1993** *January 20*: William Jefferson (Bill) Clinton becomes U.S. president.

*January 25*: A Pakistani lone-wolf terrorist shoots and kills two CIA employees at the entry to CIA headquarters in Virginia.

*February*: A truck bomb explodes in the underground garage of the WTC, killing six and wounding more than a thousand.

*March–June*: The FBI and NYPD arrest perpetrators of the WTC bombing and forestall a plot to destroy New York landmarks such as the Holland and Lincoln tunnels.

**1994** *January*: Attorney General Janet Reno appoints a special prosecutor to investigate Whitewater.

*March*: After losing two Black Hawk helicopters and eighteen soldiers, Clinton withdraws U.S. forces from Somalia.

*November*: For the first time in forty years, Republicans capture majorities in both houses of Congress.

**1995**   *January*: Philippine police discover an Islamist plot, popularly labeled "Bojinka," to blow up a dozen U.S. transpacific airliners simultaneously.

*February*: WTC bombing suspect Ramzi Yousef is captured in Pakistan and brought to the United States.

*April*: A bomb destroys a federal building in Oklahoma City, killing 168.

*May–June*: Clinton proposes legislation to strengthen the federal government's antiterrorist authority and centralizes the coordination of counterterrorist activity under NSC aide Richard Clarke.

*July*: A classified National Intelligence Estimate analyzes the Islamic terrorist threat to the United States and warns of likely attacks on the American homeland.

*November*: A bomb in Riyadh kills five Americans and two others.

**1996**   *June*: Terrorists bomb the Khobar Towers complex in Saudi Arabia, killing 19 Americans and wounding 372.

*July?*: Khalid Sheikh Mohammed (KSM) visits UBL in Tora Bora and proposes a number of possible terrorist operations, including an early version of the 9/11 attacks.

*November*: Clinton is reelected, but the Republicans retain control of Congress.

*December*: A congressional ethics committee finds House Speaker Newt Gingrich guilty of financial improprieties; he eventually resigns the Speakership and leaves Congress.

**1998**   *January*: Kenneth Starr, Whitewater special prosecutor, gets permission to broaden his investigation to cover allegations of perjury in connection with sexual harassment suits filed against Clinton.

*February*: UBL and two others issue a fatwa condemning U.S. actions in the Middle East and saying it is the religious duty of Muslims to kill Americans wherever they may be found.

*May*: India and Pakistan conduct surprise nuclear tests. The CIA plans and practices an operation to capture UBL, but Director of Central Intelligence George Tenet and the White House call it off.

*August 7*: U.S. embassies in Kenya and Tanzania are destroyed by bombs; surviving perpetrators confess immediately to acting for al Qaeda.

*August 17*: Clinton gives testimony under oath to Starr's grand jury; he confesses to having had a sexual relationship with White House intern Monica Lewinsky.

*August 20*: In retaliation for the embassy bombings, U.S. forces rain cruise missiles on al Qaeda training camps in Afghanistan and on a pharmaceutical plant in Sudan.

*September*: Starr delivers a Whitewater report to the House of Representatives, charging Clinton with perjury and obstruction of justice. Clarke circulates his "Plan Delenda," calling for focused efforts to destroy al Qaeda.

*December*: In response to Iraq's ousting of UN nuclear arms inspectors, U.S. forces acting for the UN stage heavy air raids on suspected nuclear, chemical, and biological warfare facilities in Iraq.

*December 19*: The House of Representatives votes two counts of impeachment against Clinton.

**1999**  *February*: UBL is spotted at a hunting camp south of Kandahar, but a cruise missile attack is not launched because of concern about possibly hitting important visitors from the United Arab Emirates.

*February 12*: The Senate vote on impeachment falls far short of the two-thirds majority required to remove a president.

*March–April*: UBL approves the "planes operation," which will become the 9/11 attack; he, Mohammed Atef, and KSM hold planning sessions in Kandahar.

*May*: UBL is sighted near Kandahar; CIA operatives urge a cruise missile attack, but Tenet decides that the intelligence is not clear enough.

*June*: The Serbian government agrees to end ethnic violence in Kosovo, and NATO suspends a two-month bombing campaign.

*December*: Jordan breaks up an al Qaeda plot to kill Americans and other tourists over the millennium weekend.

**2000**  *January*: An al Qaeda plot to strike the USS *The Sullivans* with an explosives-laden boat is aborted because the boat is overloaded and sinks. U.S. and Malayan security services learn of a gathering of terrorist plotters in Kuala Lumpur.

*October*: An explosives-laden boat plows into the USS *Cole* in Aden harbor; seventeen seamen are killed.

*November*: Democratic presidential candidate Al Gore wins a majority of the popular vote but lacks a clear majority in the electoral college.

*December*: The Supreme Court rules that Florida's electoral votes should go to Republican candidate George W. Bush; Gore concedes the election.

**2001**  *January 20*: George W. Bush becomes U.S. president.

*January 25*: Clarke briefs National Security Advisor Condoleezza Rice on terrorism; she asks him to remain on the NSC staff.

*April*: The NSC Deputies Committee begins to discuss a possible National Security Presidential Directive (NSPD) on terrorism.

*May–June*: Intelligence reports of possible al Qaeda attacks flood in; most suggest the targets will be in the Middle East.

*August 6*: A President's Daily Brief (PDB) item titled "Bin Ladin Determined to Strike in US" reviews historical evidence of possible plans for another incident like the 1993 WTC bombing.

*August 16*: Zacarias Moussaoui is arrested for visa violations after seeking pilot training in Minnesota.

*September 4*: NSC principals hold their first discussion of terrorism.

*September 10*: The NSC Deputies Committee meets to discuss a draft NSPD on terrorism.

*September 11*: The "planes operation" is carried out: two hijacked aircraft hit and destroy both towers of the WTC; a third hits the Pentagon; a fourth, probably headed for the Capitol, crashes in Pennsylvania after passengers attack the hijackers.

*September 20*: Bush addresses a joint session of Congress, effectively declaring what will be called a "global war on terror."

*October–December*: U.S. and allied forces attack Afghanistan, unseat the Taliban government, destroy al Qaeda's training camps, kill some al Qaeda leaders, and capture others.

**2002**  *February*: Congressional leaders announce that the House and Senate intelligence oversight committees will hold a joint inquiry into whether 9/11 constituted an "intelligence failure."

*June*: Representatives of the families of 9/11 victims rally in the national capital, calling for an independent investigation of 9/11.

*June 14*: The administration makes public a new National Security Strategy, which asserts that terrorism may require preemptive rather than retaliatory military action.

*November*: Bush signs a bill creating the 9/11 Commission.

**2003**  *March*: A coalition led by the United States and the United Kingdom, but without UN sanction, launches a war against Iraq.

*May*: Bush announces that major combat operations in Iraq have been completed, but guerrilla warfare continues.

*July*: The congressional joint inquiry report is finally published, with many CIA excisions.

*October*: The 9/11 Commission, in the midst of negotiations for access to PDB files, subpoenas FAA documents; Chair Thomas Kean warns of other possible subpoenas.

*November 7*: The Commission subpoenas NORAD records.

*November 20*: The administration and the Commission reach an agreement on Commission access to PDBs.

*November 24*: Max Cleland resigns from the Commission and is replaced by Bob Kerrey.

**2004** *January*: A Commission hearing makes public tapes of in-flight reports on the 9/11 hijackings.

*March 3*: House Speaker Dennis Hastert agrees reluctantly to extend the Commission's reporting date by sixty days.

*March 23–24*: Former and current cabinet members testify before the Commission.

*April 8*: After initially refusing, Rice gives public testimony before the Commission.

*April 24*: The commissioners interview the president and vice president.

*May*: The Commission takes testimony in New York City about first responses to the 9/11 attacks.

*June*: Final Commission hearings concern the performance of the FAA and NORAD on 9/11.

*July*: The Commission publishes its report.

*November*: Bush is reelected with both popular and electoral college majorities.

*December*: Bush signs the Intelligence Reform and Terrorism Prevention Act, putting into effect a number of recommendations from the 9/11 Commission.

**2005** Former members of the 9/11 Commission issue a report card on government action on Commission recommendations.

# Questions for Consideration

1. Why did Usama Bin Ladin and his associates plan and carry out the attacks of 9/11?
2. Why were the 9/11 hijackers willing to undertake suicide missions?
3. How might the U.S. government have prevented the 9/11 attacks?
4. How might actions by state and local governments or by companies or private individuals have prevented or forestalled the attacks?
5. Did the terrorist threat have high priority in the United States prior to 9/11? Why or why not?
6. Is 9/11 an example of an "intelligence failure"? Why or why not?
7. Why did the CIA and FBI have so much difficulty communicating with one another prior to 9/11? Do they still have difficulty?
8. Why was partisanship so strong in the era of 9/11 and the Commission report?
9. What sections of the report might have been written differently had the Commission consisted primarily of Republicans or primarily of Democrats or been made up of nonpartisan outsiders?
10. The Commission took many hours of closed-door testimony, during which there were no security restrictions on questions or answers. Why did it also hold nineteen days of public hearings?
11. Should the 9/11 Commission serve as a model for future government inquiries? Why or why not?
12. How might 9/11 be considered a turning point in American history?
13. What do you see as the lessons of 9/11?

# Selected Bibliography

THE COMMISSION

To read (and search) the entire text of *The 9/11 Commission Report*, go to http://www.9-11commission.gov/. This Web site also contains full texts of the seventeen staff statements issued preliminary to the public hearings and transcripts of the nineteen days of public hearings. In addition, the site has the full texts of two monographs sponsored by the Commission: one on terrorist financing, the other on terrorist travel.

An excellent overview of the Commission's work based chiefly on interviews with commissioners and staff members is "Piloting a Bipartisan Ship: Strategies and Tactics of the 9/11 Commission" (Case No. C15-05-1813.0, Kennedy School of Government Case Program, Harvard University, Cambridge, 2005). The chief author is Kirsten Lundberg, a former journalist, who is the Kennedy School's premier case writer; I was the case's overseer.

Thomas H. Kean and Lee H. Hamilton, with Benjamin Rhodes, *Without Precedent: The Inside Story of the 9/11 Commission* (New York: Alfred A. Knopf, 2006), is discreet and does not contain much new information but illustrates well how the chair and vice chair were able to speak with one voice.

Writings by or about members of the Commission include Thomas H. Kean, *The Politics of Inclusion* (New York: Free Press, 1988), which is partly an autobiography; Alvin S. Felzenberg, *Governor Tom Kean: From the New Jersey Statehouse to the 9-11 Commission* (New Brunswick, N.J.: Rutgers University Press, 2006); Richard Ben-Veniste, *Stonewall: The Real Story of the Watergate Prosecution* (New York: Simon and Schuster, 1977); Bob Kerrey, *When I Was Young: A Memoir* (New York: Harcourt, 2002); and John F. Lehman Jr., *The Executive, Congress, and Foreign Policy: Studies of the Nixon Administration* (New York: Praeger, 1976), *Making War: The 200-Year-Old Battle between the President and the Congress over How America Goes to War* (New York: Scribner's, 1992), *On Seas of Glory: Heroic Men, Great Ships, and Epic Battles of the American Navy* (New York: Free Press, 2001), and *Command of the Seas* (Annapolis, Md.: Naval Institute Press, 2001).

THE POLITICAL SETTING

On Bill Clinton's pre-presidential background, nothing has supplanted David Maraniss, *First in His Class: The Biography of Bill Clinton* (New York: Simon and Schuster, 1995). Bill Clinton, *My Life* (New York: Alfred A. Knopf, 2004), is long but not revealing. John F. Harris, *The Survivor: Bill Clinton in the White House* (New York: Random House, 2005), is a much better complement to Maraniss.

Mel Steely, *The Gentleman from Georgia: The Biography of Newt Gingrich* (Macon, Ga.: Mercer University Press, 2000), is by a onetime aide to Gingrich but manages to maintain some objectivity. Though hostile to the entire Bush clan, Kevin Phillips, *American Dynasty: Aristocracy, Fortune, and the Politics of Deceit in the House of Bush* (New York: Viking, 2004), is the most informative work so far on George W. Bush's ascent to the presidency. Phillips's subsequent *American Theocracy: The Perils and Politics of Radical Religion, Oil, and Borrowed Money in the 21st Century* (New York: Viking, 2006) is an even more unbalanced diatribe, but it is based on a wide study of public opinion polls and comparable sources and is by the one analyst to have seen far in advance the shift of Democrats into the Republican party. The most thoughtful survey of American politics at the turn of the twenty-first century is Geoffrey Hodgson, *More Equal Than Others: America from Nixon to the New Century* (Princeton, N.J.: Princeton University Press, 2004).

BIN LADIN AND AL QAEDA

Jonathan C. Randal, *Osama, the Making of a Terrorist* (New York: Random House, 2005), is a stab at a biography. Peter L. Bergen, *The Osama bin Laden I Know* (New York: Free Press, 2006), is an annotated collection of Bin Ladin's pronouncements and interviews, as well as many excerpts from firsthand descriptions of him. Lawrence Wright, *The Looming Tower: Al Qaeda and the Road to 9/11* (New York: Alfred A. Knopf, 2006) is by a *New Yorker* writer who conducted hundreds of interviews throughout the Middle East to learn personal details about Bin Ladin and his associates. It adds a good deal to the portrait of al Qaeda that appears in the Commission report. It also has some lively detail on Americans, particularly from the FBI, who investigated al Qaeda.

The most penetrating analysis of radical Islamist ideology antedates 9/11. It is Gilles Kepel, *Jihad: The Trail of Political Islam* (Cambridge: Harvard University Press, 2002), which appeared originally in French in 2000. Two interesting books are Michael Scheuer, *Through Our Enemies' Eyes: Osama bin Laden, Radical Islam, and the Future of America*, 2nd ed. (Washington, D.C.: Potomac Books, 2006), and Daniel Benjamin and Steven Simon, *The Age of Sacred Terror* (New York: Random House, 2002). Scheuer's book originally appeared in 2002 with the author listed as Anonymous. At the time, he was still in the CIA, where he had been head of the unit following Bin Ladin's movements. (He is the "Mike" of chapter 4 of the report.) He went public later. Benjamin and Simon were both on the staff of Richard Clarke, the National Security Council counterterrorism coordinator.

Works that do not replace but that in some respects update Kepel's *Jihad* include Abdel bari Atwan, *The Secret History of al Qa'ida* (London: Saqi Books, 2006); Shmuel Bar, *Warrant for Terror: Fatwas of Radical Islam and the Duty of Jihad* (Lanham, Md.: Rowman and Littlefield, 2006); Rohan Gunaratna, *Inside al Qaeda: Global Network of Terror* (New York: Columbia University Press, 2002); and Mary R. Habeck, *Knowing the Enemy: Jihadist Ideology and the War on Terror* (New Haven, Conn.: Yale University Press, 2006).

### U.S. COUNTERTERRORISM

An admirable survey is Timothy Naftali, *Blind Spot: The Secret History of American Counterterrorism* (New York: Basic Books, 2005). *Blind Spot* originated as a supporting study for the 9/11 Commission. Naftali had been my doctoral student at Harvard and at the time worked for Philip Zelikow at the University of Virginia's Miller Center, managing the transcription and publication of secret presidential tapes from the 1960s and 1970s. He has since become director of the Richard Nixon Presidential Library.

The books by Scheuer and by Benjamin and Simon cited earlier also bear on U.S. counterterrorism. Richard A. Clarke, *Against All Enemies: Inside America's War on Terror* (New York: Free Press, 2004), is a memoir by the counterterrorism coordinator. Steve Coll, *Ghost Wars: The Secret History of the CIA, Afghanistan, and Bin Laden, from the Soviet Invasion to September 10, 2001* (New York: Penguin Press, 2004), is a wonderfully detailed and vivid history, mostly of CIA operations in Afghanistan.

### 9/11 AND ITS AFTERMATH

Jim Dwyer, *102 Minutes: The Untold Story of the Fight to Survive inside the Twin Towers* (New York: Times Books, 2005), supplements chapter 9 of the Commission report. Steven Brill, *After: How America Confronted the September 12 Era* (New York: Simon and Schuster, 2003), is a diary chronicling official actions and quoting interviews with ordinary citizens.

# Index

Abdul Aziz University, 60
Abraham, 54
Abu Bara al Yemini, 97
Abu Hoshar, Khadr, 105
Abu Turab al Jordani, 122
Abu-Yasir Rifa'Israel Ahmad Taha, 172
Abu Zubaydah, 105, 175
AC-130 helicopters, 88–89
Aden, Yemen, 52, 77
Advisory Council (Shura), al Qaeda, 61
"Afghan Arabs," 60
"Afghan Eyes," 109–10
Afghanistan, 21, 29
    Bin Ladin's move to, 77–78
    hijacker training in, 122–23
    invasion plans, 88, 89–91
    *jihad* against Soviet Union, 58–61
    locating Bin Ladin in, 156
    long-term commitment to, 183
    map, 59*f*
    Muslim response to Soviet invasion of,
        58–61
    Pashtun community, 78
    pre-9/11 policy options, 156
    al Qaeda in, 62–64
    refugees, 63
    Sheikh Mohammed in, 94–95
    Soviet invasion of, 24
    Soviet withdrawal from, 52–53
    terrorist training camps, 63–64, 80, 82,
        85, 90, 105, 134, 143–44
    Tora Bora cave complex, 148
    U.S. plans to attack, 148
    U.S. plans to destroy al Qaeda in, 143–45
    U.S. strikes against terrorist training
        camps, 81–82
    USS *Cole* attack and, 111–13
*Against All Enemies* (Clarke), 13
Ahmed, Mahmud, 143
Air Force One, 49–50, 138–39
Airman Flight School, Norman, Oklahoma,
    120, 125

airplanes. *See also* hijacked airplanes
    airline industry, 140
    American Airlines Flight 11, 37–38,
        39–42
    American Airlines Flight 77, 38–39
    hijacking of, 39–47
    resume flying, following attacks, 140
    security concerns, 154
    systemic defenses in, 154
    United Airlines Flight 93, 39
    United Airlines Flight 175, 37–38
    as weapons, 152–54
airport security
    Logan International Airport, 38
    recommendations for, 178–79
airspace protection
    agencies responsible for, 47–48
    recommendations for, 181
air traffic control (ATC)
    airspace protection responsibilities,
        47–48
    Boston Air Traffic Control Center, 40, 41
Albright, Madeleine, 27, 87
Ali, Ali Abdul Aziz, 103
aliens, of "special interest," 141
Allbaugh, Joseph, 139
Allen, Charles, 27, 110
American Airlines
    Flight Services Office, 41
    flights ordered grounded, 43
    ground facilities, 13
    realization of multiple hijackings,
        44–45
    Southeastern Reservations Office,
        40–41
American Airlines Flight 11
    boarding, 37–38
    crash into North Tower, World Trade
        center, 42
    descent of, 41–42
    hijackers of, 128
    hijacking of, 39–42

American Airlines Flight 77
    boarding, 38–39
    crash into Pentagon, 44
    hijackers of, 127
    hijacking of, 43–44
Americans. *See* United States
anti-Semitism, among terrorists, 99, 100
Arab states
    economies, 57–58
    social malaise in, 57–58
    U.S. oil concerns and, 22–23
Arafat, Yasir, 24
Arizona Aviation, 121
Arlington County Fire Department, 138
Armitage, Richard, 27, 143
Arnett, Peter, 170
Arpey, Gerard, 43
Ashcroft, John, 27, 44, 142
    briefed on al Qaeda threat, 129
    Gorelick and, 14–15
    public hearing testimony, 14
    special interest immigration hearings,
        141
    terrorist identification priorities, 142
Atef, Mohammed, 27, 93, 94, 95, 111, 187
    death of, 97, 148
    "planes operation" and, 97, 102–3
    al Qaeda strategy and, 126–27
Atta, Mohammed, 27, 37–38, 40, 42, 97
    arrival in U.S., 120
    Binalshibh and, 100
    flight training, 120, 122
    hijacker teams and, 127–28
    passports and visas, 103
    "planes operation" and, 102–3, 123–25
    profile, 98–99
    role of, 103
aviation training. *See* flight training
Aziz Ali, Ali Abdul, 27
Azzam, Abdulla Yusuf, 23, 27, 37, 60, 61,
    97

Balkans, 84
Bangladesh, Jihad Movement, 172
Banihammad, Fayez, 27, 37–38
Bara al Yemeni, Abu, 27
Barksdale Air Force Base, 139
Bay of Pigs, 71
Beirut, suicide bombings, 52
Ben-Veniste, Richard, 7, 11, 14, 17, 27
Berger, Samuel ("Sandy"), 27, 75, 79, 80,
    81, 82, 84, 88, 92, 106, 109, 110
    presidential transition period, 114
    USS *Cole* attack and, 111, 112
Binalshibh, Ramzi, 27, 99
    Atta and, 100
    coordination role, 120, 123–26
    flight training, 103
    Moussaoui and, 134
    "planes operation" and, 102–3
    profile, 99–100

Bin Attash, Tawfiq. *See* Khallad (Tawfiq bin
    Attash)
Bin Ladin, Usama, 27, 33, 93, 185–89
    in Afghanistan, 60–61, 77–78, 156
    aircraft hijacking plans, 174–75
    appeal to Muslims, 54–58
    biography, 60
    Bush and, 13–14
    CIA plans to capture and/or kill, 78–80,
        86–92
    Clarke's campaign against, 84–85, 86,
        90
    Clinton and, 24–25, 75, 83, 85, 87–89,
        109, 112, 113
    covert action against, 85–88
    declarations by, 169–72
    early intelligence on, 77–78
    East Africa embassy bombings and,
        80–81, 95, 176
    as *emir* of al Qaeda, 61
    family wealth, 60
    fatwas issued by, 52, 169–70, 172
    FBI knowledge of, 67
    fealty (*bayat*) to, 64
    financial holdings frozen, 85
    financial support of, 63
    fundamentalism and, 55–56, 58
    hatred of America by, 56
    hijackers and, 121, 122, 123
    Hussein and, 22, 145
    justification for *jihad* (holy war), 65
    leadership of, 58, 61, 64
    media coverage of, 151
    motives of, 22–25
    opposition to U.S. military bases in Saudi
        Arabia, 61
    PDB's concerning, 130
    "planes operation" and, 96–97, 102–3,
        123–26
    plans to attack in U.S., 14, 130, 175–76
    Predator surveillance of, 110, 157
    presidential transition and, 113–15
    al Qaeda and, 61, 111, 126–27
    rise of, 58–61
    Sheikh Mohammed and, 94–95
    al Shifa, pharmaceutical plant, 81–82
    tannery building, Sudan, 81
    terrorism goals, 81
    threat posed by, 150–52, 155–57
    U.S. campaign against, 81–92
    U.S. Congress and, 76
    U.S. policy and, 154–57
    use of lethal force in capturing, 86–87
    USS *Cole* attack, 110–11
    world view of, 55–57
    writings
        *Declaration of War against the
        Americans Occupying the Two Holy
        Places*, 169–70
"Bin Ladin Determined to Strike in U.S."
    (PDB), 14, 130, 175–76, 188

"Bin Ladin Preparing to Hijack US Aircraft and Other Attacks" (PDB), 174–75
Bin Ladin Unit, CIA, 77, 83, 86, 116
biological terrorism, 81
biometric entry-exit screening system, 179
bipartisanship, 21
birth certificates, 180
Black, J. Cofer, 27, 116
Black Hawk helicopters, 62, 74
"Blind Sheikh," 66. See also Rahman, Sheikh Omar Abdel
"Bojinka" plot, 94, 95, 186. See also Manila air plot
Bolten, Joshua, 139, 142
bomb threats
  by hijackers of United Airlines Flight 93, 46
  by hijackers of United Airlines Flight 175, 42
Booker, Emma E., Elementary School, 48
Border Patrol agents, 69
border security, 179
Bosnia, 84
Boston Air Traffic Control (ATC) Center, 40, 41, 45
box cutters, 43, 44, 124
Brown, Aaron, 12
Brzezinski, Zbigniew, 75
Bureau of Alcohol, Tobacco, and Firearms, 69
"Bureau of Services" (Mektabl al Khidmat), 60. See also Mektab al Khidmat (MAK)
Bush, George H. W., 2, 5, 28, 72, 185, 188
Bush, George W., 28, 128, 189
  administration capabilities, 157–59
  background, 5
  communications problems, 50
  counterterrorism approach, 115–18
  Democratic opposition to, 5
  election of, 5
  intelligence briefings, 115, 129–30, 155
  Iraq concerns, 145–46, 147
  9/11 Commission and, 1, 6–10, 12
  9/11 response, 142–45, 188
  post-9/11 planning, 144–45
  response to news of 9/11 attack, 48–51
  safe location, following attacks, 138–39
  September 11 activities, 37
  September 11 response, 138–48
  strike options available to, 157–59
  transition, 113–15
  "war council," 142, 144
Bush administration
  cooperation from, 8, 9, 10
  disputes with 9/11 Commission, 10–13
  public hearing testimony, 13–14
  terrorism priorities, 13–14, 22

caliph (Muslim leader), 54–55
Caliph of Baghdad, 24

Canadian border controls, 109
CAP. See combat air patrol (CAP)
capabilities failures, 157–59
Capitol, as 9/11 target, 123
car bombs, 62
Card, Andrew, Jr., 9, 12, 28, 48, 49, 115, 142
cargo carriers plan, 95
Castro, Fidel, 71
CBS News, 11
CENTCOM. See U.S. Central Command (CENTCOM)
Central Intelligence Agency (CIA), 25, 32. See also Counterterrorism Center (CTC)
  "Afghan Eyes," 110
  Afghanistan strike, 148
  agency capabilities, 158
  Bin Ladin capture plans, 78–80, 85–89, 91–92
  Bin Ladin Unit, 77, 78, 83, 86, 116
  Clandestine Service, 71, 73
  Clarke's criticism of, 118
  collateral damage concerns, 79, 86, 90, 91
  cooperation from, 8, 10
  covert operations, 70–71, 85–88
  culture of, 72
  Directorate of Intelligence, 72
  Directorate of Operations, 71, 77, 78–79
  early efforts, 72–73
  employees killed by terrorists, 185
  functions of, 70–71, 75
  funding of, 109
  institutional management, 161
  management issues, 161
  millennium plots and, 109
  offices, 18
  PDBs and, 11
  policy challenges, 156
  post-9/11 intelligence and covert operations, 144
  reforms of, 180–81
  report of nerve gas at al Shifa pharmaceutical plant, 81
  2001 intelligence briefings, 129–30
  "virtual station," 77
chemical terrorism, 81
Cheney, Lynne, 50
Cheney, Richard B., 28, 113, 115
  Democratic opposition to, 5
  evacuation to underground bunker, 50
  Homeland Security Council and, 140
  meeting with Commissioners, 12
  response to 9/11 attacks, 48–51, 138–39, 140, 142
  shootdown orders authorized by, 51
Chertoff, Michael, 182
Chinese embassy, Belgrade, 92
chronology, 185–89
Church, Frank, 71
CIA. See Central Intelligence Agency (CIA)

citations, 18–19
Civil Aviation Security, 152
civilian casualities. *See* collateral damage
civil liberties, 181
Civil Liberties Protection Officer, 181
Clandestine Service, CIA, 71, 73
Clarke, Richard A., 21, 28, 75, 77, 79, 81, 83,
    88, 92, 107, 109, 186–88
  aircraft concerns of, 154
  apology to 9/11 victims' families, 13
  Bin Ladin and, 84–85, 86, 89, 90
  Bush administration and, 113–17
  criticism of CIA by, 118
  criticism of counterterrorism methods
    by, 117–18
  "Plan Delenda," 20, 84, 115, 187
  policy and, 155
  Predator and, 110
  presidential transition period, 113–15
  public hearing testimony, 13, 20
  al Qaeda concerns, 151–52
  terrorism alerts, 129
  terrorism priorities, 115–18
  2001 intelligence briefings, 129–31
  USS *Cole* attack and, 111, 113
classified information, 9, 18, 173
Cleland, Max, 7, 8, 28, 189
Clinton, Bill, 20, 28, 91, 185–87
  administration capabilities, 157–59
  background, 2–3
  Bin Ladin and, 24–25, 83, 85, 87–89,
    104–5, 109, 112, 113
  Bush transition and, 113
  conservative opposition to, 3–5
  counterterrorism coordination by, 75
  domestic politics and, 155
  East African embassy bombings and, 21,
    80, 187
  FBI and, 68
  impeachment proceedings against, 4
  Iraq air strikes, 84
  meeting with Commissioners, 12
  Pakistan bombing, 88
  political authority of, 21–22
  presidency, 3
  public hearing testimony, 13
  reelection of, 4
  strike options available to, 157–59
  terrorism priorities, 75, 105, 114
  USS *Cole* attack and, 112, 113
  World Trade Center bombing and, 66
Clinton, Hillary Rodham, 3
CNN, 12, 48, 170
coalition strategy, 164
Coast Guard, 129
Cohen, David, 77, 87, 89, 158
Cohen, William, 28, 84
collateral damage, Bin Ladin capture plan
    and, 79, 86, 91
combat air patrol (CAP), 32, 50–51
"commerce" (terrorist attacks), 175

communications
  Bush administration, 50
  Clinton administration, 162
  information sharing issues, 159–61, 181
  millennium plots and, 162–63
  responsibility for, 160
  security policy and, 158
compassionate conservatism, 5
"Compound Six," 123
Congress, U.S.
  Bin Ladin and, 76
  Homeland Security Committees, 182
  oversight responsibilities, 76, 182
  public opinion and, 76
  recommended reforms, 182
  terrorism and, 76
conservatives, 3–5
Contract with America, 3, 4
counterintelligence. *See also* intelligence
  Defense Department role, 74
  executive office role, 74–75
  Justice Department role, 67–70
  military role, 74
  State Department role, 73
  2001 threat reports, 128–31
counterterrorism, 65–76. *See also* terrorism
  Bush and, 115–18, 147–48
  Clarke's criticism of, 117–18
  Clinton and, 75
  coalition proposed, 142
  early CIA efforts, 72–73
  failure to share information about, 158
  foreign *vs.* domestic, 131
  government reorganization for, 165
  Justice Department activities, 67–70
  law enforcement agencies and, 67–70
  legal system and, 66, 67
  millennium plots and, 162–63
  priorities for, 146
  recommended strategies, 163–64
  strike options, 157–59
  unity of effort, 165
  World Trade Center bombing and, 65–66
Counterterrorism Center (CTC), 32, 72–73,
    163
  Bin Ladin capture plan and, 79
  Kuala Lumpur terrorist meeting and, 108
  management issues, 161
  Northern Alliance and, 90–91, 92
  telltale indicators for surprise attacks,
    153–54
Counterterrorism Security Group (CSG),
    32, 75, 77, 84, 107, 116, 131, 158, 163
  presidential transition period, 114
  2001 terrorism alert levels, 129
criminal investigations, intelligence
    activities and, 69
cruise missiles
  Bin Ladin capture plans and, 88, 90, 91
  fired at al Shifa pharmaceutical plant, 82
  Tomahawk, 80

CSG. *See* Counterterrorism Security Group (CSG)
CTC. *See* Counterterrorism Center (CTC)
cultural programs, 184
Customs Service, 69, 129, 132

DCI. *See* Director of Central Intelligence (DCI)
*Declaration of War against the Americans Occupying the Two Holy Places* (Bin Ladin), 169–70
Deek, Khalil, 28, 105–6, 107
"Defeating the Terrorist Threat to the United States," 144–45
Defense Department
  agency capabilities, 158
  counterintelligence activities, 74
  institutional management, 161
  intelligence activities, 70
*delenda*, 84
"Delenda Plan," 20, 84, 115, 187
Delta Force, 74
Democratic Commissioners, 1, 6–8, 35
Democratic Party, 2
Dempsey, Joan, 161
Deputies Committee, 114, 115, 188
"Desert One," 74
detainees
  lack of Commission access to, 10
  treatment of, 141
DHS. *See* Homeland Security Department
"Direction and Control of Emergencies in the City of New York," 136
Director of Central Intelligence (DCI), 70, 72, 91, 115. *See also* Tenet, George
  institutional management, 161–62
Director of National Intelligence (DNI), 180
domestic intelligence gathering
  by FBI, 67–68
  post-9/11, 141–42
Donovan, William J. "Wild Bill," 71
Drug Enforcement Administration, 69
Dulles International Airport, 38–39, 43

East Africa, U.S. embassy bombings in, 21, 64–65, 80, 130, 155–56, 176, 186, 187
economic policies, 183–84
*Economist, The*, 82, 85
economy, oil production and, 57–58
education support, 184
Egyptian Islamic Jihad (EIJ), 172, 175
emergency preparedness, 164
  9/11 Commission recommendations, 177–78
emergency response, 135–38
  9/11 Commission recommendations, 177–78
  Pentagon, 137–38
  World Trade Center, 135–37
*emir*, of al Qaeda, 61
EMPTA, 81

*Encyclopedia of Jihad* (Deek), 105–6
"Enduring Freedom" operation, 148
executive office, counterterrorism role, 74–75
executive privilege, 10, 11, 12

FAA. *See* Federal Aviation Administration (FAA)
Family Steering Committee, 8
Farouq mosque, Brooklyn, 66
fatwas, 22, 186
  to drive Americans out of Saudi Arabia, 52, 171–72
  to evict U.S. troops from Somalia, 61–62
  issued by Bin Ladin, 52, 169–70
  issued by World Islamic Front, 52, 171–72
  for murder of Americans, 52, 169–70
FBI. *See* Federal Bureau of Investigation (FBI)
FDNY. *See* New York City Fire Department (FDNY)
fealty (*bayat*), 64
Federal Air Marshals, 159
Federal Aviation Administration (FAA), 32, 121, 129
  access to records, 11
  agency capabilities, 159
  airspace protection responsibilities, 47–48
  Civil Aviation Security, 152
  Dulles Airport investigations, 39
  hijackings and, 44–45, 48
  Moussaoui and, 132–33
  shootdown orders and, 51
  unpreparedness of, 51–52
Federal Bureau of Investigation (FBI), 25, 32, 129
  agency capabilities, 158–59
  Bin Ladin capture plan and, 79
  Bin Ladin-related investigations, 176
  communications issues, 161–62
  counterterrorism activities, 67–69
  criminal investigations, 69
  domestic intelligence gathering, 67–68, 162
  extremists in U.S. and, 106–7
  field offices, 67, 69, 131, 133
  intelligence activities, 67–69
  legal constraints on, 68–69
  millennium plots and, 107, 109, 162–63
  Minneapolis Field Office, 131, 133
  Moussaoui and, 132–34
  national security workforce, 180
  New York Field Office, 67, 69
  "office of origin" system, 67
  presidential transition period, 114
  public hearing testimony, 14
  recommendations for, 165
  terrorism responsibilities, 75

Federal Bureau of Investigation (FBI)
    (*cont.*)
    threat advisory, 130
    "the wall," 69, 142
    World Trade Center bombing
        investigation, 65, 185
    federal emergency assistance, 140
Federal Emergency Management Agency,
    139
Felzenberg, Al, 18
Fielding, Fred F., 7, 28
financial markets, 140
first responders. *See also* emergency
        response
    radio spectrum for, 177
FISA. *See* Foreign Intelligence Surveillance
        Act (FISA)
flight attendants, 13
flight simulator computer games, 98
flight simulator training, 125
flight training, 103, 119–22, 125
    understanding significance of, 154
Florida Flight Training Center (FFTC),
    120
Foreign Intelligence Surveillance Act
        (FISA), 32, 69, 107
    search warrant requirements, 132–33
foreign policy recommendations, 183–84
"four moms from New Jersey," 8
Franks, Tommy, 28, 112, 144, 148
Freeh, Louis, 21, 28, 68, 114
fundamentalism
    Bin Ladin and, 55–56, 58
    defined, 55
    history of, 57
    in Pakistan, 62–63
    Sunnis, 57

Gabriel, 54
Gama'at al-Islamiyya, 173
Genoa, G-8 summit, 128, 129
Ghamdi, Ahmed al, 28, 37–38
Ghamdi, Hamza al, 28
Ghamdi, Saeed al, 28, 39
Gingrich, Newt, 3, 4, 28, 186
Giuliani, Rudolph, 28, 136
Golden Chain, 60, 63
Gonzales, Alberto, 9, 10, 11, 12
Gonzalez, Nydia, 13, 41
Gordon, John, 86, 92
Gore, Al, Jr., 5, 12, 28, 82, 113, 187
Gorelick, Jamie S., 7, 8, 28, 173
    access to PDBs, 11
    Ashcroft's attack on, 14–15
    report review by, 17
Gorton, Slade, 7, 8, 14, 17, 28
Government Printing Office, 18
GPS equipment, 125
G-8 summit, Genoa, 128, 129
guerrilla warriors (mujahideen). *See*
    mujahideen (holy warriors)

Hadith, 54, 55
Hadley, Stephen, 28, 114, 115, 116, 129–30,
    131, 142
Haji Habash house, 86
Hamburg group
    flight training, 120–22
    members of, 98–108
Hamilton, Lee, 7, 8, 9, 28, 173
    access to PDBs, 11
    effectiveness of, 12
    public hearings and, 13–14
    report design and, 16
    report outline and, 16
    report publication and, 18, 19
    working relationship with Kean, 8–9
Hamzah, Shaykh Mir, 172
Hanjour, Hani, 28, 38–39, 124, 145
    flight training, 121
Hanson, Lee, 42–43
Hanson, Peter, 42–43
Hastert, Dennis, 28, 189
    9/11 Commission reporting deadline and,
        12
    report publication and, 19
Hazmi, Nawaf al, 29, 38–39, 97, 98, 108,
    123, 124, 159–60
    arrival in U.S., 118–20
Hazmi, Salem al, 29, 38–39, 108, 159–60
Haznawi, Ahmad al, 29
hijacked airplanes. *See also* airplanes
    American Airlines Flight 11, 39–42
    American Airlines Flight 77, 43–44
    cockpit doors, 124
    FAA and NORAD protocols for, 48
    flight attendants, 13
    in-flight reports, 13
    pilots, 120–22
    al Qaeda's plan to use as weapons, 96–98
    selection of, 124
    shootdown orders for, 51
    United Airlines Flight 93, 44–47
    United Airlines Flight 175, 42–43
    weapons used on, 42, 43, 44, 46
hijackers
    contingency plans, 124
    final preparation, 124–25
    flight simulator training, 125
    knowledge of hijacking plan, 123
    movement to departure cities, 127–28
    muscle hijackers, 122–23, 124–25
    pilots, 120–22
    planning for, 124–25
    training, 122–23, 174
hijacking, of airplanes
    Bin Ladin's plans for, 174–75
    al Qaeda and, 95–96
    suicide missions, 152–54
Hijazi, Raed, 29, 106, 107
homeland security. *See also* national
        security
    funding allocations, 178

9/11 Commission recommendations, 177–80
Homeland Security Committees, 182
Homeland Security Council, 140
Homeland Security Department, 32, 178, 182
Honoré, Russel, 20
Hoover, J. Edgar, 68
Hussein, Saddam, 14, 29, 84, 185
    Atta and, 99
    Bin Ladin and, 22, 145
    9/11 attacks and, 145–46

imagination failures, 149–54
Immigration and Naturalization Service (INS), 32, 69, 109, 129
    Moussaoui and, 132
    post-9/11 arrests, 141
immigration laws, 109
immigration violations, 141
Incident Command System, National Capital Region, 138
incident command systems
    Pentagon, 138
    recommendations for, 178
    World Trade Center, 136–37
indicators, for surprise attack, 152–53
"Infinite Resolve" strike options, 112, 144, 148
infrastructure assessment, 178
INS. *See* Immigration and Naturalization Service (INS)
institutional management
    assessment of, 161–62
    9/11 Commission recommendations, 180–82
intelligence. *See also* counterintelligence
    accuracy of, 92
    examples, 173–76
intelligence budget, 182
intelligence community
    adequacy of, 73
    criminal investigations and, 69
    FBI activities, 67–69
    federal agencies involved in, 70–73
    information management problems, 36
    recommendations for, 180–82
    understanding of Bin Laden, 151
international broadcasting, 184
International Terrorism Operation Section (ITOS), 133
International Youth Opportunity Fund, 184
Inter-Services Intelligence Directorate (Pakistan) (ISID), 32
Iran
    Islam in, 24
    Shi theocracy, 57
    support of Saudi Hezbollah by, 62
Iraq, 187
    air strikes against, 84
    economic sanctions against, 22

9/11 attacks and, 145–46
    post-9/11 attack considered, 145–47
    U.S. air strikes against, 85
Iraq War, 188–89
    opposition to, 5, 13
    al Qaeda and, 14
ISID. *See* Inter-Services Intelligence Directorate (Pakistan) (ISID)
Islam. *See also* Muslims
    beliefs of, 54–55
    Bin Ladin's use of, 54
    branches of, 54
    as code of conduct, 55
    fundamentalism, 55–56, 57, 58, 62–63
    golden age of, 23
    in Iran, 24
    *jahiliyya vs.*, 56
    meaning of word, 23, 54
    religious beliefs, 23–24
    spread of, 55
Islamic Army Shura, 61
"Islamic Extremist Learns to Fly," 133, 154
Islamic terrorism. *See also* terrorism; terrorists
    preventing growth of, 164
Israel
    al Qaeda and, 61
    terrorists' hatred of, 94
    U.S. support of, 22, 171–72

*jahiliyya*, 56
Jalil, Abdul, 111
Jamiat-ul-Ulema-e-Pakistan, 172
Jarrah, Ziad, 29, 39, 45, 46–47, 127
    flight training, 103, 120, 122
    passports and visas, 103
    "planes operation" and, 102–3
    profile, 101–2
"Jeff," 79
Jerusalem, 22
Jesus Christ, 54
Jihad Movement, Bangladesh, 172
*jihads* (holy wars)
    in Afghanistan, against Soviet Union, 58–61
    Bin Ladin's justification for, 65
    declared against U.S., 170
    *mujahideen* (holy warriors), 24, 170
    al Qaeda and, 61
"John," 134
Johnson, Lyndon B., 73
Joint Chiefs of Staff, 114, 158
joint operations, 161
Joint Terrorism Task Force (JTTF), 32, 69, 109
Jordan, 105, 107, 187
JTTF. *See* Joint Terrorism Task Force (JTTF)
Justice Department
    counterintelligence activities, 67–70
    counterterrorism activities, 67–70

Justice Department (*cont.*)
9/11 detainees and, 141
terrorism responsibilities, 75
World Trade Center bombing
investigation, 65–66

Kahtani, Mohamed al, 45
Kandahar, 86, 91–92
Kansi, Mir Amal, 75, 78
Kaplan, Stephanie, 17
Kean, Thomas, 6, 7, 173, 189
effectiveness of, 12
leadership by, 8, 9
PDB access and, 11
public hearings and, 13–14
report design and, 15–16
report outline and, 16
report publication and, 18, 19
working relationship with Hamilton, 8–9
Kean, Thomas H., 29
Kennedy, John F., 71, 73
Kenya, U.S. embassy bombings, 64–65, 80,
95, 176, 186, 187
Kerrey, Bob, 7–8, 17, 29, 189
Khaldan terrorist camp, 105
Khalilzad, Zalmay, 145
Khallad (Tawfiq bin Attash), 29, 97, 98, 109
Khattab, Ibn al, 132
Khobar Towers bombing, 62, 83, 186
King, Martin Luther, Jr., 68
Kissinger, Henry, 6, 73
knives
hijacker training in use of, 122
purchase of, 125
used by American Airlines Flight 77
hijackers, 43, 44
used by United Airlines Flight 93
hijackers, 46
used by United Airlines Flight 175
hijackers, 42
Kojm, Christopher, 8, 9, 16, 17, 29
Kosovo, 84, 187
KSM. *See* Sheikh Mohammed, Khalid (KSM)
Kuala Lumpur, 108, 159, 187

Lake, Anthony, 29, 75
"landmarks plot," 66, 185
law enforcement agencies, 67–70
legal system, counterterrorism and, 66, 67
Lehman, John F., 7, 14, 17, 29
Lemack, Carie, 8
Lewin, Daniel, 40
Lewinsky, Monica, 4, 5, 21, 82, 187
Libby, Lewis (Scooter), 51
library programs, 184
Libya, air strikes against, 74
Lodhi, Maleeha, 143
Logan International Airport, 37–38, 42, 128
security checkpoints, 38
Los Angeles International Airport, 162, 175
millennium plots, 106

mace, used by United Airlines Flight 175
hijackers, 42
MacEachin, Douglas, 16, 29
MAK. *See* Mektab al Khidmat (MAK)
management
failures, 159–63
institutional, 161–62
millennium plots and, 162–63
operational, 159–61
teamwork problems, 159–60
Manila air plot, 77, 94, 95, 147, 186
Marcus, Daniel, 8, 17, 29
Marquis, Craig, 41
"marriage" (terrorist attacks), 175
Masri, Abu Hafs al, 93
Massoud, Ahmed Shah, 29, 91
assassination of, 127
May, Ernest R., 1–2
report design and, 15
report drafting and, 17
report outline, 16
report review by, 17
McCain, John, 6, 12, 29
McCarthy, Mary, 81
McNamara, Robert, 73
McVeigh, Timothy, 77
Mecca, 22, 23
media
Bin Ladin coverage by, 151
Commission member discussions with,
9–10
millennium plots coverage, 162–63
Medina, 22, 23
Mektab al Khidmat (MAK), 32, 60, 61
Memorandums of Notification (MON), 32,
78, 85, 86, 87, 91
metal detectors, Dulles International
airport, 39
Middle East map, 53*f*
Mihdhar, Khalid al, 29, 38–39, 97–98, 103,
108, 159–60
arrival in U.S., 118–19, 123
"Mike" (Michael Scheuer), 29, 77, 86, 90
Bin Ladin capture plan and, 79
*Milestones* (Qutb), 66
military bases, in Saudi Arabia, 22, 61
military measures, 74
against Taliban, 143–44
failure of, 156
millennium plots, 105–10
CIA and, 109
counterterrorism effectiveness, 162–63
FBI and, 107, 109
media coverage of, 162–63
National Security Agency and, 108, 109
significance of, 175
U.S. disruption efforts, 109
Mineta, Norman, 139
Minihan, Kenneth, 161
Minneapolis Joint Terrorism Task Force,
131, 133

Mohammed, 23, 52, 54, 55, 56
MON. *See* Memorandums of Notification
(MON)
Moqed, Majed, 29, 38–39
moral beliefs, partisan conflict over, 2
Moussaoui, Zacarias, 29, 141, 188
    arrest of, 125, 132, 133, 154
    aviation training, 120
    Binalshibh and, 134
    failure to see as threat, 132–34
    FISA and, 132–33
    flight simulator training, 125
    flight training, 125, 131–32
    investigation of, 131–34, 159
    "planes operation" role, 125–26
    al Qaeda connections, 133–34
Mueller, Robert, 29, 49, 142
mujahideen (holy warriors), 24
    Bin Ladin's preparation of, 61
    financial support for, 60
    suicide operatives, 170
muscle hijackers, 122–23
    final preparation, 124–25
    knowledge of hijacking plan, 123
    selection of, 122
    training, 122–23
Musharraf, Pervez, 29, 143
Muslim Brotherhood, 55–56, 93
Muslims. *See also* Islam
    Bin Ladin's appeal to, 54–58
    hatred of U.S. by, 22–25, 56
    religious beliefs of, 23–24
    U.S. as oppressor of, 66
Myers, General (Richard), 142, 145–46

Nairobi, al Qaeda cell, 61
Nami, Ahmed al, 29, 39
National Command Authority, 47
National Commission on Terrorist Attacks
    upon the United States. *See* 9/11
    Commission
National Counterterrorism Center (NCTC),
    165, 180
national crisis management, 48–52
National Infrastructure Protection Plan,
    178
National Institute of Standards and
    Technology, 135
National Intelligence Director, 165
National Intelligence Estimate, 77, 83, 150,
    186
national security. *See also* homeland
    security
    civil liberties and, 181
    failures of, 36
National Security Act of 1947, 70
National Security Agency (NSA), 32
    functions of, 70–71
    institutional management, 161
    millennium plots and, 108
    operational management issues, 159–60

National Security Council (NSC), 32, 79,
    162, 188
    cooperation from, 10
    creation of, 73
    files, 20
    intelligence briefings, 129
    interagency process, 158
    "phase two" discussion about Iraq,
        146–47
    public hearing testimony, 13
    response to 9/11 attacks, 139, 142–43
National Security Law Unit, 132
National Security Presidential Directive
    (NSPD), 32, 188
    number 9, 144–45
National Security Strategy, 188
National Strategy for Transportation
    Security, 178
NATO, 84, 187
nerve gas, suspected production of, Sudan,
    81–82
Newark Liberty International Airport, 39,
    44
    security checkpoints, 39
New York City, "landmarks plot," 66, 185
New York City Fire Department (FDNY),
    32
    emergency response, 135–37
New York City Police Department (NYPD),
    32, 185
    emergency response, 135–37
New York Field Office, FBI, 67, 69
*New York Times*, 11, 151
9/11 Commission
    access to PDB, 10–11
    Bush administration and, 8, 9, 10–13
    documents reviewed by, 36
    establishment of, 1, 6–10
    expectations for failure of, 1–2, 6, 7
    factors affecting success of, 8
    families of victims and, 8, 9
    *Final Report on 9/11 Recommendations*,
        177–84
    goals of, 36
    independence of, 36
    interviews conducted by, 36
    leadership of, 8
    management of, 8
    members of, 6–10
    public hearings, 13–15, 36
    purpose of, 1, 6
    recommendations, 25
    reporting deadline extension, 12
*9/11 Commission Report*
    classified information review, 18
    condensation, 23, viii
    contents, viii
    criticism avoided in, 21–22
    as history, 15–16
    length of, vii
    motivations for 9/11 attacks, 22–25, 56

*9/11 Commission Report (cont.)*
  narrowness of focus, 19–21
  preface, 35–37
  publication of, 18–19
  purpose of, 35–36
  recommendations, 177–85
  report design, 15
  report outline, 16–17
  shortcomings of, 19–25
  value of, vii–viii
  writing of, 15–19
Nixon, Richard, 2, 73
nongovernmental organizations (NGOs),
  60
nonproliferation, 9/11 Commission
  recommendations, 182
North American Air Defense Command
  (NORAD), 32, 189
  agency capabilities, 158
  airspace protection responsibilities,
    47–48
  protocols for hijackings, 48
  unpreparedness of, 51–52
Northeast Africa map, 53*f*
Northern Alliance, 29
  Counterterrorist Center and, 90–91, 92
  leadership of, 91
  Taliban and, 127
Norton, W. W., 18, 19
NSA. *See* National Security Agency (NSA)
NSC. *See* National Security Council (NSC)
NYPD. *See* New York City Police
  Department (NYPD)

"office of origin" system, 67
Office of Strategic Services (OSS), 71
Offutt Air Force Base, 139
oil production
  economy and, 57–58
  U.S. concerns, 22–23
Olsen, Barbara, 43–44
Olsen, Ted, 43–44
Omar, Mullah Mohammed, 29, 37–38, 63,
  127
Omar, Ramzi, 100. *See also* Binalshibh,
  Ramzi
Omari, Abdul Azziz al, 29, 40
O'Neill, John, 30, 107
Ong, Betty, 13, 40–41
operational management, 159–61
Operation Desert Fox, 84
Operation Infinite Reach, 88
Operation Infinite Resolve, 88
Orlando International Airport, 45

Pakistan
  accidental bombing by U.S., 88
  Afghan refugees in, 63
  Bin Ladin campaign and, 89
  Islamic fundamentalism in, 62–63
  al Qaeda refuge in, 148

  terrorists in, 94
  U.S. relations with, 143, 183
  Wahhabism in, 63
Palestine Liberation Organization (PLO),
  24, 72
Palestinian refugee camps, 23
Palestinians, 23
Pan Am Flight 103, 74, 96
Pan Am International Flight Academy, 121,
  125
PAPD. *See* Port Authority Police
  Department (PAPD)
Pashtuns, 78, 90
passport security, 179
Pataki, George, 49
Pavitt, James, 30, 78–79, 155, 160–61
PDB. *See* President's Daily Brief (PDB)
Pentagon
  crash of American Airlines Flight 77 into,
    37, 44, 49
  incident command, 138
  as 9/11 target, 123, 124
Persian Gulf War, 185
personal information, government sharing
  of, 181
Philippines, Manila air plot, 77, 94, 95, 147,
  186
Pickard, Thomas, 30, 133
Pike, Otis, 71
pilots, hijackers, 120–22
Pirenne, Henri, 23
"Plan, the," 92
"Plan Delenda," 20, 84, 115, 187
"planes operation." *See also* September 11,
  2001 terrorist attacks
  chronology, 187–88
  cockpit doors, 124
  contingency plans, 124
  coordination of, 123–26
  financing, 104
  flight training, 103, 119–22
  hijacker training, 122–23
  muscle hijackers, 122–23
  pilots, 120–22
  planning, 95–98
  preparation for, 118–20, 123–26
  requirements for, 104
  targets, 123–24
  U.S. visas, 103
policy failures, 154–57
"Political-Military Plan Delenda" (Clarke),
  84
political partisanship
  9/11 Commission reporting deadline and,
    12
  in 1990s and early 2000s, 2–6
  report design and, 16
Port Authority Police Department (PAPD),
  32
  emergency response, 135–37
Portland, Maine, airport, 128

Powell, Colin, 30, 114, 115, 139, 142, 143, 146
Predator, 110, 157
Presidential Decision Directive 62, 63, 75
presidential election (2000), 113
President's Daily Brief (PDB), 32, 72, 83–84, 129, 188
  "Bin Ladin Determined to Strike in U.S.," 14, 130, 175–76, 188
  "Bin Ladin Preparing to Hijack US Aircraft and Other Attacks" (PDB), 174–75
  Commission access to, 10–11
  declassification of, 173
  al Qaeda attack warning in, 11
Principals Committee, 75, 114, 115, 117, 143
  millennium plots and, 109
Privacy and Civil Liberties Oversight Board, 181
privacy issues, 181
private sector preparedness, 178
public diplomacy recommendations, 184
Public Discourse Project, 25, 177
public hearings, 13–15
Public Law 107-306, 35
public opinion, on terrorism, 76

Qadhafi, Muammar, 74
al Qaeda, 27, 29
  Advisory Council, 61
  in Afghanistan, 62–64
  airplane hijacking and, 95–96
  assumed behind 9/11 attacks, 139
  Bin Ladin and, 61, 111, 236–37
  Black Hawk helicopters shot down by, 62
  Bush and, 14, 115–18
  car bombs used by, 62
  Clinton and, 21
  defined, 1
  Department of Defense and, 158
  donations to, 60
  *emir* of, 61
  fatwa, 22
  fealty (*bayat*) to Bin Ladin, 64
  founding of, 24, 61
  funding for September 11 attacks, 104
  hatred of Americans by, 56
  infiltration of, 92
  Iraq War and, 14
  leadership of, 61, 96, 126–27
  military aid to Somalia, 61–62
  millennium plots, 105–10
  motives of, 22–25
  Nairobi cell, 61
  9/11 detainees, 10, 141
  organizational structure, 61, 93
  in Pakistan, 148
  PDB warning of attack by, 11
  "Plan Delenda" and, 20, 84, 115, 187

  post-9/11 policy toward, 143–44
  pre-9/11 response to, 77–92, 155
  presidential transition and, 113–15
  propaganda video, 111
  rise of, 58–61
  Taliban and, 126–27, 143, 147
  terrorist role of, 64
  2001 threat reports, 128–31
  U.S. knowledge about, 20–21, 83–84, 150–52
  U.S. policy and, 143–45, 154–57
  USS *Cole* attack, 110–11
  USS *The Sullivans* attack attempt, 107–8
Qur'an, 54, 55
Qutb, Sayyid, 30, 55–56, 60. *See also* Rahman, Sheikh Omar Abdel
  hatred of Western society, 56

radio spectrum, for first responders, 177
Rahman, Fazlur, 172
Rahman, Sheikh Omar Abdel, 30, 66, 176
ar-Rashid, Harun, 24
Reagan, Ronald, 2, 73, 74, 75
Reagan, Ronald, Washington National Airport, 44, 50
REAL ID Act, 180
"red team" analysis, 152
Rehnquist, William, 4
Reno, Janet, 30, 69, 82, 87, 113, 185
Republican Commissioners, 1, 6–8, 35
  executive privilege concerns, 10, 11
Republican-Democratic conflicts, 2–6
Republican Party, 2, 3–4
Ressam, Ahmed, 30, 107, 134, 162–63, 175
  arrest of, 106, 107
Rice, Condoleezza, 9, 18, 30, 48, 49, 142, 173, 188, 189
  counterterrorism approach, 115–18
  post-9/11 planning, 143, 144–45, 146, 151–52
  presidential transition period, 113–15
  public testimony, 12, 14
  response to 9/11 attacks, 139
  2001 intelligence briefings, 130
  "Richard," 116–17
Ridge, Tom, 140
Roemer, Timothy J., 7, 9, 11, 13, 30
  report outline and, 17
  report review by, 17
Rolince, Michael, 30
Roosevelt, Franklin D., 67–68, 71
Rove, Karl, 30, 48
Rumsfeld, Donald, 30, 50, 115, 142
  Iraq concerns, 146
  military plan against Taliban, 143–44
  post-9/11 response, 142–43
  al Qaeda and, 158

Sadiq 'Awda, Muhammad, 174
Salameh, Mohammed, 30, 66, 94
sarin nerve gas, 81

Saudi Arabia
  assistance to Afghanistan, 60
  fatwa issued to drive Americans from, 52,
    171–72
  Khobar Towers bombing, 62
  National Guard facility bombing, 62
  U.S. military bases in, 22, 61
  U.S. relations with, 23, 183
  Wahhabism in, 57
Saudi Hezbollah, 62, 77
Scheuer, Michael ("Mike"), 29
scholarship programs, 184
Schoomaker, Peter, 30, 88, 89
Schroen, Gary, 30, 80, 86, 90
Screening Coordination Office, 179
Secret Service, 69, 129
  Moussaoui and, 132
  response to 9/11 attacks, 49, 139
Securities and Exchange Commission, 140
security clearances, 182
Senguen, Aysel, 30, 101, 102
Senior Executive Intelligence Brief, 72
Sensitive Compartmental Information
    Facility (SCIF), 18
September 11, 2001, terrorist attacks. *See
    also* "planes operation"
  Bush's response to, 48–51
  capabilities failures revealed by, 157–59
  Cheney's response to, 48–51
  circulation of information about, 48
  comprehension of, 149–50
  devastation of, 149
  emergency response, 135–38
  events of September 11, 37–52
  fatalities, 135, 138
  imagination failures revealed by, 149–54
  immediate domestic response, 139–42
  impacts of, vii
  management failures revealed by, 159–63
  motivation for, 22–25, 56
  "planes operation," 95
  planning, 93, 95–98
  policy failures revealed by, 154–57
  preparation for, 118–20
  Saddam Hussein and, 145–46
  Sheikh Mohammed's role in, 93–94
  victim compensation, 140
  World Trade Center bombing and, 65–66
Serbia, 84, 85
Shanksville, Pennsylvania, United Airlines
    Flight 93 crash in, 47
Sharia, 24, 54, 57
Sharif, Nawaa, 88
Shehhi, Marwan al, 30, 37–38, 42, 123, 124,
    128
  arrival in U.S., 120
  flight training, 120, 122
  passports and visas, 103
  "planes operation" and, 102–3
  profile, 100–101
Shehri, Mohand al, 30, 37–38

Shehri, Wail al, 30, 37–38, 40
Shehri, Waleed al, 30, 37–38, 40
Sheikh Ali camp, 90
Sheikh Mohammed, Khalid (KSM), 30–31,
    32, 111, 119, 121, 128, 173, 174, 176,
    186, 187
  family, 93
  hatred of U.S. by, 93
  Moussaoui and, 125
  "planes operation" and, 95–98, 104
  planning role, 125
  role in September 11 attacks, 93
  terrorist activities, 93–95
Shelton, Hugh, 31, 80, 87, 88, 109, 112, 114,
    142, 157
Shia Muslims, 54
  in Iran, 57
al Shifa pharmaceutical plant, 81–82
Shinrikyo, Aum, 81
shootdown order, United Airlines Flight 93,
    50–51
Shultz, George, 73
sleeper cells, in the U.S., 109
Small Group, 84–85, 112
social malaise, in Arab states, 57–58
SO/LIC. *See* Special Operations and Low-
    Intensity Conflict (SO/LIC)
Somalia, 52, 77
  Black Hawk helicopters shot down in, 62,
    74, 186
  fatwa demanding eviction of U.S. troops
    from, 61–62
  al Qaeda aid to, 61–62
Southern U.S., political parties in, 2
Soviet Union
  Afghanistan invasion, 24, 58–61
  withdrawal from Afghanistan, 53
Special Forces, 148
"special interest" detainees, 141
Special Operations and Low-Intensity
    Conflict (SO/LIC), 20, 32
Special Operations Command, 88–89
"Spooky," 88
Starr, Kenneth, 4, 186, 187
State Department
  counterintelligence activities, 73
  Moussaoui and, 132
  terrorism responsibilities, 75
  TIPOFF [terrorist] watchlist, 108–9
Steinberg, James, 31, 85
Sudan, 21, 62–64
  Bin Ladin's tannery in, 81
  al Shifa, pharmaceutical plant, 81–82
  terrorist activities in, 94
suicide bombings, fatwa praising, 52
suicide hijackings
  pre-9/11 analysis of, 152–54
  protection against, 154
suicide operatives
  flight training for, 103
  Hamburg group, 98–108

mujahideen (holy warriors), 170
al Qaeda's concerns about, 96
selecting, 97, 153
training, 97–98
U.S. visas for, 103
Sunni Muslims, 54
fundamentalists, 57
Wahhabism, 57
Suqami, Satam al, 31, 37–38, 40
surprise attack
methods of forestalling, 152
tell-tale indicators for, 152–53
"Survey of Intelligence Information on Any
Iraq Involvement in the September
11 Attacks," 145
Sweeney, Brian David, 42
Sweeney, Louise, 42, 43
Sweeney, Madeline "Amy," 40–41

Tajiks, 90
*takfiri*, 58
Taliban
Afghan training camps, 63–64, 80, 82
ethnic composition, 90
military plan against, 143–44
Northern Alliance and, 127
Pakistani interest in, 63
al Qaeda and, 126–27, 143, 147
U.S. and, 111–12, 157
Tanzania, U.S. embassy bombings, 64–65,
80, 95, 176, 186, 187
Tarnak Farms, 78, 80, 110
Tenet, George, 31, 76, 79, 80, 82, 86, 87, 91,
113, 115, 142, 155, 186, 187
East Africa embassy bombings and,
80–81
institutional management, 161–62, 163
intelligence assessment by, 92
post-9/11 intelligence plans, 144
presidential transition period, 114
public hearing testimony, 20
response to 9/11 attacks, 139
2001 intelligence briefings, 129–30
USS *Cole* attack and, 111
terrorism. *See also* counterterrorism
Bush priorities, 13–14, 115–18
Clinton priorities, 75, 105, 114
Congressional role, 76
domestic threat response, 131
eliminating, 142–45
extremist religious groups and, 68
motivation for, 56
nature of, 150–52
preparing for, 164
preventing growth of, 164
protecting against, 164
public opinion and, 76
al Qaeda role, 64
recommended strategies, 163–64
2001 threat reports, 128–31
U.S. policy and, 154–57

terrorists
anti-Semitism of, 99, 100
attacking, 164
detainees, 10, 141
detention standards, 183
financing, 184
motivations of, 82
purpose of, 36
sanctuaries of, 164, 183
Taliban training camps, 63–64, 80, 82, 85,
90
training camps, Afghanistan, 80, 97–98
in U.S., 106–7, 109
use of hijacked airlines by, 47
Thompson, James R., 7, 15, 31
Thompson, Larry, 31, 142
*Thousand and One Nights, The*, 24
TIPOFF [terrorist] watchlist, 108–9
Tokyo, sarin nerve gas attack, 81
Tomahawk cruise missiles, 80
Tora Bora, 148
"traffic analysis," 70
transportation security, 178–79
Transportation Security Administration
(TSA), 178–79
Treasury Department, 69, 140
truck bombs, at Khobar Towers, 62
Turab al Jordani, Abu, 31
Twin Towers, 37, 137

UAE. *See* United Arab Emirates (UAE)
UBL. *See* Bin Ladin, Usama
Ummah (Muslim community), 54
unemployment, of young men, in Arab
states, 58
United Airlines, realization of multiple
hijackings, 44–45
United Airlines Flight 93
boarding, 39
cell phone calls from, 45–46
cockpit voice recorder, 46
crash, Shanksville, Pennsylvania, 47
flight data recorder, 45
hijackers of, 127
hijacking of, 44–47
passenger revolt, 46–47
shootdown order, 50–51
take-off delay, 44
United Airlines Flight 175
boarding, 37–38
crash into South Tower, World Trade
Center, 43
hijackers, 128
hijacking, 42–43
United Arab Emirates (UAE), 33, 90, 127
United States
Afghan resistance and, 60
Bin Ladin's desire to attack, 170, 186
Black Hawk helicopters shot down, 62,
74
campaign against Bin Ladin, 81–92

United States (*cont.*)
  East Africa embassy bombings, 21,
    64–65, 80–81, 95, 155–56, 176,
    186
  extremists in, 106–7, 109
  fatwa to drive Americans from Saudi
    Arabia, 52, 169–70
  fatwa to evict U.S. troops from Somalia,
    61–62
  fatwa to kill Americans, 52, 169–70
  international broadcasting, 184
  leadership vision, 184
  military bases in Saudi Arabia, 22, 61
  Muslim hatred of, 56
  as oppressor of Muslims, 66
  terrorists' hatred of, 94
United States Marines
  Khobar Towers bombing, 62
  suicide bombings of, 52
U.S. Air Force
  combat air patrol (CAP), 50
  Predator, 110, 157
U.S. Army, Delta Force, 74
U.S. Central Command (CENTCOM), 32,
    88, 112, 128, 144
U.S. embassies
  East Africa bombings, 21, 64–65, 80–81,
    95, 130, 155–56, 176, 186
  Yemen, 128, 155–56
U.S. Fifth Fleet, 128
"U.S. Hard Put to Find Proof Bin Laden
    Directed Attacks," 151
U.S. Marine Corps, 128
U.S. Marshals Service, 69, 141
USA PATRIOT Act, 142
USS *Cole*, 29
  Afghanistan and, 111–13
  attack on, 187
  al Qaeda responsibility for attack, 110–11,
    147, 157
  U.S. response to attack, 111–13, 116,
    117–18, 157
USS *The Sullivans*, 107–8, 187
US-VISIT system, 179

victims' relatives and friends
  Clarke's apology to, 13
  compensation of, 140
  federal emergency assistance to, 140
  investigation demanded by, 1
  lobbying by, 8
  public hearings and, 13
  relationship to 9/11 Commission, 8, 9
  research by, 8
Vietnam War, 71

"virtual station," CIA, 77
VX (nerve gas), 81

*Wag the Dog*, 82
Wahhabism, 57, 63
"wall, the," 69, 142
"war council," 142, 144
Watson, Dale, 31, 107, 114, 133
weapons of mass destruction (WMD), 33,
    182
Western society, hatred of, 56
White House, as 9/11 target, 44, 123, 124
Whitewater investigation, 4, 21, 185, 186
WMD. *See* weapons of mass destruction
    (WMD)
Wohlstetter, Roberta, 149
Wolfowitz, Paul, 31, 129, 146
  Iraq concerns, 146–47
Woodward, Bob, 11, 31, 146
Woodward, Michael, 41
World Islamic Front, 65
  fatwa issued by, 52, 171–72
World Trade Center, 33, 37
  American Airlines Flight 11 crash into, 42
  bombing of, 65–66, 75, 93–94, 95, 150,
    173, 185, 188
  collapse of, 137
  emergency response at, 135–37
  evacuation of, 135–36
  fatalities, 135
  incident command, 136–37
  as 9/11 target, 123, 124
  United Airlines Flight 175 crash into, 43
World Trade Organization (WTO), 33
WTC. *See* World Trade Center
WTO. *See* World Trade Organization (WTO)

Yemen, 61, 128
Yousef, Ramzi, 31, 65–66, 93–94, 95, 147,
    174, 175, 186
Y2K concerns, 162–63

Zawahiri, Ayman al, 31, 111, 172
  fatwa issued by, 52
Zelikow, Philip D., 8, 9, 31, 173
  access to PDBs, 11
  classified information and, 18
  report design and, 15
  report drafting and, 17
  report outline, 16
  report publication and, 18
  report review by, 17
Zinni, Anthony, 31, 80, 86, 88, 89
Zionist-Crusaders, 169
Zubaydah, Abu, 31